AF804762

LAWYERING FOR THE RULE OF LAW

Lawyering for the Rule of Law introduces a new model of government lawyering in which government lawyers function as an ancillary mechanism that enables the court to expand its influence on policy-making within the political branches by forming out-of-court settlements. It discusses the centrality of government lawyers with regard to judicial mobilization and the enforcement of social reforms through adjudication, and sheds light on particular functions of government lawyers as adjudicators and facilitators of institutional arrangements. It also discusses the ethical and professional dilemmas of government lawyers in judicial review and the relationship between lawyers' professional morality and outcomes in litigation.

YOAV DOTAN is Edwin A. Goodman Professor of Law and former Dean of the Faculty of Law at the Hebrew University of Jerusalem.

CAMBRIDGE STUDIES IN CONSTITUTIONAL LAW

The aim of this series is to produce leading monographs in constitutional law. All areas of constitutional law and public law fall within the ambit of the series, including human rights and civil liberties law, administrative law, as well as constitutional theory and the history of constitutional law. A wide variety of scholarly approaches is encouraged, with the governing criterion being simply that the work is of interest to an international audience. Thus, works concerned with only one jurisdiction will be included in the series as appropriate, while, at the same time, the series will include works which are explicitly comparative or theoretical – or both. The series editors likewise welcome proposals that work at the intersection of constitutional and international law, or that seek to bridge the gaps between civil law systems, the US, and the common law jurisdictions of the Commonwealth.

Series Editors
David Dyzenhaus
Professor of Law and Philosophy,
University of Toronto, Canada
Adam Tomkins
John Millar Professor of Public Law,
University of Glasgow, UK

Editorial Advisory Board
T. R. S. Allan
Cambridge, UK
Damian Chalmers
LSE, UK
Sujit Choudhry
Toronto, Canada
Monica Claes
Maastricht, Netherlands
David Cole
Georgetown, USA
K. D. Ewing
King's College London, UK
David Feldman
Cambridge, UK
Cora Hoexter
Witwatersrand, South Africa
Christoph Moellers
Goettingen, Germany
Adrienne Stone, Melbourne, Australia
Adrian Vermeule, Harvard, USA

Books in the series:

Lawyering for the Rule of Law: Government Lawyers and the Rise of Judicial Power in Israel Yoav Dotan

Balancing Constitutional Rights: The Origins and Meanings of Postwar Legal Discourse Jacco Bomhoff

Judges on Trial: The Independence and Accountability of the English Judiciary Shimon Shetreet and Sophie Turenne

Proportionality and Constitutional Culture Moshe Cohen-Eliya and Iddo Porat

The Politics of Principle, The First South African Constitutional Court, 1995–2005 Theunis Roux

The New Commonwealth Model of Constitutionalism, Theory and Practice Stephen Gardbaum

Searching for the State in British Legal Thought, Competing Conceptions of the Public Sphere Janet McLean

Judging Social Rights Jeff King

Proportionality, Constitutional Rights and their Limitations Aharon Barak

Parliamentary Sovereignty, Contemporary Debates Jeffrey Goldsworthy

LAWYERING FOR THE RULE OF LAW

Government Lawyers and the Rise of Judicial Power in Israel

YOAV DOTAN

CAMBRIDGE
UNIVERSITY PRESS

CAMBRIDGE
UNIVERSITY PRESS

University Printing House, Cambridge CB2 8BS, United Kingdom

Published in the United States of America by Cambridge University Press, New York

Cambridge University Press is part of the University of Cambridge.

It furthers the University's mission by disseminating knowledge in the pursuit of education, learning and research at the highest international levels of excellence.

www.cambridge.org

Information on this title: www.cambridge.org/9781107625907

© Yoav Dotan 2014

This publication is in copyright. Subject to statutory exception and to the provisions of relevant collective licensing agreements, no reproduction of any part may take place without the written permission of Cambridge University Press.

First published 2014

Printed in the United Kingdom by CPI Group Ltd, Croydon CR0 4YY

A catalogue record for this publication is available from the British Library

Library of Congress Cataloguing in Publication data
Dotan, Yoav.
Lawyering for the rule of law : government lawyers and the rise of judicial power in Israel / Yoav Dotan.
pages cm. (Cambridge studies in constitutional law; 9)
ISBN 978-1-107-03899-8 (hardback) ISBN 978-1-107-62590-7 (paperback)
1. Political questions and judicial power–Israel. 2. Government attorneys–Israel. I. Title.
KMK2244.D68 2013
347.5694–dc23
2013023923

ISBN 978-1-107-03899-8 Hardback
ISBN 978-1-107-62590-7 Paperback

Cambridge University Press has no responsibility for the persistence or accuracy of URLs for external or third-party internet websites referred to in this publication, and does not guarantee that any content on such websites is, or will remain, accurate or appropriate.

DAMAGED

For Shlomit

CONTENTS

ACKNOWLEDGMENTS

This book is a product of many years of research in the archives of the Israeli Supreme Court and the Ministry of Justice. Throughout the years and the various stages of the project I have benefited from the dedicated help of my research assistants whom are too numerous to be indicated by names. I am also thankful to the Ministry of Justice for allowing me access to their files and to the many lawyers and judges who agreed to be interviewed for this project. During the stage of writing the text I have benefited immensely from the assistance of Moshe Ostrovsky and Shira Gartenberg. I am also deeply indebted to Gali Aviv Weisman for her invaluable assistance as a statistical advisor and to Diana Rubanenko for her dedicated assistance as language editor.

FIGURES

TABLES

Introduction: The government's lawyer

Why study government lawyers? The main theme of this book is that government lawyers play a predominant role in both public law litigation and administrative policy-making. Studying the work of government lawyers is therefore essential for the study of litigation as a technique aimed at bringing about social reforms. I also argue that the study of government lawyers enables us to re-evaluate many concepts related to the study of the legal profession at large.

Lawyers in the public sector form a significant portion of the legal profession.[1] Lawyers are involved in every aspect of government work. They have a major impact on legislation, policy-making, implementation, and enforcement. Even more significant is the involvement of government lawyers in litigation. Government lawyers appear on a regular basis before all courts of law, and in many jurisdictions they form the group of lawyers who most frequently take part in high court litigation.[2] Government lawyers and their agency clients have also been shown – by research conducted in various countries – to be the most successful litigants in most

[1] For data on the relative number of government lawyers in the United States see the US Department of Labor Statistics at www.bls.gov/oes/current/oes231011.htm#nat; for Great Britain see "Trends in the Solicitors' Profession" (Annual Statistical Report 2011 prepared by Nina Fletcher Research Unit for the Law Society 2011); for Quebeq see "Lawyers in Private Practice in 2021" (Report of the Committee on Current Issues in Private Practice and the Future of the Profession, Barreau du Quebec, 2011, at 57).

[2] For example, the Solicitor General is by far the most frequent litigant before the United States Supreme Court: see R. M. Salokar, *The Solicitor General: The Politics of Law* (Philadelphia, PA: Temple University Press, 1992), 3; D. M. Provine, *Case Selection in the United States Supreme Court* (University of Chicago Press, 1980), 89. The same situation is reported with regard to the United States Court of Appeal, District of Columbia Circuit, see P. M. Wald, "'For the United States': Government Lawyers in Court," 36 *L. & Contemp. Probs.* 107, 107–108 (1998) and note 2. By the term "government lawyers" I refer to lawyers employed by the central government as opposed to lawyers who work for local authorities or independent agencies. Since the main focus of this book is on lawyers representing the government in public law litigation, I will often use the term "government lawyers" to refer to this specific group.

judicial forums, including in litigation in the high courts.[3] Accordingly, government lawyers play a major role in shaping public policy through litigation.

Despite their substantial size as a group within the legal profession and their prominent role in high court litigation, until recently academic literature has tended to neglect public sector lawyering in general and government lawyering in particular. The literature on the legal profession focuses on private sector lawyering as the prominent (if not the ultimate) model of lawyers' practice.[4] The literature on public law litigation tends, on the other hand, to view "the government" as a single-unit entity that

[3] The question of what constitutes "success" in litigation is complicated and is discussed in more detail in Chapter 3. At this stage, by "success" I refer to the immediate outcomes of the litigation (i.e. to the question of whether a petition or appeal was allowed or dismissed etc.). From this perspective there is a general consensus that governments are ultimately the most successful litigants in high court litigation. This is the case for virtually all studies that examined the outcomes of litigation in various countries and judicial forums. See for the United States Supreme Court: Provine, *Case Selection*, above note 2; Salokar, *The Solicitor General*, above note 2, at 23–31; R. S. Sheehan, W. Mishler and D. S. Songer, "Ideology, Status and Differential Success of Direct Parties Before the Supreme Court," 86 *Am. Pol. Sci. Rev.* 464 (1992). For the United States Courts of Appeals, see D. R. Songer and R. S. Sheehan, "Who Wins on Appeal? Upperdogs and Underdogs in the United States Courts of Appeals," 36 *Am. J. Pol. Sci.* 235 (1992). For states' supreme courts, see S. Wheeler, B. Cartwright, R. A. Kagan and L. M. Friedman, "Do the 'Haves' Come Out Ahead: Winning and Losing in State Supreme Courts, 1870–1970," 21 *Law & Soc'y Rev.* 403 (1987). For the House of Lords in the UK, see B. M. Atkins, "Alternative Model of Appeal Mobilization in Judicial Hierarchies," 37 *Am. J. Pol. Sci.* 780 (1993). For the Supreme Court of Canada see P. McCormick, "Party Capability Theory and Appellate Success in the Supreme Court of Canada 1949–1992," 26 *Can. J. Pol. Sci.* 523, 526 (1993). For South Africa see S. L. Haynie and J. Devore, "Judging in an Unjust Regime: South Africa's Appellate Division, 1950–1990," 17 *Am. Rev. Pol.* 245–263 (1996). For the Supreme Court of the Philippines, see S. L. Haynie, "Resource Inequalities and Litigation Outcomes in the Philippine Supreme Court," 56 *J. Pol.* 752 (1994). The case of Israel is no exception in this respect, see T. Eisenberg, T. Fisher and I. Rosen-Zvi, "Israel's Supreme Court Appellate Jurisdiction: An Empirical Study," 96 *Cornell L. Rev.* 693, 717–799 (2011) (reporting that the government is far more successful than other litigants both in civil and criminal appeals before the Supreme Court). See also the discussion in Chapter 3. For a comprehensive study on the overall influence of the Solicitor General in the United States on all aspects of the Supreme Court's decision-making see R. C. Black and R. J. Owens, *The Solicitor General and the United States Supreme Court* (Cambridge University Press, 2012).

[4] See e.g. R. L. Abel and P. S. C. Lewis (eds.), *Lawyers in Society: An Overview* (Berkeley: University of California Press, 1995); R. L. Abel and P. S. C. Lewis (eds.), *Lawyers in Society: The Common Law World* (Berkeley: University of California Press, 1988); S. M. Linowitz and M. Mayer, *The Betrayed Profession: Lawyering at the End of the Twentieth Century* (Maryland: Johns Hopkins University Press, 1994); A. T. Kronman, *The Lost Lawyer: Failing Ideals of the Legal Profession* (Cambridge, MA: Belknap Press of Harvard University Press, 1993); M. Davis and F. A. Elliston (eds.), *Ethics and the Legal Profession* (New York: Prometheus Books, 1986).

forms a unanimous party in litigation. It often disregards the fact that the government's "representative" in court is – in itself – an important player participating in the litigation, while its positions and interests do not fully correspond with those of its client agency.

It is the purpose of this book to focus on the unique function of government lawyers in high court litigation. Recently the amount of academic research performed on legal institutions within government is increasing, and much research has been conducted on major institutions such as the attorney general and the solicitor general of the United States.[5] It seems, however, that what is missing from this literature is a comprehensive discussion of the relationships between government lawyering, judicial review,[6] and policy-making in democracies.

The group I focus on in this book is a relatively small group of elite lawyers who serve in one department within the Office of the Attorney General (OAG) in Israel. This group of lawyers is in charge of representing almost all government agencies before the Supreme Court of Israel on

[5] See e.g. D. L. Horowitz, *The Jurocracy: Government Lawyers, Agency Programs and Judicial Decisions* (Washington, D.C.: Lexington Books, 1977); J. Einstein, *Counsel for the United States: U.S. Attorney General in the Political and Legal System* (Maryland: Johns Hopkins University Press, 1978); L. Caplan, *The Tenth Justice: The Solicitor General and the Rule of Law* (New York: Knopf, 1987); C. W. Clayton, *The Politics of Justice: The Attorney General and the Making of Legal Policy* (New York: M. E. Sharpe, 1992); Salokar, *The Solicitor General*, above note 2; R. L. Pacelle, *Between Law and Politics: The Solicitor General and the Structuring of Race, Gender and Reproductive Rights Litigation* (Texas: A&M University Press, 2003); N. V. Baker, *Conflicting Loyalties: Law and Politics in the Attorney General's Office 1789–1990* (University Press of Kansas, 1992); C. W. Clayton (ed.), *Government Lawyers: The Federal Legal Bureaucracy and Presidential Policies* (University Press of Kansas, 1995). For a discussion of the status of the Attorney General in the UK, see J. Ll. J. Edwards, *The Attorney General and the Public Interest* (London: Sweet and Maxwell, 1984). See also articles in N. Devins (ed.), Government Lawyering 61(1–2) *Law & Contemp. Probs.* 1 (1998); Symposium: Legal Ethics for Government Lawyers, 9(2) *Widener J. Pub. L.* 199 (2000). For a discussion of Government Lawyers in Canada see J. B. Kelly, "Bureaucratic Activism and the Charter of Rights and Freedoms: The Department of Justice and Its Entry into the Centre of Government," 42 *Can. Pub. Admin.* 476 (1999); J. B. Kelly, "Canada: Legal Services and the Role of Government Lawyers" (Paper presented at the Annual Meeting of the Law and Society Association, Budapest, July 4–7, 2001, copy with the author).

[6] The term "judicial review" carries different meanings in different legal systems. In the United States the term often refers to the *constitutional* review of statutes, while in the United Kingdom the meaning of this term is much broader and includes also review of *administrative* decisions by the courts (see e.g. S. A. De Smith, H. Woolf, J. L. Jowell and A.P. Le Sueur, *Judicial Review of Administrative Action*, 5th edn., vol. I (Sweet & Maxwell, 1995)). Throughout this book I use the term judicial review in its broad meaning to include all activities by courts to supervise acts and decisions made by both the legislature and administrative agencies.

public law matters (and, in this respect the function of this department is largely equivalent to the office of the Solicitor General in the United States). As I shall demonstrate they perform a wide range of unique functions related to the process of judicial review. The study of this group of lawyers provides insights into the unique position of government lawyers within the legal profession, and, at the same time, is the key to understanding the process of judicial review.

A. Government lawyers and lawyering

Any discussion of the ethical, social, and moral dilemmas of the legal profession needs to deal with the conflicting commitments of lawyers. Lawyers are often described as "double agents," since at the heart of law practice lies the conflict between their commitment to their clients, and their commitment to (at least some basic) general values of the system within which they operate.[7] Therefore, any lawyering (i.e. even in the private sector) is inherently embedded in the clash between the lawyer's commitment to the party they represent in litigation and their duty as "an officer of the court."[8] The dilemmas entailed in public lawyering are, however, different and far more complex. The government lawyer's commitment to their "client" agency is – in many cases – much less visible and

[7] See e.g. Kronman, above note 4, Chapter 1 (discussing the "Lawyer-Statesman" model); L. Fuller and J. D. Randall, "Professional Responsibility: Report of the Joint Conference," 44 *Am. Bar Ass'n. J.* 1159, 1161 (1958); A. S. Blumberg,"The Practice of Law as Confidence Game," in V. Aubert (ed.), *Sociology of Law* (1969) 321, 328; R. Gordon, "The Ideal and the Actual in the Law: Fantasies and Practices of New York City Lawyers, 1870–1910," in G. W. Gawalt (ed.), *The New High Priests: Lawyers in Post-Civil War America* (1984) 51; D. C. Langevoort and R. K. Rasmussen, "Skewing the Results: The Role of Lawyers in Transmitting Legal Rules," 5 *S. Cal. Interdisc. L.J.* 375, 414 (1997); E. E. Ugarte, "The Government Lawyer and the Common Good," 40 *S. Tex. L. Rev.* 269, 275 (1999).

[8] See e.g. D. Mellinkoff, *The Conscience of a Lawyer* (St. Paul, MN: West Publishing Company, 1973); M. H. Freedman, *Lawyers' Ethics in an Adversary System* (New York: The Bobbs-Merrill Company Inc., 1975); B. A. Babcock, "Defending the Guilty," 32 *Clev. St. L. Rev.* 175 (1983); C. Fried, "The Lawyer as Friend: The Moral Foundations of the Lawyer-Client Relation," 85 *Yale L.J.* 1060 (1976); D. Luban, "The Adversary System Excuse," in D. Luban (ed.) *The Good Lawyer: Lawyers' Roles and Lawyers' Ethics* (Totowa, NJ: Rowman & Allenheld, 1983) 83; W. H. Simon, "The Ideology of Advocacy: Procedural Justice and Professional Ethics," *Wis. L. Rev.* 29 (1978); G. J. Postema, "Moral Responsibility in Professional Ethics," 55 *N.Y.U. L. Rev.* 63 (1980); M. E. Frankel, "The Search for Truth: An Umpireal View," 123 *U. Pa. L. Rev.* 1031 (1975); R. Wasserstrom, "Lawyers as Professionals: Some Moral Issues," 5 *Hum. Rts.* 1 (1975); M. H. Rubin, "The Ethical Negotiator: Ethical Dilemmas, Unhappy Clients, and Angry Third Parties," 26 *Constr. Law.* 12, 24 (2006); K. P. Lewinbuk, "Let's Sue All the Lawyers: The Rise of Claims Against Lawyers for Aiding and Abetting a Client's Breach of Fiduciary Duty," 40 *Ariz. St. L.J.* 135, 137 (2008).

intensive than in the case of a private client. In some circumstances – such as in the case of criminal prosecutors – the lawyer has no tangible client except the abstract entity of the general public.[9] The dilemmas between commitment to the client and duty to the public interest at large exist, however, even outside the criminal realm, even when the government lawyer does have a concrete client, such as an administrative agency in judicial review.[10]

Questions such as to whom exactly do government lawyers owe a duty of fidelity, and which values should guide their professional activities receive conflicting answers both in official pronouncements and in the literature. One proposal is the "Single Client Model" in which government attorneys owe their duties to their direct supervisors and should serve their client's interests at the same level of zealousness as any other lawyer.[11] At the other end of the spectrum, the "Public Interest Model" holds that the true client of government attorneys is the general public and therefore government lawyers should direct their actions toward the broad public interest, rather than for the benefit of an individual member of government.[12]

One manifestation of the conflict between the duty to the specific client agency and the commitment to the public interest at large is evident in the relationships between government attorneys and the courts before which they appear as litigators. The government lawyer's commitment to the court and to the public interest (as manifested through the judicial process) is presumed to be much stronger than in the case of private attorneys. Under the doctrine of separation of powers, the judiciary and the executive in modern democracies are regarded as wholly independent of

[9] See e.g. N. D. Polikoff, "Am I My Client?: The Role Confusion of a Lawyer Activist," 31 *Harv. C.R.-C.L. L. Rev.* 443 (1996).

[10] See e.g. S. K. Berenson, "Public Lawyers, Private Values: Can, Should, and Will Government Lawyers Serve the Public Interest?," 41 *B. C. L. Rev.* 789 (2000); Note, "Government Counsel and their Obligations," 121 *Harv. L. Rev.* 1409 (2008).

[11] See G. P. Miller, "Government Lawyers' Ethics in a System of Checks and Balances," 54 *U. Chi. L. Rev.* 1293 (1987), and see also note – Harvard, above note 10, at 1413.

[12] See B. A. Green, "Must Government Lawyers 'Seek Justice' in Civil Litigation?" 9 *Widener J. Pub. L.* 235, 235–237 (2000); Berenson, above note 10; S. K. Berenson, "The Duty Defined: Specific Obligations that Follow from Civil Government Lawyers' General Duty to Serve the Public Interest," 42 *Brandeis L.J.* 13 (2003). See also P. J. Utz, "Two Models of Prosecutorial Professionalism," in W. F. McDonald (ed.), *The Prosecutor* (Beverly Hills, CA: Sage, 1979) 99 (distinguishing between "adversarial" and "magisterial" ideology of prosecutors and suggesting that the latter model is characterized by emphasis on broad commitment by the prosecutor to the general public interest rather than on narrow ambition to maximize the rate of convictions).

each other. This independence is, however, much confuted by the reality of the close relationship between government lawyers and judges. Some aspects of their close ties are institutional and professional, while others can be explained on social and ideological grounds.[13] Government lawyers appear before certain judicial forums more frequently than any other group of lawyers, and the court system's ability to operate effectively often depends on the capacity of those two groups of professionals to cooperate. Judges often depend – to a large extent – on cooperation from the government in order to assure strict compliance with their decisions, particularly in complicated or sensitive issues. The careers of judges and government lawyers are often closely intertwined, since both types of position are regarded as "public sector" legal careers.[14]

For some, this reality may appear as an inevitable or even benign aspect of an effective legal system.[15] Others may argue that close cooperation between government attorneys and judges is not only alien to the fundamental values of the adversarial legal system, but also violates the principle of separation of powers (if not reminiscent of non-democratic regimes, such as the former Eastern European systems).[16] The question whether this phenomenon of close ties between government lawyers and judges is benign or harmful will be one of the main questions discussed in this book.[17] It is hardly doubted, however, that this sense of "common public service enterprise" for both government lawyers and judges exists in many legal systems, including those traditional common-law systems that are often characterized as adversarial by nature.[18]

On top of these conflicting commitments, government lawyering raises some additional questions of an ethical, moral, and legal nature. One question touches upon the relationship between the lawyer's commitment toward their client, and their own personal ideological convictions.

[13] Thus, for example, Lincoln Caplan described in detail the social affinity of various Solicitor Generals and Supreme Court justices in the United States (See Caplan, above note 5, at 20) while Pamela Utz discussed the institutional conditions that explain the evolvement of the "magisterial" ideology of prosecutors in Alameda County (see Utz, above note 12, at 115–118).

[14] See Wald, *For the United States*, above note 2, at 109. A good illustration of the intensity of these relationships is Lincoln Caplan's characterization of the Solicitor General in the United States as "The Tenth Justice." See Caplan, above note, and see also D. A. Strauss, "The Solicitor General and the Interests of the United States," 61 *Law & Contemp. Probs.* 165 (1998).

[15] See Wald, *ibid.* [16] See e.g. Miller, above note 11, at 1297. [17] See Chapter 4.

[18] See Wald, above note 2, at 109; and above note 10. See also Y. Dotan, "Judicial Rhetoric, Government Lawyers, and Human Rights: The Case of the Israeli High Court of Justice During the *Intifada*," 33 *Law & Soc'y Rev.* 319 (1999).

Traditional theory of the legal profession regards lawyers as value-neutral professional agents hired by their clients to foster the latter's interests. This model of lawyers as "hired guns" has recently been challenged by growing academic interest in the phenomenon of "political" or "cause" lawyering. Lawyers who answer to this vision of the profession consider their legal activity as a vehicle to promote certain moral or social objectives. Therefore they choose cases, clients, and careers according to what they stand for, rather than what fosters the immediate private interest of their client.[19]

One strand of the growing literature on political lawyers focuses on lawyers who operate in the non-governmental public sector, i.e. lawyers who work for voluntary organizations (NGOs).[20] While the parameters that distinguish cause lawyering from other sorts of legal practice are by no means fully clear or agreed upon among scholars,[21] one may wonder whether and to what extent ideological preferences influence lawyers' practices and decisions within the sphere of the governmental public sector. Research on government lawyers has pointed out some interesting similarities shared by government lawyers and lawyers working for NGOs. Much like classic cause lawyers, government lawyers sometimes feel committed to certain values of the organizations to which they belong (for example, a bureau that is in charge of enforcing environmental standards in a given field). The career patterns of NGO lawyers and government lawyers may also be closely intertwined, even though those lawyers often meet each other on different sides of the litigation battlefield.[22] The same can sometimes be said about the social affiliations of these two groups of lawyers. While these facts should not disguise the fundamental differences between lawyers who serve government and lawyers operating in the non-governmental public sector, they do justify an effort to examine government lawyers within the context of political lawyering.

19 A. Sarat and S. Scheingold, "Cause Lawyering and the Reproduction of Professional Authority: An Introduction," in A. Sarat and S. Scheingold (eds.), *Cause Lawyering: Political Commitments and Professional Responsibilities* (New York: Oxford University Press, 1998) 3.

20 See *ibid.*, and the other articles appearing in this volume.

21 See Sarat and Scheingold, above note 19, at 5–8; Y. Dotan, "Public Lawyers and Private Clients: An Empirical Observation on the Relative Success Rates of Cause Lawyers," 21 *Law & Pol'y* 401 (1999).

22 See Y. Dotan, "Cause Lawyers Crossing the Lines: Patterns of Fragmentation and Cooperation between State and Civil Rights Lawyers in Israel," 5 *Int'l J. Legal Prof.*193 (1998).

Last, but not least, there is one additional factor that distinguishes government lawyers from their private counterparts. Government lawyers are not only lawyers, they are also – in most cases – *government officials*.[23] They work for the government as employees under a specific legal regime that bestows on them special powers and duties. Their commitment toward their clients may well stand in conflict with their duties as public officials under the constitution and the statutes of the relevant legal system. Additionally, and more than for any other public official, this commitment toward legal values may contradict their duty to obey the instructions of their superiors within the hierarchic structure of the bureaucracy.

Thus, more than other lawyers, government lawyers are subject to a complex array of conflicting commitments. This quadrangle of conflicting commitments toward the court before which they appear, their client agency, their personal moral convictions, and their duties as public officials will be the heart of the discussion in this book. Throughout this book I discuss the tensions between these conflicting commitments by focusing on one group of lawyers who represent the Israeli government before the Israeli Supreme Court. The model of lawyering in which those lawyers engage is by no means representative of all, or even most, government lawyers (in general, and in Israel as well). Rather, this kind of lawyering takes to the extreme some aspects of government lawyering on account of others. Nevertheless, a discussion of these law practitioners allows us, I believe, to learn much about the complexities of government lawyering and the relative advantages and disadvantages of the possible choices that government lawyers confront.

B. Government lawyers, litigation and social change

The study of government lawyers is important not only from the perspective of studying the legal profession. It is also essential for understanding litigation as a technique for social reform. Across the world we are witnessing a constant increase in courts' involvement in all aspects of public life. The phenomenon of judicial activism has long ceased to be viewed as uniquely American. Litigation is rapidly becoming a predominant technique used by individuals, organizations, and politicians in order to influence political processes and initiate social reforms.[24] While the literature

[23] See Horowitz, above note 5, at 1; Green, above note 12, at 245.

[24] See e.g. C. N. Tate and T. Valinder (eds.), *The Global Expansion of Judicial Power* (New York University Press, 1995); L. Epstein and J. F. Kobylka, *The Supreme Court and Legal*

dealing with judicial activism is abundant, it focuses almost exclusively either on the work of the courts themselves or – to a much lesser degree – on the work of organizations (governmental or non-governmental) who take part in public law litigation. The role of government lawyers in the process of public law litigation, as well as in the process of initiating and implementing social reforms through litigation, is much neglected.

One of the main purposes of this book is to demonstrate the important role of government lawyers in the process of public law litigation. Government lawyers play a central role in the process of the litigation itself. In many cases the outcome of the litigation depends on government lawyers, no less than on the judges who sit on the bench. Sometimes, their influence may even exceed that of the judges since in many cases the government lawyer has considerable latitude. They can settle the case before any judicial decision is made; they can bring their client to adopt a position that would render the litigation redundant. They are also able to adopt a given position in the litigation that will shape the framework of the anticipated litigation. Thus, the government lawyer is often able to influence the range of possible outcomes, well before the court even reads the file.

Apart from their paramount function in the litigation itself, government lawyers have an even greater role *in the process that follows the litigation*. It is hardly a secret that the courts' ability to initiate social reform is highly compromised by an array of institutional constraints. The literature discussing the social impact of judicial decision-making strongly suggests that courts *alone* can seldom bring about social change.[25] Courts normally need *cooperation* from other players within the governmental

Change: Abortion and the Death Penalty (Chapel Hill, NC: North Carolina University Press, 1992); R. Hirschl, *Towards Juristocracy: The Origins and Consequences of the New Constitutionalism* (Cambridge, MA: Harvard University Press, 2004). Judicial "Activism" is not a simple concept and there are various meanings for this term. I will discuss this in Chapter 1 Section C, p. 31.

[25] For the discussion of the institutional limitations of courts see e.g. D. L. Horowitz, *The Courts and Social Policy* (Washington, D.C.: Brookings Institution Press, 1977); R. A. L. Gambitta, M. L. May and J. C. Foster (eds.), *Governing Through Courts* (Beverly Hills, CA: Sage, 1981). For studies discussing courts' ability to bring about social change, see e.g. S. Scheingold, *The Politics of Rights: Lawyers, Public Policy, and Political Change* (New Haven, CT: Yale University Press, 1974); G. N. Rosenberg, *The Hollow Hope: Can Courts Bring About Social Change?* 2nd edn. (University of Chicago Press, 2008); M. W. McCann, *Rights at Work: Pay Equity Reform and the Politics of Legal Mobilization* (University of Chicago Press, 1994); M. M. Feeley and E. L. Rubin, *Judicial Policy Making and the Modern State: How the Courts Reformed America's Prisons* (Cambridge University Press, 1998).

sector in order to successfully transform their declarations into an actual process of social change. Courts are also well aware of this fact. Government lawyers are the most immediate candidates to supply the court with this necessary aid in transforming the court decision into an administrative process of reform. Without their cooperation, social reform through litigation is unlikely– or even completely impossible. Courts often *expect* the legal bureaucracy of the government to serve as *their* "agents" to ensure compliance and implementation.

While initially litigation could have been regarded as merely a channel through which external pressures are exerted on governments, in the world of judicial activism it has become a predominant framework for policy-making in itself. There is hardly a policy-making process in present-day democracy that disregards the question of whether the proposed decision or practice would withstand judicial review. Moreover, in many cases the policy-making process begins as a result of litigation, or is being conducted while litigation is pending and under the supervision of the judicial forum.[26]

Activist courts today have the ambition (or at least the willingness) to be involved in policy-making, despite the fact that they suffer from serious institutional limitations in this regard. Courts are passive institutions that have relatively little control of their agenda. Adjudication is a highly formal and inflexible decision-making process. Policy-making by courts is piecemeal and incremental. Courts have no means for systematically collecting data, evaluating the broad effects of a given decision (such as the price of implementing a certain court order), assessing priorities, and so forth. Courts also lack the ability to monitor over time a process that follows certain decisions and thus cannot evaluate its correctness.[27] The question is, then, how – if at all – courts can remain effective political actors despite these institutional constraints. Throughout this book, I will argue that courts in Israel have managed to overcome many of these boundaries by creating ancillary mechanisms that allow them to function

[26] See e.g. Feeley and Rubin, *ibid.*, and Chapter 5.

[27] See Horowitz, above note 25; D. J. Galligan, *Discretionary Powers: A Legal Study of Official Discretion* (Oxford: Clarendon Press, 1986); R. A. Kagan, "Adversarial Legalism and American Government," 10 *J. Pol'y Analysis & Mgmt.* 369 (1991); R. Baldwin and C. McCrudden, *Regulation and Public Law* (London: Weidenfeld and Nicolson, 1987); J. F. Handler, *Down from Bureaucracy: The Ambiguity of Privatization and Empowerment* (New Jersey: Princeton University Press, 1996); M. Shapiro, *Who Guards the Guardians?: Judicial Control of Administration* (Athens, GA: University of Georgia Press, 1988); R. J. Pierce, "Two Problems in Administrative Law: Political Polarity on the District of Columbia Circuit and Judicial Deterrence of Agency Rulemaking," *Duke L.J.* 300 (1988).

as policy-makers. I also demonstrate the central role that government lawyers play within these mechanisms.[28]

Government lawyers thus form a unique and essential part within the process of public law litigation. Rather than being merely the transparent representative of the government agency in litigation, they form an essential link between the judiciary and the executive branch. The study of this role is essential for obtaining an understanding of the social process of public law litigation. I demonstrate this importance through a discussion of the role of the lawyers representing the Israeli government before the Israeli Supreme Court. Since the 1980s this court has adopted a robust version of judicial activism. The court's strategies were based, to a great extent, on the cooperation formed by the court with the lawyers representing the Israeli government in litigation. It is the understanding of the interplay between these two groups of professionals that provides an explanation for the phenomenon of judicial activism and its impact on society.

C. The plan of the book

This book discusses the evolution of a particular model of government lawyering within which the lawyers who represent government agencies in litigation function both as affiliates of the court and as a vital component of the mechanism of judicial review. This model may not be unique to Israel.[29] But the evolvement of such a model is related to some characteristics of the political and legal system and the structure of the legal bureaucracy. Accordingly, in the first two chapters I describe the main features of the Israeli legal system. Chapter 1 describes the structure of the judicial system in Israel and the historical development of judicial review. In particular, I describe the main judicial institution that performs judicial review: the High Court of Justice (HCJ). In its capacity as the HCJ, the Israeli Supreme Court serves as the first and last instance for a considerable segment of judicial review actions against public agencies in the country. This peculiar fact – that the Supreme Court in essence must function as a trial court – bears important implications for almost every aspect of its policies and practices as a court of law, but also for its relationship with the legal bureaucracy, which is the subject of the current study.

In Chapter 2 I describe in detail the institution that represents the Israeli government before the HCJ: the Office of the Attorney General (OAG) and the High Court of Justice Department (HCJD).

[28] See Chapter 5. [29] See e.g. above note 13.

Chapters 3 and 4 deal with the principal activity of the HCJD: the representation of all governmental agencies before the HCJ. Chapter 3 is descriptive and quantitative. It describes the litigative activities of the HCJD and draws on a large-scale quantitative study of HCJ files. In Chapter 4 I discuss the main findings of the empirical study and its implications for understanding the phenomenon of government lawyering. In particular, I discuss the fundamental dilemma of government lawyers: the need to serve both as representatives of their client agencies, but also to function as the servants of the principle of the rule of law that is manifested, from their point of view, by the judicial institution that performs judicial review over those agencies.

Chapters 5 and 6 deal with some particular activities of the HCJD beyond litigation. In Chapter 5 I discuss various activities in which government lawyers perform supervisory and managerial tasks on behalf of the Justices of the HCJ. By carrying out these activities the lawyers in the HCJD enable the court to significantly extend its control over governmental policy-making and thus to broaden its political leverage on the government. In Chapter 6 I describe another practice of the HCJD, in which its members perform a role that is in essence adjudicative. This practice is known as "pre-petitions," complaints or petitions issued *directly* to the HCJD and disposed by the government lawyers instead of being filed to the Court. I conclude with some additional comments regarding the past, present and future of the model of government lawyering in Israel.

D. Methodology

The initial idea for this book came to me when I served for six months in 1994 as a lawyer at the HCJD. My work at the department gave me ample opportunity to study from inside the working practices of the HCJD (and to some extent other departments in the OAG). The materials gathered during this participant observation were complemented through the years by several in-depth interviews with HCJD members (past and present), other lawyers within the OAG, judges, bureaucrats, lawyers in governmental agencies whom the HCJD represents in court, and lawyers in NGOs who often face the HCJD in court.[30] The department also allowed me access to various documents including reports, internal files, memos, and statistics it used during its regular course of operation. The "price"

[30] All the initials of the names of the interviewees in the books are coded.

for this comfortable access to bureaucratic materials was my commitment to keep the names of all my interviewees coded and to receive the Department's permission for publishing any contents of its internal materials (refusals to use such materials were rare and, in my opinion, insignificant for the overall results of the research).

The quantitative parts of the research are based primarily on a large sample of HCJ files. The sample includes over 1,000 HCJ files from the 1990s and around 600 files from the 1970s which compose around 10 percent of all court files during these periods.[31] The HCJD represented the respondents in over 70 percent of all cases in this sample while in the rest the respondents (mostly local municipalities) were represented by other lawyers. The sampling process was conducted on *actual court files* located in the Supreme Court archives. This method of sampling is extremely cumbersome and onerous, but gave me the possibility of achieving maximum information on the files sampled. Each file is coded according to many factors, including the identity of the judges, the parties to the litigation, their lawyers, their ethnic and institutional affiliation, and so forth. The database also includes ample information on the litigation: its duration, its subject matter, its outcome, the content of the pleadings, remedies, and so on. This method of sampling also enabled me to study not only cases that were disposed by court decisions but also cases disposed by out-of-court settlements and to accurately codify the content and conditions of settlements. In addition I also created a sample of internal adjudicative files which are disposed by the HCJD itself (pre-petitions) (which are discussed in Chapter 6).

[31] Additional samples were taken from HCJ files dating from recent years.

1

The Israeli legal system and the rise of judicial activism in the High Court of Justice

A. General elements of the Israeli legal system

1. *Israel's "half baked" constitution*

In many countries around the world the word "constitution" means a single formal document that was officially and solemnly ratified through an extraordinary procedure at one stage of history, and which contains most of the fundamental institutional arrangements of the government system including a bill of rights. If this is the meaning of the word constitution, then Israel is one of the very few nations that at the beginning of the twenty-first century is yet to have one. Indeed, at the Declaration of Independence of Israel (which was solemnly introduced to the people of the State on the date of Establishment on May 15, 1948), the founders of the State provided that the people of Israel would elect a "Constituting Assembly" that would form a constitution for Israel. After the Assembly was elected, however, it soon decided to turn its name into the First Knesset (i.e. Parliament), and to postpone the preparation of the constitution for a later stage. Later on, a decision was taken by the Knesset – in the famous Harrari Resolution of 1950 – to postpone the adoption of a constitution as one document, and instead to prepare it piecemeal – chapter by chapter – in a series of basic laws to be enacted by future Knessets, which would eventually be brought together to form the constitution.[1]

The omission to form a constitution was not casual. It resulted partly from the severe security pressures under which Israel was founded and partly from

[1] A. Zysblat, "Introduction: The System of Government," in I. Zamir and A. Zysblat (eds.), *Public Law in Israel* (Oxford: Clarendon Press, 1996), 1–17 (Zamir and Zysblat); I. Zamir, "Rule of Law and Civil Liberties in Israel," 7 *C.J. Q.* 64, 65 (1988). For a thoughtful analysis of the background for this incremental approach to constitutionalism see G. J. Jacobsohn, *Apple of Gold: Constitutionalism in Israel and the United States* (Princeton University Press, 1993), 100–110.

the deep divisions among the founders on central issues such as religion and state. For the same reasons subsequent Knessets over the years have hardly been expeditious in fulfilling their constitutional mission. By 1990 there were eleven basic laws that were accepted but these were all laws that dealt with structural issues such as the composition of the Knesset, the powers of the government, the judiciary and so forth. None of these laws contained a bill of rights or any reference to basic civil rights and not one of them dealt with the issue of judicial power to review ordinary statutes of the Knesset. Moreover, these basic laws were accepted through a procedure that was practically identical to any other statute of the Knesset.[2] Accordingly, The Israeli Supreme Court – faithful to the English premise of Parliamentary Supremacy (see below) – was willing to acknowledge the constitutional supremacy of these basic laws only on rare occasions and on narrow grounds. It did so in a series of cases during the 1970s and the 1980s where it acknowledged the power of the Knesset to entrench certain clauses in the basic laws by which any legislation deviating from these clauses should stand the requirements for special majority specified in the entrenched clauses.[3]

This situation was changed, to some extent, in 1992 when the Twelfth Knesset, shortly before the termination of its tenure, accepted two additional basic laws: Basic Law: Human Dignity and Liberty and Basic Law: Freedom of Occupation. These new basic laws differed from those accepted at early stages for a number of reasons. They contained a list – albeit partial – of civil rights that were acknowledged as constitutionally protected; they dealt directly with the relationship between their orders and subsequent legislation that may infringe on these basic rights, and they contained a reference – albeit minimal – to the question of entrenchment against the possibility of their nullification by subsequent Knesset legislation.[4] Following the acceptance of these new basic laws the Supreme

[2] See e.g. Basic Law: The Knesset; Basic Law: The President of the State; Basic Law: The Government; Basic Law: The Army. For the full list of the basic laws and their English translation see www.knesset.gov.il/description/eng/eng_mimshal_yesod1.htm (last accessed July 16, 2013).

[3] HCJ 98/69 *Bergman* v. *Minister of Finance and State Comptroller* [1969] IsrSC 23(1) 693, available in English at http://elyon1.court.gov.il/files_eng/69/980/000/Z01/69000980.z01.pdf (last accessed October 8, 2012); HCJ 148/73 *Kaniel* v. *Minister of Justice* [1973] IsrSC 27(1) 794; HCJ 246/81 *Agudat Derekh Eretz* v. *Broadcasting Authority* [1981] IsrSC 35(4) 1, available in English at http://elyon1.court.gov.il/files_eng/81/460/002/Z01/81002460.z01.pdf (last accessed October 8, 2012); HCJ 141/82 *Rubinstein* v. *Chairman of the Knesset* [1983] IsrSC 37(3) 141, available in English at http://elyon1.court.gov.il/files_eng/82/410/001/Z01/82001410.z01.pdf (last accessed October 8, 2012).

[4] See note 7 below.

Court reversed its previous position about the question of judicial review. In a landmark case from 1995 it proclaimed that all basic laws enjoy a constitutional status that is inherently superior to ordinary legislation and that it is the function of the judiciary to intervene and strike down any statute that contradicts the orders of a basic law, unless the basic law itself provided for such contradiction.[5]

These developments, however, did not clear up many questions about the status of the Israeli constitution and did not bring to an end the heated political debate concerning the powers of the judiciary to review statutes of the Knesset. The list of basic rights included in the new basic laws is extremely limited. While The Basic Law: Human Dignity and Liberty asserts the right of every person for personal dignity and privacy, its text does not list fundamental political rights such as freedom of speech, freedom of religion and freedom of assembly that are essential for any bill of rights in a modern liberal democracy.[6] The protection that is given to the rights that are included in the laws is somewhat shaky and much less comprehensive than what is normally provided for by modern constitutions.[7] Moreover, the new basic laws are devoid

[5] CA 6821/93 *United Mizrahi Bank Ltd* v. *Migdal Cooperative Village* [1995] IsrSC 49(4) 221, available in English at: http://elyon1.court.gov.il/files_eng/93/210/068/z01/93068210.z01.pdf (last accessed October 8, 2012).

[6] Nevertheless these rights enjoy some limited constitutional protection according to the rulings of the Supreme Courts, see page 34 below. The list of rights included under the protection of The Basic Law: Human Dignity and Liberty includes the right for preservation of the human body and dignity, privacy, freedom of movement, freedom to leave the State of Israel and to enter it (see the text of the basic law at: www.knesset.gov.il/laws/special/eng/basic3_eng.htm, last accessed July 16, 2013).

[7] The new basic laws provide that they are binding on every state authority and bestow on the courts the power to strike down any legislation that infringes on the basic rights included in these laws. The Knesset is, however, entitled to reform, repeal, or change this law with no need for special majority, as long as the reform is done under the title of a "basic law." The Basic Law: Freedom of Occupation requires – on the other hand – that any legislation that contradicts its orders will be accepted by a special majority of 61 MKs (i.e., more than 50 percent of the members of the house). The fact that the Basic Law: Freedom of Occupation, which is the less important of these two laws, enjoys procedural protection against contradicting legislation that is stronger than the main law of Dignity and Liberty, is, in itself, an anomaly, which demonstrates the hasty and casual process by which the two laws were accepted, see J. Karp, "Basic Law: Human Dignity and Liberty: A Biography of Power Struggles," 1 *Mishpat Umimshal [Law and Government]* 323 (1993). Another shortcoming of the Basic Law: Human Dignity and Liberty is that it only binds on legislation that was passed after its formation, while legislation that was passed prior to 1992 is almost completely immune from its orders. See D. Kretzmer, "The New Basic Laws on Human Rights: A Mini-revolution in Israeli Constitutional Law?," in Zamir and Zysblat, above note, at 141, 146–147.

of any explicit reference to the principle of equality. Therefore equality arguments against the legislation of the Knesset need to be based on the vague statement in these laws concerning their purpose to further "the values of the State of Israel as a Jewish and democratic state."[8] In addition these basic laws were accepted by a narrow majority in the Knesset, without wide political consensus or any extraordinary public process previous to their acceptance.[9]

The most important implication of these constitutional settings for our purposes relates to the position of the judiciary at large and the process of judicial review in particular within the Israeli legal system. As I will demonstrate below, the Israeli judiciary enjoys a high level of autonomy vis-à-vis the executive and the legislative branches. This autonomy, however, is based on structural as well as on political and cultural factors. It does not consist of any firm constitutional protections on the formal level. While the Basic Law: The Judiciary solemnly provides for "complete" judicial autonomy,[10] this basic law itself is always subject to the possibility – at least in theory – of nullification or change by the Knesset.

Moreover, due to their incomplete content and unsteady status, the new basic laws did not bring about any positive change to this insecure constitutional status of the judiciary. Arguably, they seem to have done the reverse. They gave the judiciary the power to review legislation but without providing the courts with the necessary protections for their own constitutional status. The Israeli Supreme Court, on its part, was quick to pick up the glove that the Knesset had thrown to it in 1992 and to use

[8] See Basic Law: Human Dignity and Liberty (Art. 1A): "The purpose of this Basic Law is to protect human dignity and liberty, in order to establish in a Basic Law the values of the State of Israel as a Jewish and democratic State." The term "Jewish and democratic" appears both in the new basic laws and in other legislation of the Knesset, and its meaning was subject to much debate among scholars, see e.g. R. Gavison, "Jewish and Democratic? A Rejoinder to the 'Ethnic Democracy' Debate," 4 *Isr. Stud.* 44 (1999).

[9] See Karp, above note 7, at 326–343. The acceptance of the new Basic Laws in 1992 is often described by commentators as an attempt to preserve the political hegemony of Israel's secular-bourgeoisie elites against the erosion of their power within the political system after the political change following the 1977 elections and the rise of the right-wing religious coalition formed by Prime Minister Menachem Begin. See e.g. R. Hirschl, *Towards Juristocracy: The Origins and Consequences of the New Constitutionalism* (Cambridge, MA: Harvard University Press, 2004), 21–22; T. Ginsburg, *Judicial Review in New Democracies: Constitutional Courts in Asian Cases* (Cambridge University Press, 2003), 57–58.

[10] Section 2 of the Basic Law: The Judiciary provides that "A person vested with judicial power shall not, in judicial matters, be subject to any authority but that of the Law." This basic law contains many more provisions that deal with judicial independence. See below.

the new basic laws to further broaden its judicial review powers. By doing so, however, it did not secure the status of its judicial review powers, but rather made the debate concerning the legitimacy of judicial review more tense than ever before.[11]

2. *The court system and the HCJ*

The origins of the Israeli system are tied to the British legal system that was formed in Palestine during the era of the British Mandate (1917–1948). Despite the fact that Israeli courts have stopped being subject to the appellate jurisdiction of the Privy Council immediately after 1948, the judicial system of Israel continued to be heavily influenced by the British legal order for many years after the establishment of the Israeli State. While terminating British rule immediately after establishment, the founders of Israel preserved 99 percent of the elements of the former system created by the British authorities before the establishment (with the exception of some statutes that inhibit Jewish immigration to Palestine or were in other ways directly contrary to the interests of the new Zionist government). This means that the whole structure of the court system established under the British Mandate was kept intact (although new judges were appointed by Israel). Apart from preserving the material body of law and the procedural fundamentals of an adversarial system, the Israeli legal system preserved also its professional affiliation with the English legal tradition. This is probably because the legal education of most lawyers and judges in the newly born state was acquired in England (or along the lines of the English tradition in the only law school in Palestine).[12] Therefore, the English common law continued to be an important legal source for Israeli judges long after the establishment and in fact, the structure of the Israeli judicial system has been preserved to a great extent up to the present day.[13]

The court system of Israel is based on three levels: the Supreme Courts, District Courts and Magistrates' Courts. The two latter levels are trial courts and they are distinguished according to the gravity of the matter. Thus, in the criminal sphere, the jurisdiction of the Magistrates' Courts is restricted to matters of limited maximum sentences. In civil law, their

[11] See Hirschl, above note 9, at 68–71; Y. Dotan, "Constitution to Israel? The Constitutional Dialog After the 'Constitutional Revolution'," 28 *Mishpatim [Law]* 149 (1997).

[12] See A. Likhovski, "The Invention of 'Hebrew Law' in Mandatory Palestine" 46 *Am. J. Comp. L.* 339, 346 (1998).

[13] See Zysblat, above note 1, at 2–3.

jurisdiction is limited according to the amount of the claim and to claims that do not refer directly to ownership of immovable property. The jurisdiction of the District Courts is residual and includes "any civil or criminal matter that is not within the exclusive jurisdiction of another tribunal." In addition, the District Courts rule on "appeals from judgments and other decisions of the Magistrates' Courts."[14]

The Supreme Court of Israel has three different functions. First, it serves as an appellate court for those cases that were disposed by the District Courts as trial courts. Secondly, it serves as a court of cassation for those cases that were disposed by the Magistrates' Courts at first instance and then appealed to the District Court. In such cases the party that lost on the appellate level is entitled to apply for special leave for a (second) appeal to the Supreme Court.[15] Thirdly – and most importantly for our purposes – it is the High Court of Justice (HCJ). In this capacity the Supreme Court serves in essence as the primary trial court for judicial review cases, that is, as a first and last instance for all the cases which fall under its jurisdiction.

This function of the Supreme Court as HCJ is peculiar. Unlike civil disputes or criminal cases that are disposed by a lower court at the first instance, controversies in which public agencies are involved as respondent, make their way *directly* to the Supreme Court. This is true for any judicial review case unless a specific statute provided for another forum to dispose judicial review cases in the relevant field or unless the Supreme Court otherwise ordered. In recent years, and due to the heavy caseload on the Supreme Court, there is a gradual process of moving certain administrative controversies to the lower echelons. This was done first by rulings of the Supreme Court itself and later on by legislation. Nevertheless, even today the HCJ continues to function as the first and last instance for a substantial part of all administrative actions in Israel.[16]

[14] See Courts Law (Consolidated Version) 1984, section 40, and Zysblat, above note 1, at 13–14. Apart from the regular law courts there are some tribunals with jurisdiction on special matters. The most prominent of these are the Religious Courts that enjoy exclusive jurisdiction on matters of marriage and divorce. They also have jurisdiction on other matrimonial issues and on matters related to personal status which is not exclusive. Other important tribunals are the military tribunals and the labor tribunals, see Zysblat, above note 1, at 11–13.

[15] Courts Law (Consolidated Version) 1984, section 41(2).

[16] During the 1990s the Supreme Court stated in a number of cases that it had the power to direct that certain administrative law issues will be disposed by the regular courts (see e.g. HCJ 1921/94 *Soker* v. *The Commission for Building and Industry* [1994] IsrSC 48(4) 237; HCJ 991/91 *Pasternak* v. *Minister of Housing and Building* [1991] IsrSC 45(5) 50). In 2000 the Knesset passed the Administrative Law Courts Act (2000). This statute provides

This extraordinary structure of the judiciary in the public law field is not the result of a pre-planned process. Rather, it is the result of a set of circumstances that amounts to a historical coincidence. As mentioned before, the newly born State of Israel inherited the judicial structure of the British Mandate. The institution of the HCJ is, in principle, parallel to the institution of the English High Court of Justice, that is to the "High Courts" in England that serve even today as the principal forum for judicial review cases.[17] The High Courts in England carry their name to distinguish them from Magistrates' Courts and other lower tribunals. They are not, however, the highest judicial echelons in England.[18] In the mandatory Palestine, however, the British rulers purposely arranged so that petitions for judicial review would be referred to the Supreme Court (which was set to be the High Court of Justice). The reason for this was that unlike the District Court and the Magistrates' Courts which were populated mainly by "native" judges (i.e. native Jews or Palestinians), the Supreme Court was composed of judges of British origin (or, otherwise, judges with strong affiliation to the Mandatory regime). In other words, the British regime of Palestine was willing to allow the lower courts that disposed ordinary civil and criminal cases to be populated by "native" judges. It made sure, however, that judicial review cases – i.e. petitions

that judicial review applications, appeals against administrative decisions, and other administrative claims in the fields specified by the statute should be issued to the District Court (sitting as "Court for Administrative Matters"), while the HCJ would serve as an appellate division for these matters. The new legislation, however, refers only to matters specified in the statute, such as licensing, decisions of municipalities, zoning committees etc., while preserving the residual function of the HCJ to serve as a trial court in all other fields of administrative controversies. The list of matters in which the administrative courts have original jurisdiction under the statute has been expanded since the early 2000s. Still, the HCJ has original jurisdiction in all matters that have not been specified in this list. In addition the statute preserves the original jurisdiction of the HCJ to dispose issues of particular importance (such as in petitions that refer to the validity of regulations), even in those fields specified in the statute (see the Administrative Law Courts Act (2000), section 5). Moreover, the new law provides that the HCJ is entitled to seize jurisdiction on every administrative action, even in fields dealt with by the statute, should it so decide (the Administrative Courts Law, 2000, section 6 and HCJ 2208/02 *Salame* v. *Minister of the Interior* [2002] IsrSCs 56(5) 950). In addition, the Administrative Courts Law provides that cases disposed by the Administrative Courts (at first instance) may be appealed to the Supreme Court (see the Administrative Law Courts Act (2000), section 11).

17 See I. Zamir, *Adjudication in Administrative Cases* (The Harry Sacher Institution, 1975), 80–84.

18 Rather, the High Courts in England are trial courts whose decisions are subject to appeal to the Court of Appeal and to the Supreme Court (formally The House of Lords), see The Constitutional Reform Act 2005, section 7.

issued *against the crown* – would be tried by judges of British origin who were nominated to the Supreme Court and whose loyalty to the government was beyond any doubt.

This was the state of affairs when Israel was born. During the first few years after establishment Israel was busy enough with its bitter war against its Arab neighbors, as well as with its struggle with a difficult economic crisis and a huge wave of Jewish immigration that flouted the State. No wonder that at that stage nobody in the newly born state had the time or energy to deal with structural reform in the judiciary. During the 1950s, however, this unplanned judicial structure, and more particularly the institution of the HCJ, soon became a powerful and successful judicial institution. Therefore, any plans to reform the system were soon confronted by strong opposition, both on the part of legal professionals that pointed to the (albeit unplanned) advantages of the institution and on the part of political circles that viewed the court as a central pillar of Israeli democracy.[19] The peculiar structure of the Israeli judiciary is, therefore, the combined result of historical distortion and political reality. This structure bears, of course, a series of important consequences that will be discussed below.

3. *Judicial independence*

The Israeli judiciary enjoys a high level of independence and autonomy vis-à-vis the other branches of the government.[20] Judicial independence is guaranteed by the Basic Law: The Judiciary. Independence is also strengthened by the fact that the judges of all levels are appointed for a permanent tenure that continues until retirement at the age of 70. Judges enjoy salaries that are very high in comparison to other public employees. They cannot be removed from office except by a decision of the Court of Discipline, consisting of judges appointed by the Chief Justice of the Supreme Court, or upon a decision of the Judges' Election Committee at the proposal of the Minister of Justice or the Chief Justice of the Supreme Court. The canon of judicial autonomy in Israel is, however, the system of appointment of judges. The appointments of judges at all levels are made by the Judges' Election Committee. The committee is composed of nine members. It

[19] See Zysblat, above note 1, at 14; S. Shetreet, "Reflections on the Protection of the Rights of the Individual: Form and Substance," 12 *Isr. L. Rev.* 32, 34 (1977); Zamir, above note 17, at 125–128.

[20] See generally S. Shetreet, *On Adjudication: Justice on Trial* (Jerusalem: Yedioth Aharonot, 2004), 206.

includes the Chief Justice of the Supreme Court and two other Supreme Court Judges, the Minister of Justice and one other minister (traditionally a jurist by training), two members of the Knesset (of whom one is traditionally a member of the opposition) and two representatives of the Israeli Bar. This composition assures that the process of appointment is largely immune from any pressures or influences on behalf of the government, political parties or any other organization outside the judiciary itself, since the majority in the committee are not party politicians.[21] Furthermore, a convention has existed throughout the years that a candidate for the Supreme Court will not be selected if the choice is not acceptable to the representative of the court. This convention is but one aspect of the dominance of the Supreme Court in the process of selecting judges. The whole process is bureaucratic and until recent years it was largely hidden from the public eye or media coverage.[22] The names of the potential candidates remain secret until a very late stage, and the content of the committee's discussions remains covert.[23] The three representatives of the Supreme Court appear in the committee after coordinating their positions with all other members of the Supreme Court, and therefore are able to speak with unanimity in the committee.[24] All these factors result in a situation in which

[21] M. Edelman, "The Judicial Elite of Israel," 13 *Int'l Pol. Sci. Rev.* 235, 237 (1992); S. Shetreet, "The Critical Challenge of Judicial Independence in Israel," in P. Russel and D. M. O'Brien (eds.), *Judicial Independence in the Age of Democracy: Critical Perspectives from around the World* (2001), 233; M. L. Volcansek, "Exporting the Missouri Plan: Judicial Appointment Commissions," (in: "Symposium: The Fallacies and Fixables of Merit Selection and the Constituencies that Support Missouri Plan Reform") 74 *Mo. L. Rev.* 783, 787 (2009).

[22] In recent years the appointment process receives much more attention on behalf of the media than before, see e.g. T. Zarchin, referring to a then candidate to the Supreme Court, "This is how Noam Solberg's Road is Paved to the Supreme Court," *Ha'aretz* October 27, 2011.

[23] Zysblat, above note 1. The practice of the committee to avoid publishing the names of the candidates for judicial appointment until after the commission has made its decision was challenged in 1993 before the HCJ. The court dismissed the petitions indicating that it found no reason to interfere with the practices of the committee (HCJ 5771/93 *Zitrin* v. *Minister of Justice* [1993] 48(1) 661). Nevertheless, shortly after this decision the committee reformed its practices to some extent, so that the names of candidates are currently published twenty-one days before the committee discusses their candidacy.

[24] This practice has been criticized as a violation of the duty of each member of the committee to maintain independence in their judgment. In 2004 the law was amended to ensure the independence of each committee member, see Courts Law (Consolidated Version) 1984, section 6a; A. Rubinstein and B. Medina, *The Constitutional Law of Israel* (Tel Aviv: Shoken, 2005), 131. In 2008 the Knesset added a requirement for a qualified majority of seven members of the committee to approve new judicial appointments (see Courts Law (Consolidated Version) 1984, section 7(c)(2)). Since there are three acting justices on the

the selection of judges is heavily influenced by the Justices themselves with relatively little influence from the political branches or any other external forces. Last but not least, the high level of public support and relative popularity of the judiciary within the Israeli public buttresses the independence of the judiciary. This latter factor assures that while the government is capable, in principle, of infringing the independence of the judiciary by resorting to legislative reforms in the Knesset, it would be slow to take such an initiative.[25]

B. The High Court of Justice (HCJ)

In its capacity as the HCJ, the Israeli Supreme Court functions as the first and last instance for most judicial review (and other actions against public agencies) in the country. This peculiar fact, that the Supreme Court has to function in essence as a trial court, has important implications for almost every aspect of its practices. Some of the most prominent aspects of the HCJ on the procedural and structural levels will be discussed in this section. Other aspects that are more related to the court's normative positions and political postures will be discussed in the sections below.

1. *Caseload*

The Supreme Court of Israel is an extremely busy judicial institution. In most countries, the supreme court's primary (and usually exclusive) function is as court of cassation. In addition to this function, the Israeli Supreme Court serves – as mentioned above – as a court of appeal. On top of this, it serves as a trial court for thousands of judicial review cases per year in its HCJ function. Not surprisingly, the caseload of this court is enormous and much heavier than its counterparts in other countries. Thus, for example, in 1993, the court dealt with over 1,400 appellate cases, a similar number of cassation cases and over 1,000 other lawsuits, quite apart from the 1,171 HCJ petitions which were disposed by it during that year. The number of cases increases constantly each year. And in 1997 the Court disposed 1,463 HCJ petitions as part of an overall docket of

committee, this amendment ensures that, as a practical matter, no judicial appointment would be made against the consensus of the acting justices.

[25] See e.g. Hirschl, above note 9, at 69. Additional factors influencing judicial autonomy relate to the autonomy of the legal–bureaucratic apparatus of the state and will be discussed in Chapter 2.

over 6,800 files. In 2003 the Court disposed almost 1,700 petitions and the overall number of files exceeded 11,000.[26]

As Figure 1.1 demonstrates, the caseload in the Israeli Supreme Court is heavy, much heavier than in many other countries.[27] The important question that the data in Figure 1.1 raises is how the fifteen justices of the Israeli Supreme Court cope with such a huge caseload of thousands of appeals, petitions and other types of cases which are brought before them every year.[28] One point that should be mentioned at the outset is that the Supreme Court of Israel (also in its capacity as the HCJ, see below) normally sits in panels of three justices and only rarely sits *en banc* or in panels larger than three.[29] In this respect the Israeli Court differs from other supreme judicial institutions, such as the Supreme Court of the United States, which sits *en banc* in each and every case that is accepted for the full review of the Court.[30] Moreover, the above-mentioned number of

[26] *Source:* The Central Bureau of Statistics (CBS) for the years 1970–1998 and the Research Department of the Judicial Authority for 1998 onward. It should be noted that the measurement methods of the CBS and the Judicial Authority are somewhat different and therefore the comparison between the years before and after 1998 may not be completely accurate. Also, due to the transition of responsibility between these two agencies data for the years 1999–2002 is incomplete.

[27] This is certainly the case if one compares the Israeli Supreme Court to the US Supreme Courts that grants *certiorari* (for full hearing) to less than 100 cases each year (see generally, L. Baum, *The Supreme Court*, 6th edn. (Washington, D.C.: CQ Press, 1998), 121–27). Likewise the Supreme Court of the United Kingdom disposed a total of 220 cases in 2010 (see United Kingdom Ministry of Justice, Judicial and Court Statistics 2010, 148, available at: www.justice.gov.uk/downloads/publications/statistics-and-data/courts-and-sentencing/judicial-court-stats.pdf, last accessed July 16, 2013), while the Supreme Court of Canada disposed around 500 cases in 2010 (see Supreme Court of Canada: Statistics 2002 to 2012, 4, available at: www.scc-csc.gc.ca/case-dossier/stat/index-eng.aspx, last accessed July 16, 2013). The Federal Constitutional Court of Germany, on the other hand, disposed 6422 cases in 2010 (the vast majority of them (6251) were "constitutional complaints") available at: www.bundesverfassungsgericht.de/en/organization/gb2011/A-I-4.html (last accessed July 16, 2013).

[28] According to section 25 of the Courts Law (consolidated version) (1984) the number of the Supreme Court Justices is to be determined by a decision of the Knesset. In 2003 the Knesset decided to increase the number of Supreme Court Justices from twelve to fifteen, see Rubinstein and Medina, above note 24, at 132 and note 19.

[29] According to section 26 of the Courts Law (consolidated version) (1984) the Chief Justice of the Supreme Court has the power to extend panels in certain cases of particular importance, but this power is used, in practice, only in a handful of cases each year.

[30] Likewise the Supreme Courts of Canada sits *en banc* in all cases which are granted leave for appeals (see reference in above note 27) and so does the *Conseil Constitutionnel* in France (available at: www.conseil-constitutionnel.fr/conseil-constitutionnel/english/presentation/presentation.25739.html, last accessed July 16, 2013). The German Constitutional Court sits in two panels (available at: www.bundesverfassungsgericht.de/en/organization/organization.html, last accessed July 16, 2013).

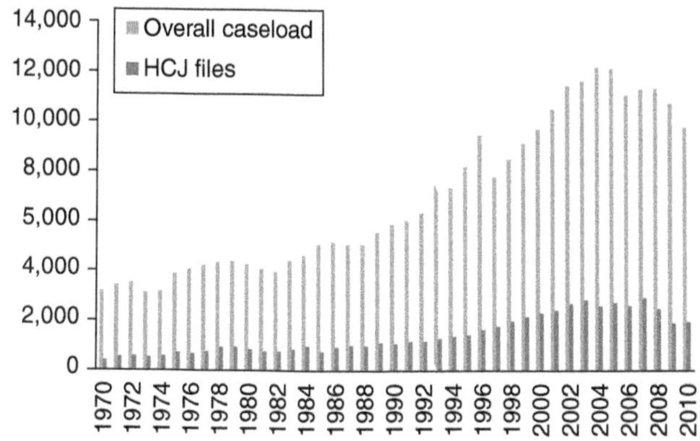

Figure 1.1 HCJ files and overall caseload in the Supreme Court 1970–2010
Source: The Central Bureau of Statistics (CBS) for the years 1970–1998 and the Research Department of the Judicial Authority for 1998 onward.[31]

cases brought to the Israeli Supreme Court is somewhat misleading, since a great proportion of these cases are applications for leaves for appeal and other "miscellaneous requests" that are normally disposed by one judge. Even in appeal cases, not all cases are fully disposed by all three justices on the bench since in some types of cases there are procedures that allow the Court to shift most of the burdens of such cases to one of the justices, while limiting the amount of work the other two members of the panel need to invest in those cases.[32] Even so the burden that this caseload puts on the justices is extraordinary.

This burden is particularly cumbersome in the case of the HCJ, since in this capacity the Court has to function as a trial court for around 2,000 cases per year. How do the justices of the Supreme Court cope with this caseload? Part of the answer to this question lies in the HCJ's procedures and practices, and will be dealt with in the current chapter. The other part of the answer relates to the function of the government lawyers who appear before this court, and this will be dealt with as we move to the next chapters.

[31] The data regarding HCJ files for the years 1999–2002 is an estimation, see above note 26. The data referring to HCJ files after 2002 includes also administrative appeals (i.e. appeals against administrative petitions disposed of by the Courts for Administrative Matters, see above note 16).

[32] See e.g. section 448 of the Code of Civil Procedures Regulations (1984) that enables the court to order that the procedure be based on written arguments without oral hearing.

2. *Procedures and (in)formalities*

The procedures in the HCJ are characterized by simplicity, brevity, and expediency. A petition to the HCJ can be written by a layman, and at no stage of the proceedings is representation by a lawyer required.[33] Any person who has reason to believe that a particular public agency denies their legal rights may petition the court and apply for a conditional order (order *nisi*). A single judge reviews the petition. The judge may order a preliminary hearing before three justices to take place, requiring the respondent to supply the court with a concise statement as to the reasons and background for the relevant governmental action. Alternatively, the judge may issue a conditional order, requiring the respondent to appear in court and show why a particular action should or should not be performed. A full hearing before three judges would then be held before the court reaches its final decision. Hearings are based on the parties' affidavits and on their oral arguments. Unlike in civil or criminal cases, oral testimonies as well as cross-examination are rarely allowed.[34] The court is able to grant petitioners immediate relief and to issue orders and injunctions, either interim or absolute, at any stage.

This highly informal and relatively simple and concise procedure may also serve as an explanation for the expediency of the HCJ as a trial court. In fact, the above-mentioned description does not tell the whole story of this expediency. From reading the HCJ procedure regulations one may get the impression that each and every case that reaches the HCJ is being processed through *both* stages that are included in the regulations, i.e. the *preliminary* hearing by the single judge *and* the *full* hearing before the panel of three justices after the parties' affidavits are issued. The reality, however, is quite different. The vast majority (around 80 percent) of cases dealt with by the HCJ are disposed at the stage of the preliminary hearing without any order *nisi* being issued.[35] This means that most petitions to

[33] Despite the lack of formal requirement for legal representation most petitioners to the HCJ are represented by lawyers (see Y. Dotan, "Do the 'Haves' Still Come Out Ahead? Resource Inequalities in Ideological Courts: The Case of the Israeli High Court of Justice," 33 *Law & Soc'y Rev.* 1059, 1071–1073 (1999) and see Chapter 3, Table 3.1 and accompanying text).

[34] According to the High Court of Justice Procedure Regulations (1984), section 18, cross-examination requires the approval of the court. In practice cross-examination in the HCJ is extremely rare. See I. Zamir, "Evidence in the High Court of Justice," 1 *Mishpat Umimshal [Law and Government]* 295, 312 (1993).

[35] Thus, for example, according to the data of the Central Bureau of Statistics of Israel, out of 4,266 cases disposed by the HCJ between 1985 and 1993, an order nisi was issued in

the HCJ are disposed through the following procedure. First, the petitioner issues the written petition that should be supported by a written affidavit. Then, the relevant agency against whom the petition is issued is required by the court to issue a responding notice in which it should answer the arguments raised by the petition. Then, the petition is brought to the preliminary hearing before three justices. This preliminary hearing is normally very short and concise, seldom taking more than one hour and often ends after a couple of minutes.[36] Only then does the court decide whether to issue a conditional order (i.e. to order the case to be heard through the full procedure) or whether to terminate the procedure at the preliminary stage – which it normally does. This means that about 80 percent of the petitions to the HCJ are being disposed through an extremely short hearing. Moreover, this concise procedure is almost completely devoid of *any* testimony on behalf of the respondents, since the responding notice is normally not required to be supported by an affidavit on behalf of the respondents.[37]

This procedure can without doubt be described as "concise" and "expedient" and can well serve as an additional explanation as to how the HCJ copes with its huge caseload. But before praising this procedure for its "expediency" one might raise serious questions as to its effectiveness. Can a process that is so short and devoid of procedural protection serve as an effective shield for the rights of the petitioner? And how, if at all, can the court reach sufficient understanding of the issues at stake through a procedure that is so different from the normal procedures that are accepted

just 886 cases. (*Source:* Central Bureau of Statistics). See also Zamir, above note 33, at 300. Accordingly, in our database for cases disposed by the HCJ during the 1990s conditional orders were issued in around 21 percent of all cases. During the 1970s, however, the relative number of cases disposed by such orders was significantly higher (around 37 percent). This issue will be discussed in detail in Chapter 3 below.

36 Accordingly, the overall time for the disposal of petitions in the HCJ is much shorter than in other civil proceedings in the Supreme Court. Thus, for example, in 1993 the median time for petitions in which a conditional order was not issued was 2.4 months (as compared to around 5 months for petitions in which a conditional order was issued). The median time for civil appeals in the same year was 20.1 months (*Source:* Central Bureau of Statistics). Accordingly, in our database (see Chapter 3 Section B) around 60 percent of all petitions issued during the 1970s in which the court did not issue a conditional order were disposed of within less than a month, while during the 1990s one third of such petitions were disposed of within less than a month and around 55 percent were disposed of within less than three months.

37 See the High Court of Justice Procedure Regulations (1984), section 7(b1). The implications of this point will be further discussed below, see Chapter 4, p. 127.

in adversarial legal systems? As I will argue throughout this book, the answer to these questions has much to do with the role of the government lawyers and other mechanisms working within the HCJ.

In order to conclude the descriptions of the procedures of the HCJ there is one additional factor that should be referred to. This is the highly informal and flexible nature of the procedure. As mentioned before, the procedure in the HCJ is extremely simple and devoid of cumbersome and complicated requirements.[38] There are no rigid requirements as to the form of the pleadings or as to the behavior within the courtroom. The justices on the bench have almost absolute control over every aspect of the function of the court. Nor is the court binding itself to the ordinary constraints of the rules of evidence. While, formally, the arguments by the parties are required to be supported by affidavits, on many occasions the arguments of the petitioners are based on information taken from the press or on official or semi-official reports not admissible in regular courts of law. The powers of the court and the limits of its jurisdiction were prescribed by the legislature in a wide and open language.[39] The few limitations that do exist in statute have been washed away by the highly "liberal" interpretation by the HCJ itself.[40] The result is that, today, there are hardly any formal limitations for the HCJ if it decides that it wishes to

[38] The point may be illustrated by comparing the number of procedural regulations. The number of clauses included in the Code of Civil Procedure Regulations consists of over 500 different (and sometimes complex) clauses. The High Court of Justice Procedural Regulations is a short set of regulations containing no more than twenty-three clauses. Section 20(c) allows the court to refer to the Code of Civil Procedure Regulations as complementary, but the court seldom takes advantage of this option.

[39] Section 15 of the Basic Law: The Judiciary provides as follows: (c) The Supreme Court shall sit also as a High Court of Justice. When so sitting, it shall hear matters in which it deems it necessary to grant relief for the sake of justice and which are not within the jurisdiction of another court (beit mishpat or beit din). (d) Without prejudice to the generality of the provisions of subsection (c), the Supreme Court sitting as a High Court of Justice shall be competent – (1) to make orders for the release of persons unlawfully detained or imprisoned. (2) to order State and local authorities and the officials and bodies thereof, and other persons carrying out public functions under law, to do or refrain from doing any act in the lawful exercise of their functions or, if they were improperly elected or appointed, to refrain from acting. For the full text of this basic law see www.knesset.gov.il/laws/special/eng/basic8_eng.htm (last accessed July 16, 2013).

[40] Thus, for example, section 15(c) of the Basic Law: The Judiciary grants the HCJ judicial review jurisdiction only in cases that "are not within the jurisdiction of another court." The HCJ has largely ignored this limitation, see e.g. HCJ 6163/92 *Eisenberg* v. *The Minister of Building and Housing* [1993] IsrSC 47(2) 229, available in English at http://elyon1.court.gov.il/files_eng/92/630/061/Z01/92061630.z01.pdf (last accessed October 8, 2012), and see also R. Gavison, M. Kremnitzer and Y. Dotan, *Judicial Activism at the High Court of Justice* (Jerusalem: Magnes, 2000), 9–11.

hear a certain case.[41] Other limitations that may normally preclude judicial review, such as time limitations or requirements for the exhaustion of alternative remedies, have also been subject to liberal interpretation that has left them largely subject to the wide discretion of the HCJ itself.[42] The Court has also developed a wide array of judicial remedies that allows itself wide discretionary latitude to cope with various scenarios in which it needs to intervene in governmental decisions.[43]

3. *Access*

Another notable aspect of the HCJ is the ease of access to the court. One must bear in mind that the HCJ is the Supreme Court of Israel functioning as a trial court for administrative matters. I doubt whether there is any other Supreme Court around the world to which the access is as easy as the HCJ. Some of the aspects regarding the ease of access have already been mentioned above: the lack of any screening by any other forum prior to the issuance of the petition and the lack of cumbersome formal requirements. Other relevant factors in this regard have to do with the substantial legal doctrines developed by the HCJ throughout the years and will be dealt with below.[44] For the present stage I will refer to some additional institutional elements that influence the ease of access.

Apart from formal procedural requirements, an important factor that influences access to judicial institutions is the costs of litigation. In this regard, litigation before the HCJ is low-cost. The court's fees are significantly lower compared to those that apply in civil matters,[45] and the simplicity of the procedures also contributes to ease the financial burden of

[41] Indeed, the court itself developed throughout the years rules and practices that preclude certain types of action from being brought to the HCJ (instead of being issued in a civil court or any other tribunal) but these rules themselves are discretionary and do not preclude the court from seizing jurisdiction in cases which it is interested to hear, see above note 16.

[42] See Gavison *et al.*, above note 39. Thus, for example, the requirement of *laches* in the HCJ is subject to the discretion of the court to entertain judicial review even when the petition has been issued long after the administrative decision at stake had been taken, see e.g. HCJ 170/87 *Asulin* v. *Mayor of Kiryat Gat* [1988] IsrSC 42(1) 678.

[43] See Y. Dotan, "Non-Delegation and the Reformulation of Legality," 42 *Mishpatim [Law]* 397 (2012).

[44] See also Section C.2 below.

[45] Currently court fees are around 1,700 NIS (equivalent to $450). During most of the research period, however, court fees were much lower (approximately the equivalent of $100) and were significantly raised after the passage of the Administrative Law Courts Act (2000), see above note 16.

litigation. While legal aid services (by the state) are scarce in public law litigation, there is a developed network of non-governmental organizations that provide legal services for many disadvantaged petitioners.[46] Moreover, petitioners to the HCJ are normally subject to only a minimal risk of being ordered by the court to reimburse the other party for their costs in the case of defeat. Normally, the Israeli system adopts the principle that the party who loses the litigation has to reimburse the winning party for the costs of litigation. In the HCJ, however, the risk of incurring these costs is minimal. While in civil litigation an order for costs against the defeated party is the normal rule, the HCJ normally refrains from issuing such orders. This is particularly so when the petitioner is an individual who issues the petitions to assert some civil liberties, or when they belong to a disadvantaged group (such as minorities, immigrants and so forth).[47] In such cases the court would seldom issue an order for costs against the petitioner, and when this is done, it will normally be after the court has warned the petitioner about the potential risk and offered an opportunity to withdraw the petition.[48] Even when costs are ordered, they are normally much lower than in civil litigation. The data concerning the costs of litigation is shown in Figure 1.2.

As we can see from Figure 1.2, in the vast majority of cases disposed of during the 1970s and the 1990s the HCJ refrained from imposing costs when petitions were dismissed. Only in around 12 percent of all petitions dismissed did the court impose costs on the petitioners. Moreover, there was a clear difference between different categories in this respect. In the case of petitions issued by commercial corporations the HCJ imposed costs in around 45 percent of all petitions dismissed by court decision while in the case of individual petitioners the court refrained from imposing costs

[46] See the discussion in Section C.2 near note 75 below and Chapter 5.

[47] See Dotan, above note 32, at 1062 and note 7 *id* (only in 8 percent of the cases disposed of between 1986 and 1995 that involved indigenous or other "have-nots" petitioners did the court impose costs when the petition was dismissed). It should be noted that recently the HCJ shows signals of a possible change in its policy regarding litigation costs. For example, the court imposed costs on NGOs that challenged the privatization of hospitals, see HCJ 2114/12 *Association of Civil Rights in Israel* v. *Government of Israel* (August 15, 2012).

[48] Practitioners who often appear before the HCJ report that the court refrains from imposing costs on petitioners in many cases of dismissals, unless the petitioner has some "fault" on their part. Such a fault may be related to misbehavior during the process (such as failing to disclose an important fact to the court), or an obstinate refusal to withdraw the petition despite suggestions on the part of the justices to do so. The court is particularly slow to impose costs on the petitioner in cases where the petition, despite its dismissal, raises an important public issue, see Dotan, above note 32, at 1062.

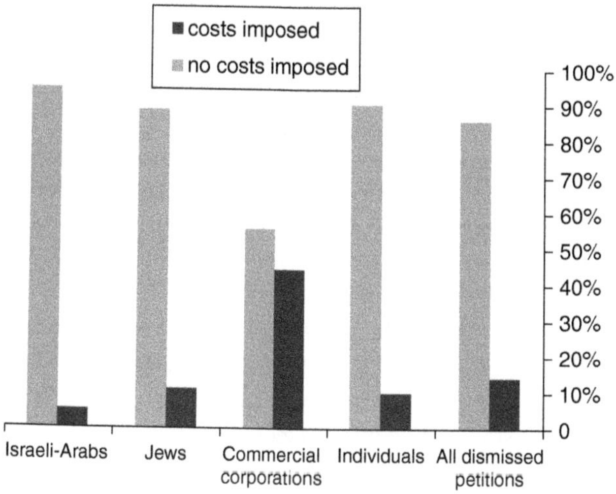

Figure 1.2 Costs imposed by the HCJ, by petitioner's identity – 1970s and 1990s
Source: HCJ files.[49]

in around 90 percent of all cases. The rate of dismissals that were accompanied by the imposition of costs was even lower in the case of minority Arab petitioners (around 5 percent).

C. Judicial activism in the HCJ

"Judicial Activism" is far from being a precise scientific concept that can be accurately defined and empirically quantified. In fact, the term is notorious for being amorphous and slippery.[50] One reason for the lack of agreement regarding the content of "activism" is that the term has acquired many distinct and even contradictory meanings.[51] The other principal reason is that the term "activist" always involves some value-based

[49] The figure refers only to petitions dismissed by the HCJ. For more details on the database and methods see Chapter 3.

[50] As one scholar noted that "as the term becomes more commonplace, its meaning has become increasingly unclear." See K. D. Kmiec, "The Origin and Current Meaning of 'Judicial Activism'," 92 *Cal. L. Rev.* 1441, 1443 (2004) and see also F. H. Easterbrook, "Do Liberals and Conservatives Differ in Judicial Activism?," 73 *U. Colo. L. Rev.* 1401 (2002).

[51] Among the various meanings of the term scholars include the following: (1) second-guessing the federal political branches or state governments; (2) departing from text and/or history; (3) departing from judicial precedent; (4) issuing broad or "maximalist" holdings rather than narrow or "minimalist" ones; (5) exercising broad remedial powers; and

judgment on behalf of the one who makes the observation and usually carries negative connotations.[52]

Those difficulties aside, there is a wide consensus among scholars that the Israeli Supreme Court has become increasingly activist since the 1980s.[53] Since one of the objectives of this book is to describe the relationship between the shifts in the practices of the HCJ in Israel in judicial review and the functions of the legal apparatus representing the state before this court, it is important to review the process of the rise of judicial activism in the HCJ throughout the research period. In the following sections I shall bring an overview of the developments in the doctrines and practices of the HCJ. In Chapter 3 I shall focus on one dimension of judicial activism, the rise in the relative number of cases in which the HCJ interfered and reversed decisions made by the elected branches.[54]

1. *The "Old Court" – from establishment to 1980*

The Israeli Supreme Court has been traditionally regarded as a strong, independent, and prestigious institution within the Israeli polity. Since the establishment of the state, and despite the absence of a written constitution (see above), the court succeeded in establishing its judicial review powers over the Israeli executive. Shortly after Israel was established, and in the middle of a war that seriously threatened the very existence of the state, the Supreme Court struck down a decision made by military authorities to detain an Arab resident of Jaffa using their powers under emergency regulations. The court ruled that the detention was illegal due to the failure of the authorities to follow the procedure set by the regulations

(6) deciding cases according to the partisan political preferences of the judges. See e.g. B. C. Canon, "Defining the Dimensions of Judicial Activism," 66 *Judicature* 236 (1983); W. P. Marshall, "Conservatives and the Seven Sins of Judicial Activism," 73 *U. Colo. L. Rev.* 1217 (2002); E. A. Young, "Judicial Activism and Conservative Politics," 73 *U. Colo. L. Rev.* 1139, 1142 (2002).

52 See C. R. Sunstein, *Radicals in Robes* (New York: Basic Books), 42; F. B. Cross and S. A. Lindquist, "The Scientific Study of Judicial Activism," 91 *Minn. L. Rev.* 1752 (2007).

53 See e.g. Gavison *et al.*, above note 39, at 5, 60; M. Mautner, *Law and Culture in Israel at the Threshold of the Twenty First Century* (Tel Aviv: Am Oved, 2008), 126 *et. seq.*; M. Edelman, "Israel," in C. Neal and T. Vallinder (eds.), *The Global Expansion of Judicial Power* (New York University Press, 1995), 403, 407; R. Posner, "Enlightened Despot," *The New Republic,* April 2007 (Review of *The Judge in a Democracy* by Aharon Barak, 2006). For more references see Mautner, above, at note 3.

54 The frequency by which judicial institutions reverse decisions of the elected branches is considered "the most common standard for evaluating judicial activism," see Cross and Lindquist, above note 50, at 1759.

and ordered the release of the detainee. Thereby it established its judicial review powers over the executive branch in general and the military authorities by stating: "The authorities are bound by the law like any other citizen in the State. And the rule of law is one of the fundamental principles of the State."[55]

This firm statement establishing the principle of rule of law was followed by a number of cases in which the courts developed doctrines to serve as tools for judicial review, such as the principle that government agencies should not exceed the powers bestowed on them by the legislator (the *ultra vires* doctrine), and the requirement that agencies should follow not only the written letter of the law but also its underlying purposes, and refrain from abuse of discretion. Other principles developed by the courts were the principle of equality and the prohibition against discrimination in administrative action, as well as procedural requirements of fairness in administrative actions.[56]

At the same time the courts used creative techniques of statutory interpretation in order to establish legal principles for the protection of individual rights. A good example is the celebrated decision in the *Kol Ha'am* case. There, the Supreme Court struck down a decision of the Minister of the Interior to order the suspension of the publication of a communist newspaper for a period of ten days. The ministerial order was issued after the newspaper published some articles that criticized the state's foreign policy and were regarded by the government as containing false information that was harmful to the public interest. The court ruled that the government is not allowed to use its powers to restrict the freedom of the press unless it can demonstrate that the restriction is necessary due to an immediate and serious danger for the security of the state or the public order. There was nothing in the language of the press ordinance, on which the Minister founded his initial action, that pointed to the creation of such a requirement. The court, however, used the Declaration of Independence as a canon of interpretation, in order to read into a British-colonial ordinance – which was enacted in order to restrict the freedom of

[55] HCJ 7/48 *El-Karbotli* v. *Minister of Defence* [1949] IsrSC 2 5, 15.

[56] HCJ 98,105/54 *Lezarovitz* v. *The Food Inspector* [1956] IsrSC 10 40; I. Zamir, "Administrative Law," in Zamir and Zysblat, above note 1, at 18. The development of the principles of judicial review during the early period was influenced by administrative law doctrines in the UK. Gradually, however, the link to UK law weakened with the rise of judicial activism, see Y. Shachar, R. Haris and M. Gross, "Reference Patterns of the Supreme Court: A Quantitative Analysis," 27 *Mishpatim [Law]* 119, 157–159 (1996) (reporting a decline in the relative number of references by the Supreme Court to UK law and a rise in the number of references to US law throughout the years and in particular after 1980).

the press – some constitutional principles taken from the jurisprudence of constitutional democracies with an established bill of rights.[57] Using similar interpretative techniques the Supreme Court developed guarantees for other human rights such as freedom of demonstration and procession, freedom of association, freedom of occupation and the right for privacy. Over the years, the willingness of the court to rigorously develop such human rights protection by using creative methods of statutory interpretation and by resorting to foreign jurisprudence of established constitutional democracies (such as the United States and Canada) has granted those principles a semi-constitutional status. In theory, these judicially acknowledged freedoms were always subject to infringement by clear-cut language of the Knesset. In practice, however, the Knesset seldom used its sovereign supremacy in order to limit those freedoms and seldom used legislative initiative in order to reverse such judicial decisions. These developments led some commentators to view this body of judicial rulings as Israel's "unwritten constitution" that contains, among other principles "an unwritten bill of rights."[58]

Notwithstanding the willingness of the Supreme Court to step in to defend human rights and to vigorously develop doctrines of judicial review, it managed to keep a very low public profile during the period between establishment and the beginning of the 1980s. Throughout this

[57] HCJ 73,87/53 *Kol Ha'am* v. *Minister of the Interior* [1953] IsrSC 7 871, available in English at http://elyon1.court.gov.il/files_eng/53/730/000/Z01/53000730.z01.pdf (last accessed October 8, 2012); B. Bracha, "The Protection of Human Rights in Israel," *12 Israel Yearbook of Human Rights* 12 (1982) 110; A. Zysblat, "Protecting Fundamental Rights in Israel without a Written Constitution," in Zamir and Zysblat, above note 1, at 47. For a detailed historic account of the development of *Kol Ha'am* jurisprudence see P. Lahav, *Judgment in Jerusalem: Chief Justice Simon Agranat and the Zionist Century* (Berkeley: University of California Press, 1997), 107–112.

[58] See D. Barak-Erez, "From an Unwritten to a Written Constitution: The Israeli Challenge in American Perspective," 26 *Colum. Hum. Rts. L. Rev.* 309 (1995); Lahav, above note 55, at 90–92. It should be noted, however, that the protections given by this unwritten bill of rights were severely limited in some respects. They could not withstand direct legislation aimed at infringing on human rights (see Section A.1 above). They were also able to ameliorate only to some extent the impact of emergency legislation (mostly British legislation that was preserved by Israel after the establishment of the State). And, they were applied by the courts in a much less activist manner in favor of Arab-Israelis and Palestinians in the context of state security than towards the Jewish population in other contexts. R. Shamir, "'Landmark Cases' and the Reproduction of Legitimacy: The Case of Israel's High Court of Justice," 24 *Law & Soc'y Rev.* 781 (1990); G. Barzilai, "Fantasies of Liberalism and Liberal Jurisprudence: State Law and Israeli Arab-Palestinian Community," 34 *Isr. L. Rev.* 425 (2000); Y. Dotan, "Judicial Rhetoric, Government Lawyers and Human Rights: The Case of the High Court of Justice during the Intifada," 33 *Law & Soc'y Rev.* 319 (1999).

period the court was careful to keep itself distanced from any involvement in political controversies or heated public debates. A number of doctrines and strategies were adopted by the court to assure minimal exposure to intensive political involvement. First, the Court imposed strict limitations on the ability of litigants to raise political issues in court. The concept of "standing" adopted by the HCJ during this period was designed to keep the court within the safe boundaries of an institution whose main function is to decide controversies between individuals and the state rather than issues reflecting clashes of interests between opposing factions in society. In order to meet the requirement of standing, the petitioner had to show direct and substantial interest in the state action at stake. The court held that a mere infringement upon religious feelings or ideological convictions of the petitioner is unlikely to satisfy this requirement.[59]

Moreover, even when petitioners could show that state actions caused them some *material* damage, they were likely to be denied standing if the same action caused similar harm to a large group of other people or to the whole sector of which they formed a part. This narrow concept allowed the court to refrain from interfering in sensitive political issues in the areas of religion and state, and law enforcement with respect to high-ranking political figures.[60] One important implication of this policy was that it reduced significantly the ability of political parties, interest groups, and other organized litigators to use the court as an arena to promote their political agenda.

The rules of standing were not the only factor inhibiting the use of litigation by organized interests. Another concept with similar effects was justiciability. During this period the Supreme Court adopted a narrow concept of justiciability. Under this concept the court decided that petitions involving issues of foreign policy, military actions, or other questions concerning sensitive political issues were considered "unsuitable" for judicial determination and therefore non-justiciable.[61] The court also adhered to a narrow concept of judicial review. In particular, the HCJ showed an unwillingness to take a close look at certain areas of state activity of major

[59] HCJ 11/79 *Mirkin* v. *Minister of Interior* [1979] IsrSC 33(1) 502; HCJ 331/80 *Hatishbi* v. *Commander of Tel-Aviv Police Station* [1980] IsrSC 34(4) 113; HCJ 287/69 *Meiron* v. *Minister of Employment* [1970] IsrSC 24(1) 337; HCJ 348/70 *Kfir* v. *Religious Council of Ashkelon* [1971] IsrSC 25(1) 685; HCJ 26/76 *Bar Shalom* v. *Israel Land Administration* [1977] IsrSC 31(1) 796.

[60] *Meiron* v. *Minister of Employment*, above note 57; *Kfir* v. *Religious Council of Ashkelon*, above note 57; *Bar Shalom* v. *Israel Land Administration*, above note 57.

[61] HCJ 561/75 *Ashkenazi* v. *Minister of Defense* [1976] IsrSC 30(3) 309; HCJ 222/68 *Hugim Leumiem* v. *Minister of Police* [1970] IsrSC 24(2) 141.

importance. Thus, even when the court was willing to deal with some matters of sensitive political implication, it developed doctrines that substantially narrowed the scope of review in those matters. For example, the court adopted a narrow concept of review regarding decisions taken by the military and other security agencies.[62] It also adhered to a remarkably narrow concept of review regarding prosecutorial decisions, stating that only in extreme cases of clear *mala-fides* would it be willing to interfere with the decisions taken by the attorney general or other prosecutorial authorities.[63] Apart from these legal principles there were a number of other informal strategies and tactics that were aimed at keeping the court away from political controversies and preserving its low public profile. For example, the opinions given by the justices were relatively short and their reasoning was often founded on professional, legal, and technical-procedural arguments rather than on broad policy statements and value judgments.[64] The justices tried to reach consensus while sitting on the bench. Political conflicts among the justices were often framed and presented as professional disagreements between legal experts rather than frictions caused by opposing moral or political convictions. The low political profile of the court was also preserved since the justices refrained almost entirely from expressing their views on legal matters as well as on other issues while not on the bench, and from appearances in the media.[65]

2. *The "New Court" – judicial activism since 1980*

The 1980s saw a major shift in almost all the aspects of judicial review mentioned above. There was a dramatic change in the principles concerning access to the courts. In its landmark decision in *Ressler* v. *Minister of Defense*, the Supreme Court reversed its prior rulings on the issues of standing and justiciability. On the issue of justiciability, Justice (later Chief Justice) Aharon Barak said:

> Every [human] action can be "contained" within a legal norm, and there is no action regarding which there is no legal norm which "contains" it. There

[62] HCJ 46/50 *El Aiubi* v. *Minister of Defense* [1950] IsrSC 4(1) 222.

[63] HCJ 156/56 *Shor* v. *Attorney General* [1957] IsrSC 11(1) 285; Y. Dotan, "Should Prosecutorial Discretion Enjoy Special Treatment in Judicial Review? A Comparative Analysis of the Law in England and Israel," *Pub. L.* 513 (1997).

[64] M. Mautner, *The Decline of Formalism and the Rise of Values in Israeli Law* (Tel Aviv: Ma'agalei Deot, 1993).

[65] Y. Dotan, "Does Israel Need A Constitutional Court," 5 *Mishpat Umimshal [Law and Government]* 117, 153–154 (1999).

> is no "legal vacuum", in which actions are undertaken without the law taking any position on them. The law spans all actions … The fact that a matter is "clearly political" cannot negate its existence as a "legal matter."[66]

Similar revisions were made on the issue of standing. In the early 1980s, the court was already willing to acknowledge the standing of a petitioner who was substantially harmed by a certain state action even if they belonged to a larger group of people who suffered similar harm. The court went on to specifically acknowledge the standing of individuals representing interests of a larger sector, such as in the case of consumer protection and environmental issues. The court also acknowledged at that stage that the ideological nature of the interest of the petitioner should not serve as grounds to deny standing.[67] It was not, however, until the decision in the *Ressler* case that the new concept of standing was presented, completely revising the older case law. In the *Ressler* case, the Court decided that whenever a petition raises an issue of important constitutional merit, or when there is a suspicion of serious governmental violations of the principle of the rule of law, *any* person is entitled to bring the petition into court, *regardless* of their personal interest in the outcome of the litigation. This decision marked a major shift in the position of the Supreme Court as to its self-image concerning its role in society. The court overtly acknowledged its duty to serve as the guardian of the rule of law, rather than merely as a forum designated for the adjudication of conflicts between the individual concerned and the state.[68]

The reform of the rules concerning the access to court was followed by a similar revision of the rules of judicial review. During the 1980s and the 1990s, the courts showed a growing tendency to expand the scope of its supervision over the administration. They developed new tools for judicial review and imposed new requirements on administrative authorities such as the duties of reasonableness, rationality of the decision-making process, and proportionality.[69] The courts also revealed a willingness to review

[66] HCJ 910/86 *Ressler* v. *Minister of Defense* [1988] IsrSC 42(2) 441, 477, available in English at http://elyon1.court.gov.il/files_eng/86/100/009/Z01/86009100.z01.pdf (last accessed October 8, 2012), para. 36. While this wide concept of justiciability was not adopted in its entirety by all other justices of the Supreme Court, it did mark a willingness on the part of the court to substantially widen the range of issues which were thereafter considered justiciable under the new approach.

[67] HCJ 217/80 *Segal* v. *Minister of Interior* [1980] IsrSC 34(4) 429, 443; HCJ 1/81 *Shiran* v. *Broadcasting Authority* [1981] IsrSC 35(3) 365.

[68] *Ressler* v. *Minister of Defense*, above note 64; Mautner, above note 51 at 167–168.

[69] HCJ 389/80 *Dapei Zahav* v. *Broadcasting Authority* [1980] IsrSC 35(1) 421; HCJ 376/81 *Lugasi* v. *Minister of Communications* [1982] IsrSC 36(2) 449; HCJ 297/82 *Berger* v.

actions of institutions which were previously held partly or wholly immune from judicial supervision, such as the military and the security services.[70] The HCJ also revised its deferential attitude towards prosecutorial institutions. It ruled that prosecutorial discretion is susceptible to judicial review as is any other administrative discretion. This ruling paved the way for a number of successful attacks on decisions of prosecutorial authorities not to prosecute prominent members of the political, military, and financial elites.[71] Moreover, the court became increasingly involved in governmental decisions concerning appointments of senior public officials in all sectors. It struck down nominations of senior government officials and military officers. The grounds for intervention were either that the nomination was motivated by party calculations rather than by professional considerations, or that the nominee was involved at some point in the past in a public scandal and therefore the nomination was unreasonable.[72] In 1993 the HCJ ordered Prime-Minister Yizthak Rabin to dismiss a minister and a deputy minister from his government after they were indicted for alleged corruption.[73] Last, but not least, in 1981 the HCJ decided that it had jurisdiction to hear petitions dealing with the internal procedures of the Knesset. This decision opened the door to a long series of petitions in which the court was asked to intervene in various kinds of decisions and activities of the Knesset, its committees, and other parliamentary organs.[74]

Minister of Interior [1983] IsrSC 37(3) 29; HCJ 987/94 *Euronet Kavei Zahav* v. *Minister of Communication* [1994] IsrSC 48(5) 412; HCJ 5510/92 *Turkeman* v. *Minister of Defense* [1993] IsrSC 48(1) 217; H.C. 3477/95 *Ben-Atiya* v. *Minister of Education, Culture and Sport* [1995] IsrSC 49(5) 1; I. Zamir, "Unreasonableness as Ground of Review" in Zamir and Zysblat, above note 1, at 327.

70 HCJ 680/88 *Schnitzer* v. *The Chief Military Censor* [1989] IsrSC 42(4) 617, available in English at http://elyon1.court.gov.il/files_eng/88/800/006/Z01/88006800.z01.pdf (last accessed October 8, 2012); HCJ 393/82 *Gama't Asachan* v. *Regional Commander of Judea and Samaria* [1983] IsrSC 37(4) 785.

71 HCJ 329/81 *Nof* v. *Attorney General* [1983] IsrSC 37(4) 326; Dotan, above note 61. HCJ 425/89 *Tsofan* v. *General Military Prosecutor* [1989] IsrSC 43(4) 718; HCJ 935/89 *Ganor* v. *Attorney General* [1990] IsrSC 44(2) 485; HCJ 7074/93 *Swissa* v. *Attorney General* [1994] IsrSC 48(2) 749.

72 *Eisenberg* v. *The Minister of Building and Housing*, above note 39; HCJ 1284/99 *Plonit* v. *Chief of Staff* [1999] IsrSC 53(2) 62.

73 HCJ 3094/93 *The Movement for Quality in Government in Israel* v. *State of Israel* [1993] IsrSC 47(5) 404, available in English at http://elyon1.court.gov.il/files_eng/93/940/030/Z01/93030940.z01.pdf (last accessed October 8, 2012); HCJ 4267/93 *Amitai – Citizens for Judicial Watch* v. *The Prime Minister of Israel* [1993] IsrSC 47(5) 441.

74 HCJ 652/81 *Sarid* v. *Chairman of the Knesset* [1982] IsrSC 36(2) 197, available in English at http://elyon1.court.gov.il/files_eng/81/520/006/Z01/81006520.z01.pdf (last accessed October 8, 2012); D. Kretzmer, "Judicial Review of Knesset Decisions," 8 *Tel Aviv U. Stud. L.* 95 (1988).

The reforms of the legal doctrines were accompanied by a wide range of changes in the style of judging. The decisions of the Supreme Court became much longer and more elaborate. The justices based their reasoning on broad principles of law, moral judgments, and social policies. Terms such as "reasonableness," "the values of the legal system," and so on became increasingly common within the court's rulings. Unlike their counterparts in the previous era, the judges of the 1980s dealt explicitly and at length with general issues of law and policy even if they were not directly related to the specific question raised by the case at stake.[75] Some judges (most notably Chief Justice Aharon Barak) were intensively involved in academic writing, and they often met in public with members of the Knesset as well as with other public figures.

One direct implication of the above-described changes was the rise of organized litigants in the HCJ. The willingness of the court to review almost any public action and any official decision without limitations such as standing and justiciability enabled interest groups as well as politicians and political parties to resort to the court on almost any public issue. The HCJ became a tempting forum for organized interests to carry out their political agenda through litigation. Apart from its activist policies there were several other characteristics of the HCJ that made the court a favorable forum from organized interests' point of view. As explained above, access to the HCJ was extremely fast, easy, and relatively inexpensive.[76] At the same time, the benefits that an interest group and other political actors could obtain through litigation were significant. During (and after) the 1980s the court enjoyed a high reputation and prestige among the Israeli public.[77] Its rulings were (and still are) obeyed by the Israeli bureaucracy and thus may influence governmental behavior (sometimes even when they include mere comments and recommendations without any official or positive orders).[78] Moreover, litigation before the HCJ is intensively covered by the media. Therefore, interest groups could derive significant symbolic benefits as well as public exposure even when they did not win the litigation itself. As a result, since the beginning of the 1980s there has been a sharp increase in the

[75] See Mautner, above note 51, at 133–136, 160–165.
[76] See Section B.3 above.
[77] G. Barzilai, E. Yuchtman-Ya'ar and Z. Segal, *The Israeli Supreme Court and the Israeli Public* (Tel Aviv: Papyrus, 1993). The same authors also published the main findings in "Supreme Courts and Public Opinion: General Paradigms and the Israeli Case," 4(3) *Law & Courts* 3 (1994).
[78] Cf. the discussion in Chapter 5.

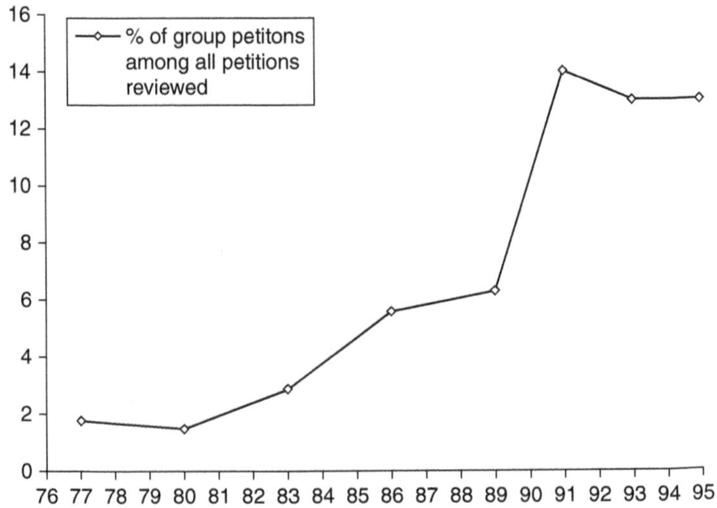

Figure 1.3 The proportion of group petitions among all petitions to HCJ (percent) 1977–1995

Source: Dotan and Hofnung 2001, below note 80.[79]

volume of organized interest litigation before the HCJ.[80] These changes are presented in Figure 1.3.

The influence of organized interests on litigation in the HCJ reaches way beyond the court's docket. Interest groups are among the more successful litigators before the Supreme Court.[81] They succeeded in challenging public policies and affecting government action through litigation in

[79] See also the discussion in Chapter 3. We found that during the 1970s only in 1% of the cases was the petitioner represented by a public organization, but by the 1990s the relative number of petitioners represented by a public action organization had risen to 11.5%. See Chapter 3 – Table 3.1.

[80] See generally, Y. Dotan and M. Hofnung, "Interest Groups in the Israeli High Court of Justice: Measuring Success in Litigation and in Out-of-Court Settlements," 23 *Law & Pol'y* 1 (2001) (Dotan and Hofnung 2001). For the same reasons a similar rise was measured in the volume of petitions issued by political parties, Knesset members and candidates in elections to the HCJ, see Y. Dotan and M. Hofnung, "Legal Defeats – Political Wins: Why Do Elected Representatives Go to Court?," 38 *Comp. Pol. Stud.* 75 (2005) (Dotan and Hofnung 2005).

[81] See Dotan and Hofnung 2001, above note 77, at 11–15 and Table 3.2. The success rate of groups was found to be much higher than the success rate of the general population in petitions (51.4 percent vis-à-vis 30 percent). See also Table 3.4 in Chapter 3. We found that petitioners represented by an organization are much more likely to succeed in litigation in the HCJ in comparison to those represented by private attorneys (odds ratio 2.62).

several cases during the 1980s and the 1990s. To mention just two notable examples (out of many): the policy of the Israeli Defense Forces disallowing women from taking combat positions was successfully challenged by a women's activist group in 1994, and the HCJ's decision brought about a wide-ranging change in the policies of the defense force regarding women soldiers.[82] Similarly, in 1999, following a petition issued by several human rights organizations, the HCJ struck down the use of torture by the Israeli General Security Services during interrogations of terrorist suspects in the Occupied Territories, thereby bringing about a significant shift in the policies of the security services.[83]

3. *The evolvement of the model of judicial hyper-activism*

In the previous sections I have described how the HCJ has become a key player within the Israeli polity since the 1980s. There is hardly a political controversy, an issue of public importance, or a contemporary moral dilemma that does not find its way, sooner rather than later, as a subject of a petition to this judicial forum. The above description, however, does not fully address the question of the mechanisms by which the court exerts

[82] See HCJ 4541/94 *Miller* v. *Minister of Defense* [1995] IsrSC 49(4) 94, available in English at http://elyon1.court.gov.il/files_eng/94/410/045/Z01/94045410.z01.pdf (last accessed October 8, 2012), in which the court struck down the refusal of the Air Force to allow the petitioner to take the exams for the combat pilot course. For other major successes of interest groups see e.g. HCJ 230/86 *Miller* v. *Minister of Interior* [1986] IsrSC 40(4) 436 (ordering the Ministry of the Interior to register as Jewish a woman who was converted to Judaism by a Reform Jewish Rabbi in the United States); HCJ 453/94 *Israel Women's Network* v. *Government of Israel* [1994] IsrSC 48(5) 501, available in English at http://elyon1.court.gov.il/files_eng/94/530/004/Z01/94004530.z01.pdf (last accessed October 8, 2012) (forcing the government to nominate more women on the boards of publicly owned companies); HCJ 240/98 *Adalah – The Legal Center for the Rights of the Arab Minority* v. *Minister for Religious Matters* [1998] IsrSC 52(5) 164 (ordering government appropriations for Muslim cemeteries in accordance with the principle of equality); HCJ 6698/95 *Ka'adan* v. *Israel Land Administration* [2000] IsrSC 54(1) 258, available in English at http://elyon1.court.gov.il/files_eng/95/980/066/a14/95066980.a14.pdf (last accessed October 8, 2012) (holding that government policy banning Non-Jewish from the right to build a house on public land in certain peripheral villages is illegal).

[83] HCJ 5100/94 *Public Committee Against Torture in Israel* v. *The State of Israel* [1999] IsrSC 53(4) 817, available in English at http://elyon1.court.gov.il/files_eng/94/000/051/a09/94051000.a09.pdf (last accessed October 8, 2012). See also HCJ 358/88 *The Association for Civil Rights in Israel* v. *The Central District Commander* [1989] IsrSC 43(2) 529, available in English at http://elyon1.court.gov.il/files_eng/88/580/003/Z01/88003580.z01.pdf (last accessed October 8, 2012) (ordering the Military Commander to conduct a hearing before issuing decisions to demolish houses for security considerations in the Occupied Territories). For a fuller account see Gavison *et al.*, above note 39, at 52–57.

its enormous influence on society and the overall social implication of its activities. By way of illustration, I shall use the following example.

On May 9, 1999, a week before the general elections the Minister for Internal Security issued, under his powers according to the Emergency Defense Regulations (1945), an order of closure of some institutions and offices of the Palestinian Authority (PA) in Jerusalem, including, most notably, the Palestinian headquarters at Orient House in East Jerusalem. Orient House had been for some years the diplomatic center of the PA and had been recognized by several foreign governments as a symbol for support of Palestinian political claims regarding the status of the city. It was also visited by many foreign diplomats and heads of state. Therefore, it was expected that the order, had it been carried out by the Israeli police, would have caused an international crisis. It was also feasible that the enforcement of the order would have stirred a wide range of violent clashes between Palestinian activists and Israeli security forces. No less clear was the fact that the timing of the issuance of this order was not fortuitous. It was issued by the Minister after heavy pressures exerted on him by the Prime Minister at that time, Benjamin Netanyahu, who was facing a defeat in the upcoming elections and sought to create a political crisis on the issue of Jerusalem.

Less than forty-eight hours after their issuance, the closure order was challenged in a petition to the HCJ. If one imagines a "normal" world of relations between the judiciary and the executive (for example, the one that existed in Israel in the pre-activist era until the late 1970s), it would have been easy to think of a wide range of practical reasons, judicial doctrines, and procedural techniques that would prevent the court from any intervention in this matter. First, it is hard to imagine a hotter potato on the court's docket. The combination of the international implications with the immediate political implications on the upcoming elections, should have – on the face of the matter – led such a court to summarily dismiss the petition without getting to the merits as non-justiciable.[84] Moreover, the petition was not issued by any person with a direct interest in the issue at stake. Neither the PA nor any of its organs were listed among the petitioners. Instead, the petition was issued by a group of Israeli left-wing activists, who had no formal connection whatsoever to the institutions against which the orders were directed. Therefore, any court in

[84] Under the "old regime" issues of grave security importance or such related to foreign affairs were often considered non-justiciable by the courts, see e.g. HCJ 186/65 *Reiner* v. *Minister of Justice* [1965] IsrSC 19(2) 485; *Hugim Leumiem* v. *Minister of Police*, above note 59, and *Ashkenazi* v. *Minister of Defense*, above note 59 and text.

this hypothetically "normal" world would have summarily dismissed the petition for lack of standing. Furthermore, on the face of the matter it was hard to see on what grounds the petition was based. According to the relevant emergency regulations the minister had wide discretion to issue the closure orders, provided only that some procedural requirements had been fulfilled. Since the relevant procedures were indeed followed, it was highly unlikely that the court would have any basis to intervene in the discretion of the minister.

Nevertheless, the HCJ did not summarily dismiss the petition. Instead, the single justice before whom the petition was brought for preliminary hearing immediately issued an intermediary writ ordering the respondents to refrain from enforcement of the closure until a further hearing had taken place. She also ordered the respondents to issue a statement regarding their position within seven days. The seven-day period was to end a day *after* the elections. In principle, such intermediate writ made *ex parte* is subject to reconsideration by the court at any stage, should the respondents move for a request for a hearing in which both parties are present. Interestingly, however, the government in this case made no attempt to appear in court in order to ask for the revocation of the intermediary order. Instead they stayed their response for a while, and some weeks later (i.e. *after* the general election) the petition was removed with consent of all parties. Therefore, the crisis created by the issuance of the closure order was prevented through the mechanism of the court's intervention.[85]

This episode, in which no final judgment of the HCJ was given, no opinion was written, and no discussion on the merits took place, illustrates some of the more subtle, but no less important, aspects of judicial activism. First, it should be noted that the court is able to have an enormous impact on the bureaucracy and the political system without the need to issue a formal judgment, and without the need for an *actual valid legal cause* on the merits in order to found such judgment. Secondly, there is the crucial issue of the *timing* of review. It should be noted that the HCJ is probably the only Supreme Court in the world that can influence any state action *while it is taking place and in real time.* Unlike most of its counterparts (such as the Supreme Court of the United States, England or Canada), the court serves as a first (and last) instance for judicial review and therefore preserves full discretion to intervene immediately in *any* public issue that is brought before it.

[85] HCJ 3123/99-A *Hilman* v. *Minister for Internal Security* (May 11, 1999, unpublished); HCJ 3123/99-C *Hilman* v. *Minister for Internal Security* (July 7, 1999, unpublished).

Moreover, over the years the HCJ has developed doctrines and techniques that are meant to ensure that it will have the formal power as well as the practical capability to immediately interfere in any public controversy. The court established its authority to review not only governmental organs and public authorities but also other supervisory bodies such as the attorney general (see above), the Military Prosecutor, all legal advisors in the various ministries, the State Comptroller and Ombudsman, as well as investigation committees of all kind.[86] It created a pyramid of legal supervision over which the court itself presides and is capable of intervening in any matter at any stage should it wish to do so. It also used a creative interpretation to free itself from any formal constraints as to its legal jurisdiction and vigorously developed an array of judicial remedies that enable it to confront different needs. The combination of all the above with the extensive media coverage which the HCJ proceedings enjoy enables the court to function as a powerful player influencing *in real time* major processes, frequently with no need to issue a formal final decision.[87] Thus, for example, the appointment of a new Chief of Staff for the Israeli Defense Forces was blocked by a petition to the HCJ on the ground that the relevant candidate (General Yoav Galant) was allegedly involved in financial misbehavior. As in the case of Orient House, the HCJ did not have to make any decision. Rather, the government, facing a public scandal and upon the intervention of the attorney general, backed off from the appointment.[88]

[86] The HCJ held that a governmental decision to appoint (or *to refrain* from appointing) an investigation commission under the National Investigation Commissions Act (1968) (as well as any other executive decision (or omissions) to appoint other kinds of commissions by the Executive) are reviewable under the general principles of public law; the court, however, stated that it would exert much deference regarding such decisions, see HCJ 6001/97 *Amitai – Citizens for Judicial Watch* v. *The Prime-minister* (October 22, 1997); HCJ 6728/06 *Ometz* v. *The Prime-minister* (November 30, 2006).

[87] For discussion of media coverage of the HCJ see Dotan and Hofnung (2005), above note 77; B. Bogoch & Y. Holtzman-Gazit, "Mutual Bonds: Media Frames and the Israeli High Court of Justice," 33 *Law & Soc. Inquiry* 53 (2008); O. Bassok, "Television Coverage of the Israeli Supreme Court 1968–1992: The Persistence of the Mythical Image," 42 *Isr. L. Rev.* 306 (2009).

[88] See HCJ 6770/10 *The Green Party* v. *The Government of Israel* (February 7, 2011, unpublished); the decision of the government *to back off* from the appointment has also been subject to an attempted attack in the HCJ, see HCJ 952/11 *Gur-Arie* v. *The Government of Israel* (February 3, 2011) and so was the decision to appoint another candidate for this senior post, see HCJ 8707/10 *Hess* v. *Minister of Defense* (February 3, 2011). In the same year another top appointment for the Chief Commissioner of the Police was blocked in a similar way on the ground of allegations regarding the candidate's involvement in a sexual

4. *The political implications of judicial hyper-activism – the 2000s*

The rising judicial activism was accompanied by a wide range of different reactions on the part of politicians and bureaucrats in Israel varying from obedience and assimilation to sharp and vocal resistance. The creation of a powerful and hierarchical mechanism of judicial review, which is able to interfere in any governmental action in real time, brought about a process of an almost complete judicialization of the Israeli bureaucracy and political processes alike. The picture of ministers, senior governmental officials, army generals, and their like marching to their offices accompanied by lawyers has become commonplace in the Israeli media. The question of whether a certain decision is capable of sustaining judicial review has become an essential part of any bureaucratic decision-making process as well as any legislative initiative. The degree of involvement of legal aspects and judicial consideration is such that it is even an essential part of the military when planning all sorts of active operations.[89]

Even more remarkable are the implications of judicial hyper-activism on the political system. Obviously, the willingness of the Supreme Court to second-guess political choices of all kinds has created strong incentives for politicians (particularly opposition members) to challenge public policy through litigation after attempts to change it through the political process have failed. Likewise, the possibility of judicial review of legislation has an impact on the ways in which both the Knesset and the government create legislation of all kinds. The intensity of the judicial involvement, however, carries much wider strategic implications. In order to demonstrate this

harassment scandal, see A. Glikman, "The Attorney General Freezes the Appointment of the Chief Commissioner," *Ynet*, November 18, 2010, available at: www.ynet.co.il/articles/0,7340,L-3986816,00.html (last accessed July 16, 2013). It is worthwhile noting that in neither case have criminal (or disciplinary) proceedings been conducted against the relevant candidates after the elimination of their candidacy.

89 See e.g. A. Straschnov, *Justice Under Fire* (Tel Aviv: Yedioth Aharonot, 1994). The question of the explanation for this rise of judicial activism in Israel is beyond the scope of the current discussion. One popular explanation refers to the immobilism of political institutions in Israel (see Edelman, above note 51, at 407–408) and the political stalemate in Israel at the end of the 1980s (see G. Barzilai, "Between the Rule of Law and the Laws of the Ruler: The Supreme Court in Israeli Legal Culture," 49 (152) *Int'l Soc. Sci. J.* 193 (1997); Mautner, above note 51, at 169–170). A different theory refers to the judicialization of politics in Israel as an attempt to preserve the political hegemony of the State's founders against the eradication in their political power and the rise of new competing political forces during the 1980s. See R. Hirschl, "The Political Origins of Judicial Empowerment through Constitutionalization: Lessons from Four Constitutional Revolutions," 25 *Law & Soc. Inquiry* 91 (2000).

let me return to the *Orient House* case discussed in the previous section. As explained, the court intervened in the closure decision only by issuing an intermediary order that could have been subject to revocation at any stage. Why was it, then, that Netanyahu's government refrained from issuing an immediate motion to revoke the judicial writ (a motion that had every chance of success)? The most probable answer is that the government was not at all interested in such a move. All the Prime Minister was looking for was a way to demonstrate his commitment to the issue of Jerusalem before the elections. This was achieved by the very fact that the orders were issued. The interference by the HCJ was well anticipated by the decision-makers. It enabled the government to have its cake and eat it, i.e., to enjoy the political benefits entailed from the very issuance of the orders, without bearing the consequences of enforcing them. In other words, the government sought the judicial intervention that allowed it to shift the blame onto the court for preventing an action that it was not interested in carrying out in the first place. The *Orient House* case demonstrates how deeply judicial review became involved in bureaucratic and political decision-making in Israel, and how such involvement may be utilized and manipulated not only by the reviewing courts and political actors that resort to the court but also by those institutions that are the subject of review.

The judicial policies of the Israeli Supreme Court have triggered not only reactions of participation and manipulation. They have also raised strong opposition on the part of several sectors in Israeli society. While during the 1980s – the decade of the breakthrough of judicial activism – the opposition to the political branches of the expansion of judicial power was minimal,[90] during the 1990s there was a growing wave of criticism by politicians and bureaucrats against the court's activist policies.[91] Thus, for example, the late Prime Minister Yitzhak Rabin was cited more than once denouncing the involvement of the HCJ in military affairs as one of the main reasons for the failure of the Israeli Defense Forces to effectively confront the Palestinian *Intifada*.[92] Similarly, the open willingness of the HCJ to intervene in internal procedures of the Knesset drew several furious reactions from the Chairman of the House as well as from other members.[93] Such reactions did not stop the phenomenon of Members of

[90] See Mautner, above note 51, at 216–218.

[91] See Y. Dotan, "Ripeness and Politics in the High Court of Justice," 20 *Iunei Mishpat [Law Studies]* 93, 122–126 (1996).

[92] See Straschnov, above note 86, at 297–300.

[93] See Dotan, above note 88, at 124–130.

the Knesset (MKs) rushing to petition the court every other day, but during the 1990s the criticism on the part of politicians became more robust and the possibility of legislative moves to curtail the scope of the court's jurisdiction was openly discussed in the Knesset.[94] Moreover, during the 1990s the court's activism began to draw growing criticism from scholars and columnists.[95]

Notwithstanding these sources of opposition to judicial activism, the most zealous opposition to the policies of the Supreme Court comes from the direction of the Orthodox and Ultra-orthodox religious and political establishment. The points of friction between the court and these social segments are numerous and intense. The strong foothold of the Orthodox regime in Israeli politics has allowed the religious parties many achievements and benefits, beginning with legislation that reflects religious sentiments and ending with executive and legislative arrangements that reflect economic preferences for the Jewish religious population. The HCJ constitutes a constant threat to these arrangements.[96] Its rulings on civil liberties have directly confronted and reversed several regulations based on religious principles.[97] Its rulings on women's equality rights cut against existing legal arrangements in the field of family law and matrimonial status.[98] The court's decisions on equality for different groups regarding

[94] See *ibid.*, at 129–130.

[95] See e.g. R. Shamir, "The Politics of Reasonableness: Discretion as Judicial Power," 5 *Theory and Criticism* 7 (1994); M. Kremnitzer, "The HCJ and Its Wide Concept of Its Role," in Gavison *et al.*, above note 39, at 165; Mautner, above note 51, at 138–144.

[96] For a general description of the relationship between the religious establishment and the courts in Israel see M. Edelman, *Courts, Politics and Culture in Israel* (University of Virginia Press, 1994), 119–130. Y. Dotan, "Judicial Review and Political Accountability: The Case of the High Court of Justice in Israel," 32 *Isr. L. Rev.* 448 (1998).

[97] See e.g. *Lezarovitz* v. *The Food Inspector*, above note 54 (striking down an order that bans the supply of pigs' meat in Jewish communities); CA 6/66 *Kalo* v. *The Mayor of Bat-Yam* [1966] IsrSC 20(2) 327 (striking down municipal tax applying to non-kosher butcheries); HCJ 3872/93 *Mitrael* v. *The Prime-minister* [1993] IsrSC 47(5) 485 (striking down policy banning the production and marketing of non-kosher meat); CrimA 217/68 *Isramex* v. *The State of Israel* [1968] IsrSC 22(2) 343 (striking down refusal to grant business license to a gas station that operated on the Sabbath); HCJ 171/78 *Ashkar* v. *Minister for Labor and Welfare* [1982] IsrSC 36(3) 141 (regulation banning business activity on the Sabbath). For a general discussion see Rubinstein and Medina, above note 24, at 339–356; D. Barak-Erez, *Outlawed Pigs: Law, Religion, and Culture in Israel* (University of Wisconsin Press, 2007).

[98] E.g. HCJ 143/62 *Funk-Schlezinger* v. *Minister of Interior* [1963] IsrSC 17 225 (recognition of marriage between Israeli citizens conducted abroad and thus enabling the circumvention of religious restrictions under Israeli law); HCJ 1000/92 *Bavli* v. *Grand Rabbinical Court* [1994] IsrSC 48(2) (applying the principle of equal property rights between spouses in case of divorce despite the lack of such principle in Jewish religious law).

access to state budgets and benefits brought about the annulment of several privileges that religious sectors had achieved through political negotiations and coalition maneuvers.[99] Even more annoying – from the perspective of the Orthodox establishment – were the court's rulings that allowed alternative branches of Judaism equal standing and representation in state-owned religious institutions.[100] Not surprisingly, religious politicians as well as chief Ultra-orthodox rabbinical leaders describe the HCJ as "enemy number 1" of the Jewish religion and repeatedly call for the curtailment of its powers and for reforming the process of appointments to the Supreme Court.[101] The outrage in the Ultra-orthodox community against the court and the judicial system at large has been reflected several times in massive public demonstrations since the 1990s.[102]

[99] E.g. HCJ 4906/98 *Am Hofshi Association* v. *Ministry of Building and Housing* [2000] IsrSC 54(2) 503 (striking down housing appropriations for ultra-religious population); HCJ 5290/97 *Ezra – The Ultra-religious Youth Movement* v. *Minister for Religious Affairs* [1997] IsrSC 51(5) 410 (striking down appropriations for Ultra-orthodox movements in violation of the principle of equality); HCJ 6741/99 *Yekutieli* v. *Minister of Interior* [2001] IsrSC 55(3) 673 (striking down municipal tax deductions to Yeshiva students); HCJ 4124/00 *Yekutieli* v. *Minister for Religious Affairs* [2010] IsrSC, available in English at http://elyon1.court.gov.il/files_eng/00/240/041/n43/00041240.n43.pdf (last accessed October 8, 2012) (striking down legislation that gave preferences in appropriations to Yeshiva students).

[100] E.g. *Miller* v. *Minister of Interior*, above note 79 (recognition of conversions ceremonies made by non-Orthodox rabbis). HCJ 257/89 *Hofmann* v. *The Supervisor of the Wailing Wall* [1994] IsrSC 48(2) 265 (acknowledging the right of women belonging to alternative movement for prayer near the Wailing Wall).

[101] See e.g. S. Ilan, G. Alon and Y. Verter, "An Extreme Ultra-orthodox Attack on the HCJ: 'Barak is the Enemy of the Jewish People'," *Ha'Aretz* (February 10, 1999); S. Ilan, G. Alon, M. Moalem and N. Krao, "Rabbi Yosef: The HCJ Justices are Villains and are the Cause of All the Suffering in the World," *Ha'Aretz* (February 11, 1999); S. Ilan, "Rabbi Ovadia Yosef: 'The HCJ Justices Are Worse than Non-Jewish Courts and Should not Be Regarded as Judges of Israel'," *Ha'aretz*, (October 8, 1996). See also Dotan, above note 88, 129–131.

[102] The protest reached its peak in February 1999 when more than 200,000 demonstrators gathered to protest against the court's policies on issues of religion and state (see S. Ilan, "An Effort to Prevent Violence in the Ultra-orthodox and Secular Demonstrations in Jerusalem Today," *Ha'Aretz*, February 14, 1999). Two years earlier dozens of supporters of the Ultra-orthodox party Shas attempted in the course of a demonstration to break into the building of the Supreme Court. They were accompanied by some MKs of the Shas party, see *Ha'aretz*, July 15, 1997; R. Hazut, "The Night on which the Supreme Court was Almost Conquered," *Yediot Acharonot*, May 14, 1997. In 2010 more than 100,000 members of the Ultra-orthodox community in Jerusalem protested against the intervention of the court to strike down policies of separation between Ashkenazy and non-Ashkenazy female students in the Ultra-orthodox town of Immanuel (see HCJ 1067/08 *Noar Kehalacha Association* v. *Ministry of Education* [2009] IsrSC, available in English at http://elyon1.court.gov.il/files_eng/08/670/010/o24/08010670.o24.pdf and Y. Etinger, "More than 100,000 ultra-orthodox took part in protest against the rule of law," *Ha'Aretz* June 18, 2010).

The wave of opposition to the court's activist policies intensified throughout the 2000s and reached its pick (at least for now) toward the end of that decade. Open attacks on the court's activism became commonplace within the Israeli media by politicians, bureaucrats, top columnists, and even law professors.[103] This wave of criticism has been accompanied by a sharp decrease in public trust in the court. While at the beginning of the 1990s over 87 percent of the Israeli public expressed a high level of trust in the court,[104] at the end of the 1990s this figure had dropped to 74 percent. The level of trust continued its decline throughout the 2000s to 72 percent in 2005, 61 percent in 2007 and in 2008 the polls showed, for the first time, that the level of trust in the court was below 50 percent.[105] The government and the Knesset, on their part, stopped fighting shy of initiatives to curtail the court's powers. In 2007, the then Minister of Justice, Daniel Friedman initiated a number of bills aimed at restricting the court's authority to intervene in matters of national security or such matters that carry heavy budgetary implications.[106] In the same year another bill by the Minister of Justice proposed to limit the court's judicial review power and to subject any decision to strike down legislation to the possibility of an overruling by the Knesset.[107] Both bills drew much criticism in the media and were not passed by the Knesset. Other more modest initiatives did, however, succeed. Thus, in 2007 the Knesset amended the law to limit the tenure of the Chief Justice to seven years.[108]

D. Conclusion

The description of the functions and policies of the Israeli HCJ leaves many questions open. The fact that this court functions at the same time as a trial court and as a court of last instance has a paramount impact

[103] See Mautner, above note 51, at 219–223.

[104] See Barzilai, Yuchtman-Ya'ar and Segal (1993), above note 75, at 69.

[105] The same polls have since shown a slight rise to over 50 percent in the level of public trust. See A. Arian *et al.*, "Auditing Israeli Democracy: Democratic Values in Practice," (The Israel Democracy Institute, 2010), available at http://en.idi.org.il/media/1664777/Auditing_IsraelI_Democracy_2010.pdf (last accessed July 16, 2013); and see also Mautner, above note 51, at 220–221.

[106] See Y. Yoaz, "The Labor Party: Friedman's Proposal Will Cause Coalition Crisis," *Ha'Aretz* (November 16, 2007) (available at www.haaretz.co.il/hasite/spages/924898.html, last accessed July 16, 2013).

[107] See Proposal for Bill: Basic Law: The Judiciary (Amendment), Section 15b (2007) (available in Hebrew at www.justice.gov.il/NR/rdonlyres/33DF4EA2-D227–4E82–8208-E88857CF3360/0/תזכירחוקיסודהשפיטהביקורתשיפוטית.pdf, last accessed July 16, 2013).

[108] See Courts Law (Consolidated Version) (1984), section 8(b).

on the court's docket. As we have seen, the court copes with this problem partly by adopting procedures that are in particular summary and simple. The adoption of such procedures, however, may severely limit the court's ability to confront the complicated issues that are brought before it. In other words, the court's ambitions to function as the ultimate supervisor on governmental actions create tension between procedural efficiency and material effectiveness. How the court resolves this problem is a question that needs investigating.

Accordingly, the hyper-activism of the HCJ raises other perplexing questions. How can the court sustain an effective system of gathering reliable information in the absence of complicated formal tools (such as oral testimonies) and given the complicated nature of the issues that are brought before it? How does the court ensure systematic enforcement of its complex and demanding orders on the Israeli bureaucracy? These are all questions that necessitate a closer look at the mechanisms of the judicial review process.

The last set of questions relates to the political aspects of the HCJ's activities. The growing judicial activism has created a serious problem of legitimacy for the Supreme Court. The court is facing a growing tension between its ambitions to continue its intense influence on the Israeli polity on the one hand, and the risk that further expansion of its intervention in sensitive political areas will bring about a counter-reaction that will infringe on its institutional autonomy. The growing resentment on the part of some political forces against judicial activism, combined with the lack of firm constitutional protection for its institutional autonomy, intensify the risks and sharpen the judicial dilemmas in this respect.

The purpose of the analysis in the following chapters is to describe the position of government lawyers within this process of judicial review. I will argue that government lawyers play a key role enabling the court to cope with its complicated tasks and to confront the severe pressures described above. In order to present this argument, however, I need first to supply a detailed description of the institutions in which the HCJD lawyers operate. This will be done in the next chapter.

2

The High Court of Justice Department (HCJD): overview and history

The purpose of this chapter is to present an overview of the High Court of Justice Department (HCJD). The department is part of the legal apparatus of the Israeli government. I shall first discuss briefly the general structure of this legal apparatus within the Ministry of Justice. I will then describe the institution of the Office of the Attorney General (OAG) and the function of the attorney general. The HCJD is subject to the direct supervision of the attorney general. The historical development of the HCJD and its current status within the legal system were heavily influenced by the developments of the function of the attorney general. Therefore, the discussion of the OAG will be somewhat detailed. In the last part of this chapter I will present an overview of the department itself: its structure, its history, the career patterns of its members, and its working practices. This description will serve as an overview for the detailed discussion of the main functions of the department and its impact on public law litigation in Israel in the following chapters.

A. The bureaucratic framework

1. *Overview: Government lawyering in Israel*

Lawyers are an integral part of most governmental units in Israel. All the ministries of the government and state agencies have legal departments that are normally headed by their chief legal counselor. The functions of these departments are to assist the relevant bureaus by providing legal opinions in matters related to decision-making processes and by taking part in legislative and regulative procedures in which the ministries are involved.[1]

[1] For a description of the history and development of the legal profession in Israel see N. Ziv, "Symposium: The Legal Profession: Looking Backward: Combining Professionalism, Nation Building and Public Service: The Professional Project of the Israeli Bar 1928–2002," 71 *Fordham L. Rev.* 1621 (2003).

Lawyers who serve in a certain government unit are employees of that unit and as such are subject to the supervision of the minister or the head of the unit. This initial responsibility of the government lawyers is compromised, however, by their duty to enforce the law and their commitment to the idea of the rule of law. This commitment to the ideal of the rule of law is reflected – on the bureaucratic level – by the duty of all government lawyers (and in essence all lawyers in any public agency in the country) to follow the directions, rulings, and opinions of the attorney general (see below). It is therefore fair to say that, despite the fact that government lawyers work for many different agencies, the structure of the legal bureaucracy in Israel is centralist.

2. *The Ministry of Justice*

The Ministry of Justice is headed by the Minister of Justice, who is a cabinet member.[2] The second figure within the bureaucratic hierarchy of the ministry is the General Manager who is in charge of all administrative aspects of the operation of the ministry. The General Manager is also in charge of all the departments of the ministry that deal with registration and licensing (such as the Companies Register and the Land Register), as well as some other services that the ministry deals with, such as the Department for Legal Aid (see Figure 2.1).

The two main functions of the Ministry of Justice are advising the government in all matters of legislation (and regulation) and representing the government before all courts of law. These two functions are part of the OAG and are therefore under the supervision of the attorney general himself[3] (who, as we shall see, is almost completely independent vis-à-vis the Minister of Justice).

There are, however, some differences in the status of these two functions (legislation and litigation) within the ministry. The functions of law enforcement and litigation are executed exclusively by the OAG, without any involvement or interference whatsoever from the minister or any functionaries outside the OAG. The situation concerning legislation is more complex. While the departments in the Ministry of Justice that deal with legislation are part of the OAG office, the minister is sometimes

[2] Traditionally, most politicians appointed to the position of Minister of Justice had legal education, and many of them were celebrated lawyers before their nomination.

[3] Thus far, all the nominees to the position of the attorney general of Israel have been male. Hence, I use "he" or "his" with regard to this position.

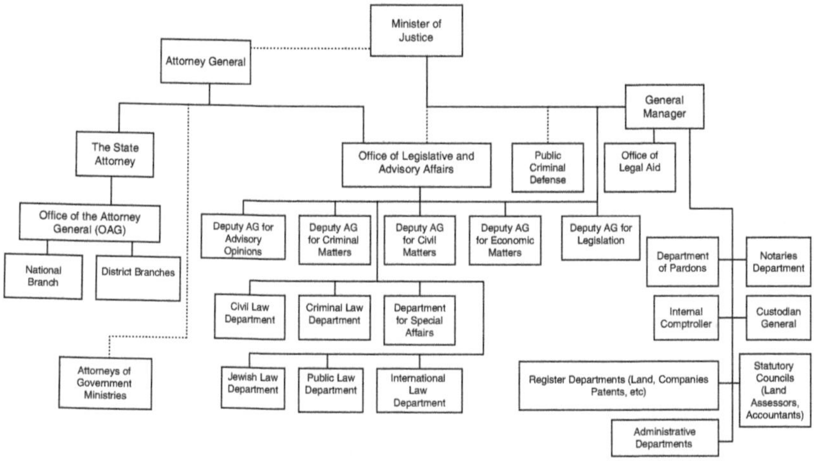

Figure 2.1 The Ministry of Justice
Source: The Ministry of Justice, available at http://old.justice.gov.il/MOJEng/Resource+Center/OrganizationalChart.htm (last accessed July 16, 2013).

involved in legislative initiatives on behalf of the government and bears the ultimate responsibility for the government's policies on legislative matters. This means that the legislative departments in the ministry are subject to the authority of the minister in matters of policy, but are subject to the supervision of the attorney general in matters of law.[4] Therefore, I shall briefly discuss the legislative functions of the ministry here, while the discussion of the functions of litigation and law enforcement will be done below with reference to the OAG.

According to the procedures of the Knesset, the government has strong hold and intensive involvement in all legislative processes in the Knesset (even where the legislation was not initiated by the government itself). Most legislative proposals in the Knesset are brought up by the government. Even when the legislation is initiated by Members of the Knesset (MKs) and not by the government (private member's bills), the government would still be involved in the process of legislation under

[4] Besides the Department of Legislation and the OAG, there are a number of other departments that assist the attorney general in fulfilling his advisory functions. These are the general advisory department and the departments for civil, criminal, and economic and fiscal matters. These departments are subject to the direct and exclusive supervision of the attorney general as long as they are not called to advise the minister on legislative policies (see Figure 2.1).

the procedural code of the Knesset.[5] Therefore, the relevant department within the ministry would be invited to advise the government with reference to the proposed legislation.[6] The ministry is also involved – under the directive of the attorney general – in the process of creating regulations initiated by any governmental department. Therefore, the relevant department within the ministry would be invited to issue an opinion on the proposed regulation, to coordinate between the different ministries affected by the proposed regulations, and to supervise the regulatory procedures.[7]

B. The attorney general

The office of the attorney general in Israel has grown from British practice.[8] There are, however, two main differences between the office of the attorney general in Israel and the comparable offices in other common law jurisdictions. First, in Israel the attorney general is not only the head of the legal service of the government and the exclusive legal advisor of the Executive, but also serves as the head of criminal prosecution and holds ultimate responsibility for law enforcement. Secondly, unlike the situation in most other countries, the attorney general in Israel is not a politician. Although he is appointed by the government and can – at least in theory – be discharged by the government at any stage, the position has always been held by professional lawyers, who are expected to exercise their powers independently of the government.[9]

While the attorney general is formally a senior official in the Ministry of Justice, he is subject to the hierarchy of the ministry (and to the supervision

[5] See Rules of Procedure of the Knesset, Sections 134–146, available in English at www.knesset.gov.il/rules/eng/bchap8.htm, last accessed July 16, 2013.

[6] See A. Rubinstein and B. Medina, *The Constitutional Law of Israel*, 6th edn. (Shoken, 2005), 732. The number of private bills has increased dramatically since the 1990s and they now form about 50 percent of the general number of bills brought before the Knesset. See S. Ilan, "Inflation of Bills: From Four to Average of 40 Bills for Each MK," *Ha'aretz* October 30, 2000.

[7] Attorney General Directive no. 60.012 (November 1985) regulates the internal procedures that regulative agencies should adopt when issuing regulations. The procedures include internal consultations with all government agencies that may have an interest in the proposed regulations, as well as with the responsible officials in the Ministry of Justice. See I. Zamir, "Secondary Legislation: Procedures and Directives," 11 *Iunei Mishpat* 339 (1986).

[8] In this part I use the term "the *office* of the attorney general" to refer to the *position* of the attorney general *himself*. This term should be distinct from the *Office of the Attorney General* (OAG) that refers to the bureaucratic organization that functions under the supervision of the attorney general and will be discussed below.

[9] I. Zamir, "The Role of the Attorney General in Times of Crisis: The Israeli Shin Bet Affair," in S. Shetreet (ed.), *The Role of Courts in Society* (Dordrecht: Nijhoff, 1988), 271.

of the minister) only on the administrative level. On the professional level he is completely independent. This means that the minister of justice has no power to give instructions to the attorney general in matters concerning law enforcement, litigation, or legal advice given to other government departments. The independence of the attorney general is not formally provided by any statute. Rather, it has developed as a constitutional convention over the years, initially acknowledged by a public committee that was appointed by the government to investigate the matter, and approved by the rulings of the Supreme Court.[10]

As the head of the legal service of the government, the attorney general fulfills four main functions. First, he is the chief legal advisor to the government. As such, he is responsible for a widespread machinery which consists of not only all the legal advisors in the ministry of justice, but also all other legal advisors in the various departments and ministries of the government. The latter are not subject to his command on the administrative level. Yet they accept – as a matter of professional tradition – his professional authority. As the legal advisor of the government, the attorney general enjoys an exclusive power to advise the government on legal issues, and his legal *opinions* are considered as binding on the government unless and until a court of law rules differently. In other words, once the attorney general has issued an opinion on a given question, his opinion is considered, as far as the government is concerned, to be the law of the land. The government may not pursue any course of action that is not in accordance with such an opinion.[11] Also, the government is not entitled to refer any legal questions to any other lawyer, such as a private attorney, without the (rarely given) consent of the attorney general.[12]

[10] See *The Report of the Committee on the Powers of the Attorney General* (1962). The Report was republished in I. Zamir (ed.), *Klinghoffer Book on Public Law* (Jerusalem, 1993), 421–449 (*The Agranat Report*); Rubinstein and Medina, above note 6, at 996; Zamir, above note 9; Y. Dotan, "Should Prosecutorial Discretion Enjoy Special Treatment in Judicial Review? A Comparative Analysis of the Law in England and Israel," *Pub. L.* 513, 519 (1997). For a detailed historical account of the early stages of the constitutional development see P. Lahav, *Judgment in Jerusalem: Chief Justice Simon Agranat and the Zionist Century* (Berkeley: University of California Press, 1997), 168–172.

[11] HCJ 73/85 *The Kach Party* v. *The Chairman of the Knesset,* [1985] IsrSC 39(3) 141, 152; HCJ 3094/93 *The Movement for Quality in Government in Israel* v. *The State of Israel* [1993] IsrSC 47(5) 404, available in English at http://elyon1.court.gov.il/files_eng/93/940/030/Z01/93030940.z01.pdf, 426 (last accessed October 8, 2012); HCJ 320/96 *German* v. *The City Council of Herzelia* [1998] IsrSC 52(2) 222, 240; Zamir, above note 9, at 272.

[12] E. Levontin and R. Gavison, "The 'Binding' Position of the Attorney General," in A. Barak (ed.), *Shamgar Book*, vol. I (2003), 221. For a comprehensive discussion see E. Levontin "*Representation of the State in Court*" (PhD dissertation, Hebrew University of Jerusalem, 2009), 23–27 (Hebrew with abstract in English) (Levontin).

It is worth mentioning that the statutes regulating the functions of the attorney general do not provide for his exclusiveness as the legal advisor of the government. Therefore, the question as to whether and to what extent the government was entitled to disagree with the attorney general on a matter of law was far from clear before 1980.[13] However, later developments – mostly on the political and bureaucratic level – led the legal (and political) system toward an acknowledgment of the exclusiveness of the attorney general's position as the legal advisor of the government. These developments are tied up with the other functions of the attorney general, and most particularly with his function as *the ultimate representative* of the government before any court of law (see below). While this exclusiveness later received the support of the Supreme Court itself, it still remains contested by some critics, and the ability of the attorney general to enforce it in practice on the government depends much on the political power of the person who holds the office and their relationship with the relevant cabinet.[14]

The second principal function of the attorney general is that he presides over the mechanism of criminal law enforcement. He is head of the national prosecution service and has wide discretion to initiate or to stay criminal investigations and prosecutions. Therefore, he has full powers to order the police to initiate investigation or to refrain from investigation of certain matters. He is entitled to order the national prosecution service and the district prosecution services to prosecute or to refrain from criminal prosecution.[15] He has the authority by law to stay any criminal

[13] In the *Agranat Report*, above note 10, the question was left moot. See I. Zamir, "Editor's Note," in I. Zamir (ed.), *Klinghoffer Book on Public Law* (Jerusalem, 1993), 419–420; Levontin, above note 12. See also the discussion at note 36 below and accompanying text.

[14] *The Kach Party* v. *Chairman of the Knesset*, above note 11; HCJ 4267/93 *Amitai – Citizens for Judicial Watch* v. *The Prime-minister of Israel* [1993] IsrSC 47(5) 441, 473. For a critique on the argument of the exclusiveness of the attorney general's advisory opinions see R. Gavison, "The Attorney General: A Critical Examination of New Trends," 5 *Plilim [Israel Journal of Criminal Justice]* 27, 76–92 (1996).

[15] Criminal Procedure Act (Consolidated Version) 1982, 36 L.S.I. 35, section 61. Normally, the decision to prosecute is taken by the staff of the OAG or by police prosecutors. Such prosecutors are appointed by the attorney general. See Criminal Procedure Act (Consolidated Version) 1982, 36 L.S.I. 35, section 62. In some cases there is a need for the prosecutor to obtain the approval of the attorney general before issuing the indictment, such as when the subject of the indictment is the prime minister (Basic Law: The Government, section 17, available in English at www.knesset.gov.il/laws/special/eng/basic14_eng.htm, last accessed July 16, 2013) or a judge (Basic Law: The Judiciary, section 12(a), available in English at www.knesset.gov.il/laws/special/eng/basic8_eng.htm, last accessed July 16, 2013). For a general description see R. Gavison, *Administrative Discretion in Law Enforcement* (Jerusalem, 1991), 136–138.

proceedings taken by any prosecutorial authority under any statute.[16] He also publishes general guidelines with regard to the prosecutorial policy of certain offences. Therefore, in principle, he has the power to lead a policy that certain criminal offences would not be enforced by the state under certain circumstances.[17]

The third function of the attorney general – as head of the litigation branch of the government – is his exclusive right to represent the government in any legal proceedings, criminal, civil, or administrative. This means that it is up to the attorney general to decide whether to institute proceedings in court on behalf of the state in any particular case. Moreover, it is up to the attorney general to decide whether to *defend* the state, the government, or any state agency when it is sued in the courts and *under what conditions or grounds*. Therefore, if the attorney general reaches the conclusion that a particular act is unlawful, and he refuses to represent the government in court, the government would remain with no legal defense before the court.[18] The possibility that the attorney general would be able to enforce his legal position on the government by refusing to defend it in court or by refusing to raise certain arguments raises serious questions. Such questions relate both to the political relationship between the attorney general and the government and to his professional and ethical duties as a lawyer toward his client (i.e., the government). The "official" position of those who support this state of affairs is supplied by Zamir, who claims that the attorney general's client is *not* the government but the "public."[19] Therefore, he concludes:

> In the exercise of these ... functions, the Attorney General does not act as a private lawyer would act for his client ... A private lawyer is only

[16] Criminal Procedure Act (Consolidated Version) 1982, 36 L.S.I. 35, section 231. The attorney general has full authority to interfere and take control of criminal proceedings initiated by private citizens, see Criminal Procedure Act (Consolidated Version) 1982, 36 L.S.I. 35, sections 71–72.

[17] The most well-known example in that respect is the attorney general's directive to refrain from the enforcement of the prohibition against homosexuality (Attorney General Directive no. 50.049 (1.1.1972)) that practically erased the offence of homosexuality from the Israeli Law Book long before the Knesset abolished the prohibition in 1990. See Rubinstein and Medina, above note 6, at 1014–1015. Unlike in England, the courts did not question the legality of such general directives dealing with non enforcement of criminal prohibitions. See Gavison, above note 15, at 177 and *ibid.*, note 175. Cf. in England: *R.* v. *The Commissioner of the Police of the Metropolis, ex parte Blackburn* [1968] 2. QB 118, and Gavison, above note 14, at 40.

[18] Zamir, above note 9, at 272; Levontin, above note 12, at Chapter 3, 89–90.

[19] I. Zamir, "The Attorney General: A Public Servant, Not a Government Servant," in I. Zamir (ed.), *Klinghoffer Book on Public Law* (Jerusalem, 1993), 451.

> responsible for his advice when it is requested. The Attorney General … [is responsible] for much more than that, it is for him to see to it that the government observes the law. He is supposed to act, not only as the government's lawyer, but also, at the same time, as the lawyer of the people, as a watchdog over the government.[20]

The discussion of the tensions between the conflicting commitments of government lawyers to their clients and to the principle of the rule of law and the public interest central to the discussion of the HCJD and will be done elsewhere.[21] We can see, however, that the origin of these tensions is the duality in the functions of the attorney general himself. Much as in the case of the first function as legal advisor, discussed above, the exclusiveness of the position of attorney general as the ultimate representative of the government before the court is not entrenched in any explicit statutory order.[22] It was adamantly criticized by politicians and academics with regard to some major cases in which the attorney general did use his power and left the government without legal representation.[23] Nevertheless, this position was endorsed explicitly by the Supreme Court

[20] Zamir, above note 9, at 272. Levontin argues that the crucial moment in the development of the concept of the full independence of the attorney general vis-à-vis the government and the right of the attorney general to refuse representation was *The Kav (Line No.) 300 Affair* (also known as *The Shin Bet Affair*). In 1984 four Palestinian terrorists hijacked an Israeli bus en route from Tel Aviv to Ashkelon (in southern Israel). A couple of hours later an IDF elite unit stormed the bus. Two terrorists were killed inside the bus during the operation while two others were captured alive but were killed shortly after by Israeli Secret Service (Shin Bet) agents. It was later revealed that senior members in the Shin Bet (including the head of the organization Avram Shalom) were personally present at the scene, and later on were involved in a coordinated effort to conceal and forge several testimonies and evidence from investigation committees appointed by the attorney general, at the time Itzhak Zamir. Zamir struggled to reveal the facts of the incident and bring to justice those responsible for it. He confronted senior cabinet members (including the prime minister), who opposed his demands and sought to avoid indictments. As the result of Zamir's efforts the Head of the General Security Service was forced to resign and the service has undergone a major reform. Zamir failed, however, to bring to justice those responsible for the cover-up operation and eventually had to leave office. The affair brought about an unprecedented crisis in the relationship between the security apparatus and the legal apparatus of the government. When the affair arrived at the HCJ the senior members of the OAG refused to represent the government. The aftermath of this affair was the appointment of an official commission (The Landau Commission) that brought about a reform in the relationship between the Shin-Bet and the attorney general. See Zamir, above note ; Levontin, above note, at 79–85. For an account of the *Shin-Bet Affair* see Wikipedia, "Kav 300 Affair" at http://en.wikipedia.org/wiki/Kav_300_affair (last accessed July 16, 2011).

[21] See Chapter 4 below. [22] Levontin, above note 12, at 27–32.

[23] See Gavison, above note 14, at 77–82. For a comprehensive critique see Levontin, above note 12, at 99–109.

in those "crisis" cases. The most notable case dealing with the question was HCJ 4267/93 *Amitai-Citizens for Judicial Watch* v. *The Government of Israel*, where the petitioners sought an order to force the Prime Minister to dismiss the Minister of the Interior after the latter had been charged with forgery and larceny. The AOG refused to defend the decision of the Prime Minster not to dismiss the Minister of the Interior. The court explicitly endorsed the position of the attorney general. While answering the argument that the Government did not enjoy proper legal representation, Justice Barak said:

> The Office of the Attorney General represented one and only client – the Prime-minister. She did so as the agent of the Attorney General ... Indeed, the position of the Attorney General was different than the position of the Prime-minister ... in such a case, the Attorney General should represent the Government according to his own legal perception. The reason for this principle is the concept, that the Attorney General is the authorized interpreter of the law *vis a vis* the Executive.[24]

Accordingly, the fact that the court supported the exclusiveness of the attorney general as the sole representative of the government made any attempts by the government to go around this principle – by hiring private attorneys to represent the government before the court – doomed to fail. This means that the attorney general and his staff enjoy a full monopoly over the representation of all government agencies in any court of law. Accordingly, government agencies are "captive clients" of the attorney general.[25]

[24] Above note 14, at 475. This case was by no means the only occasion in which the court supported the refusal of the attorney general or the HCJD to represent the government. In another case, the HCJD refused to defend a decision by the Public Censorship Committee to dismiss an application for a license to present a theater play. The court allowed the committee to be represented by a private lawyer, but intervened and quashed its decision (HCJ 14/86 *Laor* v. *Film Review Council* [1987] IsrSC 41(1) 421). For a description of other occasions of refusal on the part of the attorney general to represent the government or of divergence of their positions, see Gavison, above note 14, at 77–82; Y. Gutman, *A Storm in the G.S.S: The Attorney General Versus the Government* (Tel-Aviv, 1995); Levontin, above note 12, at Chapter 3, 85–97.

[25] I use the terminology of Donald Horowitz (which refers originally to the case of the Solicitor General in the United States; see D. L. Horowitz, *The Jurocracy* (Washington, D.C.: Lexington Books, 1977), 5–6). It should be noted, though, that in the United States the fact that government agencies are captive clients of the attorney general is the basis for the DOJ policy to allow the agencies much latitude in presenting their own policies in court, as the DOJ rarely refuses to defend challenges to agency practices (at least at the first instance, see *ibid*., at 22, 39). In Israel, on the other hand, the attorney general does make extensive use of his potential power to refuse representation. I shall discuss this point in Chapter 4.

The fourth important function of the attorney general is his statutory power to interfere in *any* legal proceedings in order to secure the public interest. This power is used by the attorney general in various contexts, such as in family law or inheritance cases in which the public or the state may have interests. Unlike the first and third functions of the attorney general (discussed above) this function is expressly provided for by statute and raises no questions of legitimacy in itself.[26] It is, however, very important for the discussion of the nature of the position of the attorney general for two reasons. First, it supports the general image of the attorney general as the ultimate representative of the public interest and the rule of law. Second, it accordingly enables the attorney general not only to refrain from *defending* the government in certain cases in which the rule of law is threatened, but also to *attack* the government in a court of law whenever the attorney general believes that the public interest is threatened and no other petitioner is willing to come forward.[27] Therefore, it gives additional support to the perception of the independence of the attorney general vis-à-vis the government.

The accumulation of all these important powers within the hands of one official is unique to Israel. It makes the attorney general the most powerful bureaucratic position within the Israeli system of government. The importance of the office of the attorney general is manifested not only by its official functions but also by its public image, professional prestige, and the history of the office. Accordingly, many attorney generals were appointed to the Supreme Court after the conclusion of their tenure.[28] Throughout the years, the people serving as attorney general developed an ideology of almost complete independence of the office vis-à-vis the government. They viewed themselves and their offices as directly committed to the fulfillment of the idea of the rule of law, as manifested by the rulings of the courts (most

[26] The Procedure Ordinance (Intervention by the Attorney General) (1968) 11 L.S.I. 282, section 1. See also Gavison, above note 14, at 45–46.

[27] This practice started in 1976. It was revealed in the media that Prime Minister Yitzhak Rabin had violated the Treasury Ministry's regulations that prohibited Israeli citizens from holding accounts in foreign banks without the permission of the regulatory authority. Officially, the power to open the proceedings against the prime minister rested, under the relevant regulations, in the hands of the treasury minister, who, for obvious reasons, was inclined not to take action. However, at this stage Attorney General Aharon Barak interfered and threatened that if the minister failed to use his prosecutorial powers the attorney general would petition the HCJ to force him to do so. Subsequently, the treasury minister was forced to indict his prime minister, and the affair soon brought the resignation of Yitzhak Rabin.

[28] Since the creation of the office five attorney generals have been appointed to the Supreme Court after the conclusion of their tenure (Chaim Cohen, Meir Shamgar, Aharon Barak, Itzhak Zamir, and Elyakim Rubinstein).

notably the Supreme Court).[29] The Supreme Court, on its part, consistently supported the efforts of the attorney general to establish independence (while at the same time developing jurisprudence to ensure that the attorney general would be subject to the court's own supervision – see below).

Not surprisingly, the development of such ideology of independence has led to many clashes between the attorney generals and politicians within the governments that they serve. The history of the office of the attorney general is, in fact, marked by a long series of confrontations and situations of crisis by which the independence of the office was shaped. Some of these clashes relate to the prosecutorial powers of the attorney general that in many cases since the 1970s have been directed against senior cabinet members and even prime ministers they served. For example, in 1977, the prosecutorial actions of Attorney General Ahron Barak (later on the Chief Justice of the Supreme Court) brought about the resignation of Prime Minister Yitzhak Rabin. In 1993, a criminal prosecution initiated by the attorney general led to the imprisonment of the former Minister for the Interior Arie Deri. In numerous other cases the attorney general initiated investigations and/or criminal proceedings against cabinet members, MKs, and senior politicians.[30] The wave of indictments against senior politicians seems to have reached a peak since the early 2000s. All four prime ministers during this period were investigated for criminal charges.[31] In 2009, Prime Minister Ehud Ulmert was forced to resign after

[29] See e.g. the statement of Itzhak Zamir, a former attorney general, at above note 19.

[30] Several cabinet ministers have been subject to criminal investigations since the 1990s, including two ministers of justice (Yaakove Neeman and Tzachi Hanegbi). One of them, Yaakov Neeman, had to resign from his office in 1996 after the attorney general at the time (Michael Ben-Yair) decided to issue an indictment against him for perjury. Nevertheless, he was finally vindicated and was appointed by Netanyahu to serve as the treasury minister after his acquittal and currently serves as the minister of justice in Netanyahu's second government. A former minister of justice, Meir Shitreet, was also subject to a criminal trial (for larceny and breach of trust of a public official) before being appointed to his post, but was acquitted by the court.

[31] Prime Minister Ehud Barak (1999–2001) was investigated for breaching campaign finance laws but in 2003 the Attorney General Elyakim Rubistein decided not to indict him. Prime Minister Ariel Sharon (2001–2006) was investigated for allegation of bribery, but the Attorney General Menachem Mazuz decided in 2004 not to forward an indictment against Sharon, but his elder son Omri Sharon was indicted and convicted for violations of campaign finance laws related to Sharon's campaign. The current Prime Minister Benyamin Netanyahu was subject to criminal investigations during his first tenure (in 1997) for misconduct related to (a failed) attempt to appoint as attorney general a party activist, but no charges were issued (see http://he.wikipedia.org/wiki/%D7%A4%D7%A8%D7%A9%D7%AA_%D7%91%D7%A8-%D7%90%D7%95%D7%9F_%D7%97%D7%91%D7%A8%D7%95%D7%9F, last accessed July 16, 2013).

being subject to a number of criminal investigations for bribery, fraud and breach of trust, and other serious criminal offences. Some of those investigations led to indictments.[32] Other occasions of clashes between attorney generals and governments have occurred in cases in which attorney generals refused to represent the government against petitions to the HCJ that were directed against the legality of the government policies or actions, and thereby brought about – almost inevitably – the interference of the court to strike down the government action.[33]

This type of tension between the attorney general and the government points to another important characteristic of the attorney general office – its tight relationship to the courts, and most notably to the Supreme Court. In other words, *there is a strong link between the independence of the attorney general vis-à-vis the government and its close relationship with the judiciary.*[34] Indeed, historically, there is a clear correlation between the rise of judicial activism during the 1980s and the rise of the independence of the attorney general's office during the same period.[35]

Before 1980, many aspects of the attorney general's authority and independence were far from being clearly established. As noted above, neither the advisory powers of the attorney general nor his power to represent the government in any legal proceedings is clearly established by statute, and no statutory provision provides for the *exclusiveness* of the attorney general's position in this respect. Therefore, before 1980, the accepted view was that the government was by no means precluded from disagreeing with the attorney general on matters of law. Correspondingly, the general view was that the attorney general was obliged to represent the government in court, even if his views on matters of law differed from those of the government.[36] Moreover, during this early period, the attorney generals were not under any pressure to adopt an independent position not in

[32] A number of criminal trials and investigations against Ulmert are still ongoing. In 2007, the Minister of Finance in Ulmert's government, Abraham Hirshezon, was convicted for grand larceny.

[33] See above note 24 and accompanying text.

[34] As we shall see (in course of the discussion of the HCJD) this close relationship is reflected in the career structure of the attorney general's office staff and in other social aspects related to the bureaucracy in the attorney general's office. See the discussion at Sections D.2 and D.3 below.

[35] See also Chapter 1 Section C.2. On the expansion of judicial review by the HCJ in Israel see Y. Dotan, "Judicial Review and Political Accountability: The Case of the High Court of Justice in Israel", 32 *Isr. L. Rev.* 448 (1998).

[36] See Gavison, above note 14, at 65; Levontin, above note 12, at 65–77 and the discussion in above note 13.

accord with the government. They knew that their legal policies (in particular in the prosecutorial field) were almost completely immune from attacks by judicial review proceedings.[37]

After 1980, however, the Supreme Court expanded its intervention in governmental actions in general, but most notably it tightened its supervision on *prosecutorial* decisions.[38] Thereby, it supplied, on the one hand, ample support for the efforts of the attorney generals in confronting the government on issues of representation or those related to the prosecution of senior politicians. On the other hand, the expansion of judicial review also placed the attorney general in a position that – in essence – *forced* him to adopt a wide and independent view of his constitutional role. Otherwise, he risked the possibility that his position would not be in accord with the activist position of the court, and therefore would be struck down by it.[39] Therefore, it was no surprise that the attorney generals during this period developed the concept that their primary responsibility as the interpreters of the law was to the "public interest" manifested by the (expected) position of the Supreme Court (before which they were expected to defend any possible rulings) and not to their initial client – the government.[40]

As the result of these developments, governments in Israel are placed in an uneasy position in their relations with the OAG. The government knows that (under the current activist tendencies of the Supreme Court) *any* action that it takes may be subject to (immediate) review by the HCJ. It also knows that the attorney general is the exclusive interpreter of the

[37] See Chapter 1, Section C.2, p. 38. [38] Dotan, above note 10.

[39] A major example of this trend is the decision of the HCJ in HCJ 935/89 *Ganor* v. *Attorney General* [1990] IsrSC 44(2) 485. The case was brought to judicial review after the Attorney General Yosef Harish decided not to bring action against a number of senior bankers in "The Bankers Affair." During the 1980s major Israeli banks manipulated the prices of their own shares. This misconduct ended up in the collapse of the banks' shares (along with the whole Israeli stock market in 1983) and the government had to step in and buy the banks in order to save them from bankruptcy. Nevertheless, Attorney General Harish decided not to issue criminal indictment against senior officials in the relevant banks. The case was brought to the HCJ and the court decided to strike down the attorney general's decision and order him to forward criminal charges, thus marking a new era of judicial supervision over the attorney general's decision-making.

[40] To this we should add that both the breakthrough of judicial activism in the 1980s and the expansion of the power of the attorney general were led by the same figures: former Chief Justice Meir Shamgar and former Chief Justice Aharon Barak. Both these figures served as attorney general before being appointed to the Supreme Court, and both are widely regarded as responsible for the expansion of the independence of the attorney general and the expansion of judicial review by the Supreme Court. The fundamentals of this model of lawyering will be further discussed in Chapter 4.

law (at least as far as the government is concerned). Therefore, if the attorney general rules that a certain action is illegal, the government is obliged, as a matter of law, to refrain from going forward. If it decides to proceed, it is likely to be taken to court, where, on the one hand, the attorney general may refuse to represent its position, and on the other hand, it is unlikely to be able to use the services of any other (external) attorney. It should be added that even if the government is allowed (by the court) to use the services of an external attorney, the contrasting position of the attorney general would be presented to the court as "the official position of the State of Israel."[41]

It is therefore hardly surprising that almost all governments in Israel since the mid-1980s have made several efforts to curtail the power and influence of the attorney general. On the face of the matter, the government should have no problem in influencing the policies of the attorney general by using its (formally) unlimited powers to nominate or discharge the attorney general. However, the high public profile of the attorney general and the strong popular support for the independence of the office served to deter the government from using these powers to infringe on the independence of the office. So far, no government has ever discharged an attorney general during the course of his tenure.[42] Moreover, an attempt made by Netanyahu's government to appoint to this elevated position a lawyer who was identified as a grass-root party activist encountered an unprecedented wave of public criticism which forced the government to back off, under the threat of intervention by the court.[43]

[41] See above note 24 and accompanying text.

[42] The only exception being the replacement of Itzhak Zamir in 1986 in the course of the events of The Shin Bet Affair. In that case, Zamir insisted on the investigation of senior officials in the General Security Service (Shin Bet) for offences of obstruction of justice and perjury in the course of a cover-up operation that the service committed with regard to the killing of two terrorists by its agents (for a description of the facts of this affair see Zamir, above note 9 and note 20 above). The heads of government, who were unanimous in their refusal to allow the attorney general to further the criminal procedures, took advantage of the fact that Zamir had announced several months before that he wished to end his tenure and would resign when the government nominated his successor, and appointed overnight Yosef Harish to the position of attorney general.

[43] See G. Alon and Y. Verter, "The Attorney General Bar-On Resigned", *Ha'aretz*, January 13, 1997; Y. Markus, "The Malice, Not the Stupidity", *Ha'aretz*, January 14, 1997. This affair also brought about a criminal investigation against Prime Minister Netanyahu, see above note 31.

C. The Office of the Attorney General

1. *Overview: The structure and functions of the OAG*

The OAG is the bureaucratic agency that assists the attorney general in carrying out his various functions and responsibilities. The office is part of the Ministry of Justice and its employees are all state employees. At the beginning of the year 2000 the office employed 501 lawyers, (as well as over 200 trainees and 136 administrative workers),[44] while in 2011 the number of lawyers in the OAG was 884.[45] The head of the office is the state attorney who is directly accountable to the attorney general. The office is composed of a central branch (known as the State Attorney Office) and a number of district branches (see Figure 2.2). The State Attorney Office operates in Jerusalem and its offices are located in the building of the Ministry of Justice. It has 10 departments employing in 2011 more than 120 lawyers. The largest departments are the Criminal Department (that represents the state in all criminal proceedings before the Supreme Court),[46] and the Department for Economic Litigation (in charge of the prosecution of complicated economic cases).[47] The two other large departments in the State Attorney Office are the Civil Department, which represents the State of Israel in all civil matters before the Supreme Court and the HCJD, which represents state agencies before the HCJ. Apart from these main departments there are an additional seven smaller departments that specialize in specific areas

[44] See Report: OAG-2000 at 17 (February 2000). The report was issued by a special committee appointed in 1997 by the then Minister of Justice Yossi Beilin. The committee was headed by the (then) State Prosecutor (and later a Supreme Court Justice) Edna Arbel. The mandate of the committee was to review the organization and practices of the OAG as well as its preparedness for its missions for the twenty-first century (OAG-2000). In Israel, there is a mandatory training period of one year for all candidates for the Bar exam. Besides the trainees there is a much smaller number of law students employed – on a part-time basis – by the OAG.

[45] Source: OAG.

[46] The Israeli Supreme Court functions as an appellate court for civil and criminal appeals that were disposed of by the District Courts at first instance, see Chapter 1 Section A.2, p. 19, and see also note 67 below.

[47] These departments are also responsible for advising all enforcement agencies on matters of law and for assisting the attorney general to carry out his powers related to law enforcement, see OAG-2000, above note 44, at 18–19. In the beginning of 2000 there were seventeen lawyers serving in the Criminal Department while in 2011 the number had risen to thirty lawyers. In 2011 twenty-six lawyers served in the economic department.

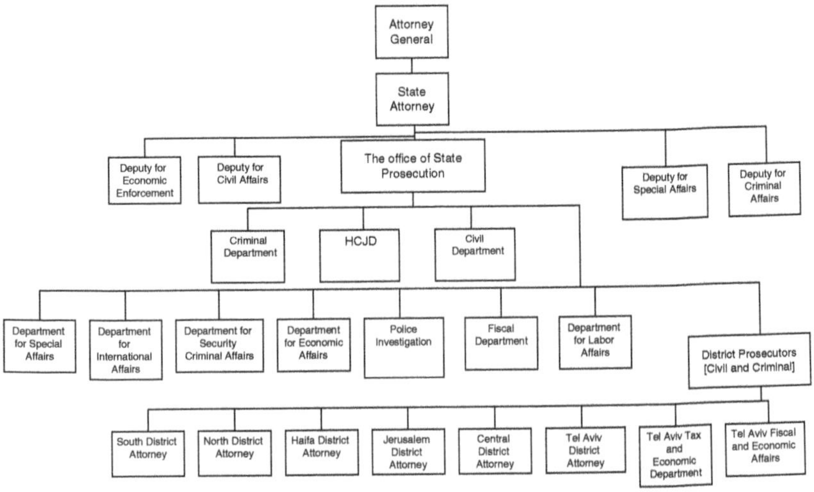

Figure 2.2 The Office of the Attorney General (OAG)
Source: The Ministry of Justice, available at http://old.justice.gov.il/MOJHeb/PraklitotHamedina/TarshimIrguni.htm (last accessed July 18, 2013).

of law (such as fiscal matters, labor law, and international law – see Figure 2.2).

Apart from the central branch the OAG has seven district branches (of which some are divided into two main offices for criminal and civil affairs). Three of them are located in the Tel Aviv area with the remaining four in other parts of Israel (see Figure 2.2). The district branches are responsible for litigation on behalf of the State of Israel before any court (criminal, civil, or administrative) – apart from the Supreme Court – and some other judicial tribunals.[48] Not surprisingly, the branches are doing most of the field work for the OAG and are responsible for the vast majority of its caseload. Correspondingly, over 80 percent of the lawyers in the OAG work in the district branches while the rest work in the State Attorney Office or in affiliated units.[49]

48 There are a number of enforcement agencies that operate under specific laws and specializing in certain areas of law, such as the Anti-trust Agency, and the Labor and Welfare Ministry that investigate and enforce safety regulations. Like the rest of the legal apparatus, these agencies are also subject to the powers of the attorney general to interfere in their operations.

49 Source: OAG. See also OAG-2000, above note 44, at 18.

2. *The OAG: Ideological and social factors*

When asked to describe her own mission the responsible senior officer of the OAG wrote the following description:

> The OAG is a *value-oriented* organization in its essence and characteristics. The people who work for the OAG have chosen the public service as *a way of life*. This is their profession, their occupation, their *life style* ... The OAG lawyer carries with her the norms and values that apply to her as a public servant and as a lawyer .... She is to represent an *impartial* and balanced approach, and she is subject to *intensified* duties of fairness and credibility. The OAG is characterized by its independence, impartiality and professionalism ... The OAG has a doctrine, a culture and a working tradition that was built, step by step, throughout many years ... It acts as the public trustee, for the public and for the interests of *the public at large* ... The public confidence bestows on the OAG its powers and independence. The prestige of the Office and the public trust in it form a public interest of the utmost importance.[50]

This self-description points to some central characteristics of the OAG. First, the career of its staff is a typical life career. Most lawyers in the OAG join the bureau at the very beginning of their professional career, i.e., immediately after graduating law school. In Israel lawyers must complete a training period of one year before taking the bar exams. Most lawyers in the OAG joined the bureau as trainees or even as student-assistants. Many of them spend their entire professional career in the bureau or stay for long periods before they leave. Those who leave the office are moving either for other bureaucratic posts within the public service, or for the bench. Leaving the OAG for a job in the private sector is relatively rare. Joining the service from the private sector at the mid-career stage or later is exceptional.[51]

A second central characteristic of the OAG is its bureaucratic autonomy. While the government appoints the attorney general himself, the political branches traditionally are not involved in nominations within the bureau. Thus, even those appointed to the highest post in the bureau – the

[50] OAG-2000, at 1–2 (italics are mine).

[51] For example, in July 2001 we found that out of sixty-one lawyers serving in the District Bureau of OAG in Jerusalem for one year or more, forty-eight (80 percent) spent their entire career in the same bureau. Another three lawyers spent some part of their career in other departments of the OAG before arriving at the Jerusalem Bureau. Of the remaining ten lawyers, only six (i.e. 10 percent) have ever worked during their career in the private sector, while only two of these lawyers spent more than half of their legal careers in the

State Attorney – have always come from within the OAG (or, in one case, from the bench).[52] Unlike in the United States changes in the political field (such as changes in the formation of the government or the substitution of the Minister of Justice) – have little effect on the careers and promotions within the OAG.

The strong sense of professional autonomy is supported by social and ideological factors that intensify the OAG's autonomy and the image of its staff as a typical professional-bureaucratic elite group. The fact that the OAG is based on life-career officers whose careers are almost completely immune from external political influences fits well with the social and ideological cohesiveness of the bureau's staff. Most OAG staff graduated from the same law schools.[53] They typically come from middle class, secular backgrounds.[54] They belong to a social reference group that includes the legal elite of Israel together with the bench and the legal academy. The structure of their career also explains why their social connections with politicians, the business elite and even the private bar are very loose.

As can be seen from the citation in the opening of this part, the OAG's staff view themselves as committed to the ideals of the rule of law and the

private sector. Another three lawyers spent some parts of their career in other government agencies, and one worked as a lawyer in England before immigrating to Israel. This state of affairs may be beginning to change in recent years mainly due to a reform, initiated by the former Minister of Justice Daniel Friedman. This reform introduced tenure limits to the positions of senior members in the OAG and forced some members to retire early into private practice.

52 The current State Attorney Moshe Lador spent most of his career as a lawyer in the OAG and served as the District Attorney of Jerusalem, He was appointed as State Attorney shortly after he retired from his previous post. His predecessor Eran Shendar also had most of his career in the OAG and served as the Head of the Department for Internal Police Investigations before his appointment. Likewise all other state attorneys who served since the 1980s came from within the OAG (with the exception of Edna Arbel who had her career at the OAG but was appointed as a district judge before she was appointed to the post). Four state attorneys (Haim Cohen, Gabriel Bach, Dorit Beinish, and Edna Arbel) were appointed to the Supreme Court after the conclusion of their tenure.

53 Until the beginning of the 1990s, there were only three law schools in Israel, but at the beginning of the 1990s there was a sharp expansion in the number of law schools and today there are fourteen such schools in the country. The proliferation of law schools does not seem to have much impact on the (rather cohesive) composition of the OAG staff. Almost all the lawyers in the HCJD through the years are graduates of either the law school of the Hebrew University or the Tel Aviv University Law School (which are considered the leading law schools in the country). For example, out of the twenty-six lawyers serving in the Department in September 2011, seventeen graduated from the Hebrew University, eight graduated from Tel Aviv University and only one came from another law school.

54 This has begun to change to some extent during the last decade as the HCJD accepted some candidates of religious background (interview with IN, September 22, 2011).

practice of law enforcement. They view all other social elite groups, and in particular members of the political and economic elite, as subject to their supervision, under the idea of the rule of law. As mentioned earlier, since the 1990s the OAG has brought to justice several senior politicians, including cabinet ministers, senior government officials, city mayors, and even prime ministers.[55] Likewise, the OAG has issued indictments against key financial figures and members of the business elite.[56]

Not surprisingly, the OAG has undergone many attacks on the part of numerous public bodies. Opponents of the judicial activism in the Supreme Court view the OAG as an essential part of the judicial apparatus and as an accessory mechanism in the process of expanding the control of the judiciary over the political arena.[57] Politicians and top business figures attack its policies in the prosecutorial field as over-zealous, over-intrusive, and detached from the realities of politics and economics.[58] Religious leaders and Ultra-orthodox politicians accuse it of being elitist, inclined toward liberal-leftist ideology, and hostile to their causes.[59] Therefore, the religious parties have consistently tried – so far mostly

[55] See above note 30 and accompanying text.

[56] See e.g. "The Bankers Affair" discussed above note 39. Similarly, the OAG recently decided to issue a criminal indictment against the former Chairman of Bank Ha'Poalim (the second-largest bank in the country) for bribery and fraud. See S. Mizrachi, "Dani Dankner to Face Indictment for Bribery and Fraud," *The Marker,* September 5, 2011 (available at www.themarker.com/law/1.1374641, last accessed July 16, 2013).

[57] See e.g. M. Moalem, "A Wave of Intimidation against OAG Staff after the Ultra-orthodox Demonstration against the HCJ," *Ha'aretz* February 17, 1999.

[58] See e.g. the attack on the State Attorney launched by the then Mayor of Jerusalem, Ehud Ulmert, after the acquittal of a senior politician and a former minister from charges of subversion of justice: A. Segal, "The Judgement of Edna Arbel [State Attorney] is Flawed," *Maariv* April 4, 2001; Ulmert continued his fierce attacks on the OAG during his criminal trial after being forced to resign from his position as Prime Minister (see above note 32 and text; and e.g. G. Grosman, "Ulmert Calls for Investigation of the OAG for Obstruction of Justice," *Walla News* June 23, 2011, available at http://news.walla.co.il/?w=/1/1699177/@@/item/printer, last accessed November 8, 2011. See also M. Zelikovitz, "Ramon: The OAG Became Coercive," *Ynet* June 12, 2008, available at www.ynet.co.il/articles/0,7340,L-3554781,00.html, last accessed July 16, 2013). Fierce criticism accompanied by various acts of (occasionally violent) protest against the OAG came on behalf of right-wing extremists with regard to law enforcement actions against Israeli settlers in the Territories. See e.g. "Yet another wave of Incitement against OAG Senior," *Globs* February 11, 2011, available at www.globes.co.il/news/article.aspx?did=1000622391, last accessed July 16, 2013.

[59] The allegations came to a head during the trial of Arie Deri, the political leader of the Ultra-orthodox Shas party. Deri had been a rising star in Israeli politics. He served as a senior cabinet member and as minister of the interior during the 1990s and was a close ally of the leaders of both the Likud and the Labor party. He was brought to justice for accusations of bribery, convicted and sentenced to two years in prison. He and his

without success – to resist the promotion of judges who came to the bench from the OAG and the Ministry of Justice.[60]

The OAG relationships with the Israeli Bar have also been tense – sometimes even confrontational – since the beginning of the rise of judicial activism during the 1980s. The leaders of the Bar have always been lawyers from private practice that were, in many occasions, affiliated with political parties or with senior politicians. Therefore, their stand in disputes between politicians and the legal apparatus of the OAG was much more favorable toward the former. Not surprisingly, they view the ever-closer relationship between the OAG and the judiciary (in particular the Supreme Court) as an inevitable threat to the influence of the Bar on judicial policies. Thus, for example, since 1980 almost half of the appointments to the Supreme Court have been of candidates who have served in the Ministry of Justice, while very few have a background in private practice (the rest were district judges prior to their appointment).[61] The leaders

supporters argued that his indictment was the result of a political conspiracy induced by the elitist establishment that feared the growing influence of Shas in Israeli politics. See e.g. S. Ilan, "Rabbi David Yosef: 'Antisemistic forces in the legal bureaucracy calls the Shas people parasites'," *Ha'aretz* February 2, 1999; S. Ilan, "Shas: Deri's Conviction is the Conviction of Shas," *Ha'aretz* March 18, 1999; A. Shavit, "An Interview with Deri," *Ha'aretz*, July 20, 2000.

60 One such attempt was to prevent the nomination of Aharon Barak (the former Chief Justice of the Supreme Court and a former attorney general) by changing the statutory rule that the veteran judge in the court would be appointed to the office after the retirement of the previous chief justice, see G. Alon, "The Government Rejects The Criticism Made by Religious MKs on Justice Barak," *Ha'aretz* December 12, 1994; D. Margalit, "Rabin and Peres of the HCJ," *Ha'aretz*, December 9, 1994. Another attempt was made in 1999 when religious politicians tried to reform this rule again in order to prevent the nomination of Justice Dorit Beinish (a former state attorney) for the same position after Barak's anticipated retirement on 2006, see G. Alon, "Ex Chief Justices Support the Seniority Rule," *Ha'aretz*, December 21, 1999. The law regarding the appointment of the Chief Justice was finally changed in 2007. See the discussion in Chapter 1 Section C.4, p. 49 and note 105.

61 Thus, for example, in 1985 four out of eleven judges of the Supreme Court were appointed from the Ministry of Justice or the legal academy (Shamgar, Barak, Elon, and Bach), while all the rest were appointed from the District Court. In 1995, out of the thirteen permanent justices of the court, five justices came from the legal bureaucracy (Shamgar, Barak, Bach, Zamir, and Dorner (military court)). The only justice in this court appointed during the 1990s to the bench as a private attorney was Mishael Cheshin. Paradoxically, however, his appointment supports the thesis of favoritism toward the legal bureaucracy in nominations to the court rather than weakening it, since Cheshin was, for most of his professional career, an OAG senior staff member. He left the Ministry of Justice after concluding his tenure as the director of HCJD and having failed to be appointed as the attorney general, and worked for a short period in private practice before his nomination. In the year 2000, five justices of the twelve permanent appointments (Barak, Zamir, Dorner, Beinish, and Englard) came from the legal bureaucracy (or academy) while none (Cheshin

of the Bar have often criticized the Supreme Court for being too occupied with theoretical and academic questions while neglecting urgent needs of the true "customers" of the courts system and the need to confront issues of efficiency.[62]

D. The High Court of Justice Department

1. *The structure and functions of the HCJD*

The HCJD is the second-largest department within the central office of the OAG. Still, it is rather a small governmental unit. It is currently composed of twenty-six lawyers, a similar number of trainees and a handful of administrative staff.[63] Despite its limited size the HCJD represents all agencies of the State of Israel before the HCJ. This includes all government ministries, departments, and units, such as the army, the police, and the security services. The HCJD also represents some independent agencies before the HCJ, although these agencies are not obliged, under the directives of the attorney general, to be represented

excluded) was appointed to the court from private practice. This picture was changed slightly during the tenure of Daniel Friedman (himself an adamant critic of judicial activism) from 2007 to 2009. He initiated the appointment of two candidates from private practice to the Supreme Court (Hanan Meltzer and Yoram Danziger). Nevertheless, in 2010, still six out of fifteen justices (Beinish, Naor, Procacia, Arbel, Rubinstein, and Fogelman) were of typical OAG background prior to their appointment.

[62] See e.g. B. Z. Zitrin, "Hoter Yishai [the then President of the Bar]: The Judicial System is Frozen and Very Conservative," *Ha'aretz*, February 25, 1997; M. Reinfeld, "The Movement for the Quality of Government to HCJ: Order the Bar to Discharge Hoter Yishai," *Ha'aretz* March 13, 1997. This criticism was also reflected in the consistent opposition of the Bar to the initiatives by the Supreme Court to introduce structural reforms in the judicial system. One such attempt was made by forming a public committee chaired by a Supreme Court Justice (Theodore Or) that prepared a report containing suggestions for the reform. The Bar fought the Committee's recommendations (which drew criticism also from other institutions) and they have undergone wide changes before reaching the Knesset (which declined to pass them into the law of the land). See e.g. H. Magen, "The Bar Rejects the Central Part of Or Commission Report," *Globs* September 9, 1997; H. Magen, "Changes in the New Proposal to Implement the Or Commission Report," *Globs* November 22, 1998. Another issue that brought up a conflict between the Bar and the court was the decision of the Bar to conduct a yearly survey among lawyers to test the level of satisfaction with the function of judges in the system. See e.g. H. Magen, "Aharon Barak: We Shall Fight Like Lions against the Individual Survey on Judges," *Globs* December 12, 2001.

[63] The number of staff in the HCJD has grown significantly over the years. In the mid-1970s the HCJD was composed of three lawyers and in the early 1980s it had five. In 1995 there were around ten lawyers in the department, while in February 2000 there were thirteen lawyers working for the HCJD. Source: OAG-2000, above note 44, at 20.

by it.[64] Moreover, the range of organs represented by the HCJ exceeds the boundaries of the Executive Branch. Until recently the HCJD represented the Knesset before the HCJ whenever a statute or any other decision of the Knesset was challenged before the HCJ.[65] It also occasionally represents any court or judicial tribunal of which a decision is attacked before the HCJ (such as military courts and religious tribunals).[66] In sum, the HCJD represents the responding agencies before the HCJ in almost all the petitions issued against public authorities, save petitions issued solely against local municipalities (which are represented before the HCJ by their own lawyers) and some other independent corporations.[67] This means that the HCJD is involved in around 75 percent of the cases litigated before the HCJ.[68] Thus, at the end of the 1990s the court's annual caseload reached 2,000 and the caseload of the

[64] Thus, for example, the HCJD represents the Israeli Broadcasting Authority (IBA) before the HCJ although the IBA is an independent statutory corporation under the law, and as such is not formally a part of the government of Israel. The representation is made in such a case according to a contract signed between the IBA and the Ministry of Justice.

[65] The practice under which the HCJ (and the attorney general) represent the Knesset in judicial proceedings evolved throughout the years as a convention, mainly as a result of the fact that in the past, proceedings against the Knesset were rare. During the 1980s, the HCJ began to hear petitions against Knesset decisions related to procedural matters (See D. Kretzmer, "Judicial Review of Knesset Decisions," 8 *Tel Aviv U. Stud. L.* 95 (1988)). This practice was kept mainly because the Knesset had no legal staff trained to litigate judicial review cases. During the 1990s and after the formation of the New Basic Laws (see Chapter 1 Section A.1) this practice was increasingly subject to criticism as a violation of the principle of the separation of powers (see e.g. Gavison, above note 14, at 84). In 2000, the Knesset amended the Law of the Knesset to authorize the Knesset Attorney to represent the Knesset in all leading procedures (see The Law of The Knesset, section 17).

[66] In most cases the tribunal that gave the decision subject to judicial review is not represented in practice, but only appears as a formal respondent to the petition. In some cases, however, there is a need to bring before the HCJ the positions of the relevant tribunals or even to present arguments on its behalf.

[67] Nevertheless, the HCJD is involved in litigation against actions of local municipalities whenever the petition involves state agencies as additional respondents, which is often the case in such petitions. Thus, for example, in 1985 out of 715 petitions disposed of by the HCJD 15 percent involved local municipalities, while all the rest were issued against state agencies and other bodies that are normally represented by the HCJD. In 1990, out of 827 petitions that were disposed of by the HCJ, 18.4 percent involved local municipalities (source: HCJD data). Since 2000, when the new Administrative Law Courts Act (2000) was passed (see Chapter 1 note 16) most petitions involving local authorities are disposed of by the administrative courts as first instances. Still a substantial number of these cases are appealed to the HCJ as an appellate court (see Chapter 1 – Figure 1.1 at p. 25 and text].

[68] Out of 1,064 files in our database for 1990–1998 the HCJD was involved (as the representative of the respondents or some of the respondents in 74 percent (source: HCJ files). See Chapter 3, Table 3.1 at p. 91 and note 8 at p. 90.

HCJD was around 1,500 court files each year. [69] In 2007 the HCJD was already handling over 2,400 HCJ cases as well as over 400 administrative appeal cases.[70]

As the representative of government agencies before the HCJ, the ultimate official function of the HCJD lawyers is to appear before the HCJ in any proceedings involving their client agencies.[71] This function includes the preparation of written briefs and the presentation of oral arguments in court. It also includes correlative advisory functions, such as advising its client agencies with regard to their chances in a given proceeding and taking part in consultations regarding the implications of HCJ proceedings. Occasionally, the HCJD may be involved in consultations even before any petition is issued to the HCJ, if the decision-makers in the relevant agency anticipate such proceedings.[72]

[69] See Chapter 1 Section B.1 and Figure 1.1 at p. 25.

[70] Source: The Ministry of Justice official site, available at www.justice.gov.il/NR/rdonlyres/DD32E243-7FEF-459C-B4AD-AF4DFE7C8932/12991/2007filesno.pdf, last accessed July 16, 2013).*Accurate* reliable numbers of petitions dealt with by the HCJD throughout the research period are not always available. The department started handling an operation to supervise its caseload in the mid-1990s for its internal purposes, but this was done unsystematically and their data is not in accordance with the data of the Central Bureau of Statistics (CBS), which was in charge of conducting statistical surveys of the judicial system in Israel until 1998. The CBS, however, has no record that refers directly to the caseload of the HCJD, but rather one has to infer this data from the records of the CBS referring to the data on the caseload of the HCJ itself. Since 1998 the Judicial Authority is conducting its own statistical surveys and so does the Ministry of Justice. Like the CBS, however, those statistics do not always include data on legal representation. Therefore, the numbers I refer to in the text here are based in some cases on estimations made on the basis of the data from a variety of sources including the CBS, The Judicial Authority, The Ministry of Justice, The OAG, and the database created for the purposes of the current study.

[71] Normally, government agencies appear before the HCJ as respondents to a petition issued by a private party. In some cases, however, the government may appear in the HCJ as the petitioner. For example, the OAG submits petitions to the HCJ against decisions of parole committees that the government regards as erroneous. In such cases the HCJD represents the government as the petitioner.

[72] See Chapters 5 and 6. Besides representing the government before the HCJ the HCJD is also responsible for representing the government before the Supreme Court in appeals against decisions of administrative courts and tribunals. Until 2000 such proceedings related mainly to a small number of appeals regarding fields in which there was a specific statute that provides for such proceedings (such as prison conditions and zoning and planning). In 2000 the Knesset passed the Administrative Law Courts Act, which authorizes the District Court to dispose of many administrative petitions, and provides for appeals against their decisions to the Supreme Court (see Chapter 1 note 16 at pp. 19–20 above). Accordingly, the number of administrative appeals in which the department is involved grew significantly.

Apart from these functions of the HCJD, which are typical of any organization in charge of litigation, the HCJD performs some important *informal* functions. These functions include, in some cases, heavy involvement in the creation of administrative policies, supervision on the work of other government agencies, and even, in some cases, an adjudicative function with regard to petitions that are issued against government agencies. These functions evolved within the HCJD as the result of the special status of the department within the Israeli bureaucracy, the special practices and ideology that were developed through the years in the department, and the special relationship between its members and the HCJD. I shall discuss them in the following Chapters.[73]

2. *Career structure in the HCJD and place within the OAG*

The career structure of the HCJD staff does not differ significantly from their colleagues in the other departments of the OAG. They are all life-career civil servants, who are appointed to their job by the state attorney, without any reference to their political affiliation, and without any interference of political or other functionaries outside the Ministry of Justice. Some of them joined the department after serving in other departments of the OAG or in legal departments of public agencies.[74] Others, however, were appointed to the HCJD immediately or soon after they completed their legal training (some, after serving in the HCJD itself as assistants while completing their internship period or as trainees of justices of the Supreme Court).[75]

[73] See Chapters 5 and 6.

[74] Interestingly, in two cases during the 1990s, the chief legal advisors of the Association of Civil Rights in Israel (ACRI) joined the HCJD immediately after completing their tenure at ACRI. See Y. Dotan, "Cause Lawyers Crossing the Lines: Patterns of Fragmentation and Cooperation between State and Civil Rights Lawyers in Israel," 5 *Int'l J. Legal Prof.* 193 (1998).

[75] There seems to have been some shift in the career structure of HCJD staff over the years. In the past, many staff members joined the HCJD after serving in another department of the OAG or even after beginning their legal career outside the Ministry of Justice (in other legal departments of public authorities or in some cases in the private sector). This practice has changed, to some extent, during the last fifteen years, when many new staff members joined the department immediately after concluding their training. It seems that the shift has much to do with the fact that the number of staff has sharply increased since the mid-1990s (see above note 63 and accompanying text). Thus, for example, out of the twenty-six lawyers serving in the department in September 2011, about half began their career as lawyers in the HCJD (usually after a one-year internship in the HCJD or in the Supreme Court) while the rest reached the HCJD after serving in other positions

Nevertheless, there are some differences between service in the HCJD and other departments within the OAG. The lawyers in the department enjoy a considerable amount of prestige both within and outside the bureaucracy. For their colleagues within the Ministry of Justice, these HCJD lawyers are those who appear solely before the Supreme Court, and are those who "control" the important arena of public law litigation. They are those who represent ministers and other high-ranked officials in court in matters that are on the public agenda, and therefore are in daily contact with them.

For the bureaucrats within the various departments of the administration, these are the people who represent them in court. From the point of view of the legal profession, the HCJD staff enjoys some of the glory of the HCJ itself. The high level of exposure of HCJ litigation in the Israeli media also contributes to the prestige of service in the department. Therefore, service in the HCJD is considered to be somewhat more prestigious than in other departments of the OAG.[76]

The strong affiliation between the members of the OAG and the judiciary is also reflected in the careers of the HCJD staff after they leave office. Many of the HCJD members leave the department for other positions within the public sector or for judicial posts. Out of seven former heads of the HCJD, only one left the service for private practice. All the rest were appointed to the bench either immediately after leaving the HCJD or after a few years (that were spent, in most cases, within the OAG). Three former heads of the HCJD were appointed to the Supreme Court of Israel (Michael Cheshin, Dorit Beinish, and Uzi Fogelman).[77] The rest were appointed to lower courts.[78] The picture does not change when we look at

within the legal bureaucracy (often in one of the district offices of the OAG). Only one of the twenty-six lawyers worked in a private firm before being admitted to the HCJD.

76 See e.g. interviews with MA and LD. For similar observations on the Office of the Solicitor General in the United States. as "cream of the crop" see R. M. Salokar, *The Solicitor General: The Politics of Law* (Philadelphia, PA: Temple University Press, 1992), Chapter 2. See also Horowitz, above note 25, at 22 ("Justice lawyers take pride in their proximity to the prestige of the courts ...").

77 An additional former member of the HCJD, Miriam Naor also currently serves in the Supreme Court. Interestingly, a similar phenomenon exists in the United States, see Salokar, above note 76, at 35 (pointing out that "[A]n appointment to the Office of the Solicitor General is commonly viewed as a stepping stone for future Supreme Court justices ...").

78 Mishael Cheshin did work for a short period as a private attorney after retiring from the OAG and before his appointment to the Supreme Court. Dorit Beinish served as the state attorney before her appointment to the Supreme Court (and later on as Chief Justice). Uzi Fogelman was appointed to the Supreme Court after serving for a short period in the

the careers of other members of the HCJD after leaving the department. Very few of them left the public service after the conclusion of their tenure. Most of them spent the rest of their career in the public service. Many were appointed to the bench.[79]

3. *Working practices*

The work of the department is characterized by professionalism. As the lawyers who appear before the HCJ in all cases involving the central government, they have naturally developed a high degree of expertise in the field of public law and judicial review. Such expertise encompasses both the knowledge of the law in the field, the procedures and practices in the court, and the internal practices within the various organs belonging to the governmental sector. Above all, the HCJD staff are profoundly experienced in appearing before the HCJ. Since the lawyers of the HCJD appear every other day before the same fifteen justices of the HCJ they have acquired an elaborate knowledge of the legal positions, the judicial policies as well as the ideological inclination of each of the judges. They are also well attuned to every "dicta" in a written decision or any oral remark from the bench which may signal a possible tendency for future decision-making or a foreseen shift in the position of the judge on a certain point of law. They are cognizant to differences of opinion on the bench as well as to the internal politics of the HCJ.

The HCJD is considered an efficient and organized institution. The heavy caseload is distributed to the lawyers by the head of the department on the basis of their specific expertise and relative work pressures. While each member of the department reports to the department's head, they normally enjoy a good deal of latitude to manage the litigation without much interference from their superiors.[80] Particularly

District Court. The other three former heads of the department were appointed either to the District Court (Felix Landau) or to The National Appellate Tribunal for Labor (Tzvi Terlo and Nili Arad). One other senior member in the HCJD, Menachem Mazuz, was appointed as attorney general in 1994.

79 For example, out of the ten members of the HCJD in 1995 three were appointed to the bench (Nili Arad, Uzi Fogelman, and Arie Romanov), three still serve in the HCJD (Osnat Mendel, Yochi Genesin, and Dana Briskman) and the rest were appointed to senior positions in the OAG or other departments in the Ministry of Justice (Meni Mazuz, Mike Blas, Yehuda Sheffer, and Orit Koren).

80 Interview with IZ. As the number of staff has grown over recent years practices of internal consultation have been formalized. Young members of staff today are assigned a case with reference to one of the more senior members, with whom they are expected to

sensitive or complex cases are dealt with by one of the senior lawyers or the head of department. In such cases, it is likely that both the state attorney and the attorney general would also be involved. The high level of autonomy given to the lawyer who is responsible for a given file is particularly important in cases where there is a difference of opinion between the lawyer and the client agency (see below). In such cases, the management of the department would normally refrain from interference in the work of the lawyer in charge and support their position vis-à-vis the client agency.

The department has highly elaborated practices for storing, indexing, and transferring information between its members. Each significant decision or any other information about developments in the field is disseminated within hours among the staff. Short and informal meetings between the lawyers take place on a daily basis. Every few weeks the trainee in charge distributes a "circulating file," which contains a list of all new cases, an abstract of every case, and short remarks about its significance. The result of these practices is that the HCJD staff are usually more informed about any development in the law than other lawyers who appear before the HCJ. In a legal environment which is rapidly changing – such as the public law field in Israel – this factor alone is sometimes crucial to the result of the litigation. The HCJD staff gather and file information not only about the court's decision but also about cases which were settled, negotiations with any other institution (whether within the governmental bureaucracy or elsewhere), and even, in some cases, oral remarks from the bench that may be significant in future litigation.[81] For the casual visitor who enters the crowded offices of the HCJD late in the evening, the institution may look more like the offices of a corporate law firm than those of a typical Israeli bureaucratic agency.

One last factor that has to be mentioned here is the strong social cohesiveness among its staff. As already mentioned, the lawyers in the OAG usually come from the same social background and share very similar lines of development in their career. Therefore, the OAG at large is characterized by close social ties among the staff. This is even more so in the case of the HCJD. Meetings between staff members out of work for social purposes are a commonplace. The department also organizes social activities

consult before they issue the briefs to the court (interviews with TL; interview with AR September 9, 2011).

[81] Cf. Salokar, above note 76, at 34.

(such as hiking trips) for its members, which come in addition to the social activities organized for the staff of the OAG in general.[82]

E. The history of the HCJD: The evolution of the "rule of law lawyer"

1. *The beginning of the HCJD – between 1948 and 1977*

During the first years after the formation of the State of Israel in 1948, there was no distinguishable department within the OAG that was in charge of litigation before the HCJ. The OAG itself was during this period a very small organization composed of a handful of lawyers and administrative staff. During the first decade after establishment the number of petitions issued to the HCJ did not exceed 200 cases per year. These petitions along with criminal and civil cases were litigated during the first half of the 1950s by the general staff of the OAG. Gradually, however, a process of work division took place within the OAG, and in 1954, there was already a senior staff member at the office, Phelix Landau, who was in charge of the field and, as such, considered by the veterans of the OAG as the first head of department of the HCJD.[83] In the same year he was joined by an additional young staff member, Tzvi Terlo, who became the head of department in 1962, when Landau left the OAG to become a district judge.

During the 1950s and the first half of the 1960s, the internal division between the HCJD and the rest of the OAG was, however, far from complete. The staff of the HCJD were occasionally called on by their superiors at the OAG to litigate civil and criminal cases. It was only in 1967, when Mishael Cheshin was appointed as head of the HCJD, that the creation of the HCJD as a separate and autonomous department within the OAG was completed.[84]

Cheshin, a distinguished jurist and a brilliant barrister, who was later appointed as a Supreme Court Justice, established the status of the HCJD as a separate and prestigious bureaucratic organ within the OAG. He joined the HCJD in 1962 and served as the head of the department between 1967 and 1977. During his long period of service Cheshin

[82] The strong social ties and mutual commitment within the HCJD were recently reflected in the tragic event of one of the lawyers, Gilad Shirman, who contracted a serious disease and eventually passed away. During his hospitalization members of the HCJD volunteered to stay by his bed in shifts (24 hours a day) for several weeks.

[83] Interview with IO (December 27, 1999); Interview with NM (March 7, 1997).

[84] Interview with IO (December 27, 1999); Interview with NM (March 7, 1997).

controlled and dominated the field of public law litigation on the part of the State of Israel almost in the form of a one-man show. Despite the fact that during this long period the number of HCJ cases more than doubled, the number of HCJD staff stayed almost unchanged. When Cheshin joined the department in 1962 there were two lawyers serving in the HCJD. It was only in 1973 that a third lawyer joined the department on a part-time basis.[85] As the head of the department (assisted for most of the period by only one staff member), Cheshin was, in essence, involved directly or indirectly in almost all cases against the State of Israel in the HCJ. Correspondingly, the whole HCJD was identified, to a large extent, with his professional prestige and vibrant personality. One reflection of the prestige and power of the department during this period was that, unlike other departments of the OAG that were subject to the primary supervision of the state attorney, the HCJD under Cheshin worked almost exclusively under the direct supervision of the attorney general himself. Cheshin acted – as one of the HCJD veterans put it – as "Special State Attorney for Public Affairs."[86]

2. *The turning point – the evolution of the New Court and the OAG*

In 1977, Cheshin concluded his tenure as head of the HCJD and moved to a senior position as the deputy attorney general within the OAG.[87] He was replaced by Dorit Beinish, a senior OAG officer who had spent most of her professional career in the criminal departments of the OAG. Beinish, a distinguished lawyer and a powerful figure within the OAG office, was appointed to her position by Aharon Barak, who was, at that stage, on the verge of concluding his tenure as the attorney general of Israel, before his appointment to the Supreme Court. The Beinish appointment signified an important shift in the status, practices, and ideology of the HCJD. The shift was closely related to the major changes in the status of the OAG and the rise of judicial activism in the Supreme Court since the beginning of the 1980s.[88]

85 In fact, the recruitment of the third staff member occurred in 1973 only due to the fact that both Cheshin and his deputy, Yoram Bar-Sela were drafted during the Yom Kipur war in October 1973 (interview with MR, January 13, 2000).

86 *ibid.*

87 Cheshin stayed in the Ministry of Justice until 1978. He resigned after he failed to be appointed as attorney general. He worked as a private lawyer, specializing in HCJ litigation, until 1992 when he was appointed to the Supreme Court.

88 See Chapter 1 Section C.2 at p. 33 et seq.

The 1970s were characterized by a steady increase in the power and status of the attorney general within the Israeli government. The three people who held the position during this period (Meir Shamgar, Aharon Barak, and Itzhak Zamir) were all distinguished lawyers who managed to establish a strong position within the administration and enforce the control of the OAG on the Israeli bureaucracy as well as on the political decision-makers.[89] The rise of the influence of the attorney general reached its peak toward the end of the tenure of Aharon Barak. Barak, initially a law professor at the Hebrew University, was appointed as attorney general in 1975, and soon established his position as one of the most influential figures in the state. He was the first to bring to justice senior politicians (including cabinet members) and top bureaucrats. He did not hesitate to initiate criminal proceedings against the Prime Minister Yitzhak Rabin which brought about the resignation of Rabin and, eventually, a political turnaround.[90] He also served as a close legal advisor for Prime Minister Menachem Begin, and was one of the architects of the Camp David peace agreement between Israel and Egypt in 1978.[91] Barak was appointed to the Supreme Court immediately after concluding his tenure as attorney general, and has served since then as the most celebrated and influential Chief Justice of the Court, who is identified more than anyone else with the judicial activism of the "New Court" era.[92]

While the enormous influence of Barak on the legal polity and society at large is well known, his enormous influence on the OAG's functions, practices, and ideology is much less noticeable. It was during his tenure that the attorney general established his monopoly as both the sole ultimate legal advisor of the government and the ultimate representative of all state units in court.[93] The concept of the independence of the OAG vis-à-vis the government had been established long before Barak took office and was significantly reinforced during the tenure of his predecessor, Meir Shamgar.[94] Barak, however, added a new dimension to this concept. Not only was the OAG independent in the sense that the government could not compromise prosecutorial discretion, but also, under Barak, the OAG

[89] See Section B above text after above note 35. See also Z. Segal, *Israeli Democracy* (Tel Aviv: Ministry of Defense, 1990), 173–179. All three were appointed to the Supreme Court, and two of them, Shamgar and Barak, were also appointed and served for long periods as Chief Justice.

[90] See above note 27.

[91] See Y. Gutman, *The Attorney General Versus The Government* (Jerusalem: Edanim, 1981), 335–342.

[92] See Chapter 1 Section C.2.

[93] See Section B above text near above note 14.

[94] See Levontin, above note 12, at 73 and Section B above.

became an organ that had as one of its primary functions to *supervise the government* and to assure that it is acting in accordance with the concept of the rule of law, thus, creating a strong tension between this function and the other traditional functions of the OAG.

The tension between the supervisory function of the OAG is particularly significant in the case of the HCJD, since it directly conflicts with the other major function of the HCJD, i.e., its duty to *represent* the government in court. Moreover, the inherent conflict of duties is also directly translated into a conflict of loyalties on the institutional level. In other words, it creates a serious question as to toward whom the HCJD lawyers are committed: toward their client (as the representative of the government in litigation) or toward the Supreme Court in the course of their duty to assure that the government is acting in accordance with the rule of law.[95]

3. *The evolution of "the rule of law lawyer" concept during the 1980s and 1990s*

The appointment of Beinish by Barak in 1977 was no surprise. Despite her relatively limited experience in the HCJD and in HCJ litigation, she was considered a distinguished lawyer, as well as a powerful bureaucratic figure within the HCJ where she had spent her professional career prior to her appointment. No less important was the fact that she was one of the people who had worked closely with Barak and was fully committed to his vision regarding the role of the OAG. As a senior member of the OAG in this period observes:

> Dorit [Beinish] was much more "public" [than Renato Yarek[96]]. She took into consideration the public interest as she understood it … much more than Renato [Yarek] would do. He [Renato] was willing to "cut corners" [for the administration] … We were always dealing with this dilemma. In Dorit's period [as the HCJD Head], the policy of opening the floor for [public] petitions in the HCJ began to develop. Mishael [Cheshin] tried to block such petitions by using every possible preliminary argument, but the floor was gradually opened. The one who led this process and inspired it was Barak, who – as the Attorney General – told the Minister of Finance that he would not defend the government against a petition in the "Foreign Account Affair" [of Rabin].[97] … He [Barak] paved the path … and created the great breakthrough [in the field of judicial review] and

[95] For further discussion of the implications of the Rule of Law Model on the professional ethics of the HCJD see Chapter 4.

[96] Renato Yarek became head of the department after Beinish, see text below near note 101.

[97] See above note 27.

> this atmosphere he imbedded in us as the AG. We felt this. We worked with him on HCJ cases … I think this had an enormous impact on Dorit [Beinish]. I think that Dorit noticed … that this is "the horse to ride on", since he was [then] already in the Supreme Court and she was in the HCJD and she "read the map" correctly, I think.[98]

Another senior member of the HCJD observes:

> It seems to me that the point where there was a certain change was when Barak became the Attorney General, and he brought with him a wider view of the rule of law concept, of what is *right* to do on the account of the duty to represent the government … he introduced a value oriented dimension … not only of what is "legal" [strictly speaking] but also what is the *proper* thing to do … Dorit [Beinish] was his student all the way since she became the Head of the HCJD and led a much more activist approach.[99]

Therefore, under Dorit Beinish as the head of the HCJD the department developed a vigorous concept of their role as government lawyers. This concept was based on the fundamental assumption that the HCJD staff were committed, on the ideological level, to the ideal of "the rule of law"; on the functional level, to their supervisory role (no less to their role as the representative of the government); and, on the institutional level, to the HCJ and the expectations of its justices, no less than to the interests of their client agencies. This concept won active encouragement and support from Barak's successor as attorney general, Itzhak Zamir, who openly expressed his support for the idea of the predominant commitment of the government lawyer to this ideal of the rule of law.[100] It also won active encouragement from the HCJ under the leadership of Barak himself. For the activist judges of the HCJ, the cooperation of the department was an important tool in the process of the expansion of their own control over the Israeli bureaucracy and political branches.

Dorit Beinish concluded her tenure as head of the HCJD in 1982 to become a deputy for the state attorney, and in 1989 she was appointed as the state attorney.[101] She was replaced by Renato Yarek, one of the HCJD

[98] Interview with NM (March 7, 1997).

[99] Interview with IZ (February 24, 1997, A-58, A-96) emphasis added.

[100] See Zamir, above note 19 and text.

[101] In December 1995, after concluding her tenure as State Attorney, Beinish was appointed to the Supreme Court. Her appointment took place despite strong opposition from politicians and some members of the academia who regarded her as a typical OAG senior bureaucrat who is strongly affiliated with the activist tendencies of Aharon Barak, see

seniors, who served as head of the HCJD from 1982 until 1987. Yarek differed sharply from Beinish with regard to his professional ideology and conceptual view regarding the role of government lawyer. He viewed the HCJD's role as primarily, if not exclusively, to represent the interest of the client agency in court and to win the litigation for its clients. He rejected the tendency of other lawyers within the HCJD and the OAG to view conflicts between private parties and government agencies from a broad "public service" perspective. He also objected to the tendencies within the HCJ to view the OAG as serving the "public interest" in that respect.

Yarek's professional ideology stood in contrast to the general ideological tendencies within the Supreme Court and the OAG. His tenure as HCJD head took place during the great breakthrough of judicial activism lead by Aharon Barak during the 1980s. Like Mishael Cheshin during the 1960s, Yarek, while appearing before the HCJ, kept raising the traditional preliminary objections (such as standing and justiciability) in any petition of a "public interest nature." These preliminary objections, however, were politely rejected again and again by the Supreme Court Justices, seeking to establish their control over the political decision-making process.[102] The same can be said of other technical arguments he raised that did not correspond with the non-formalist and "value-oriented" tendencies of the Supreme Court during the 1980s.[103]

Within the OAG, Yarek served under Attorney General Itzhak Zamir, who fully endorsed the newly created concept of "the rule of law lawyer" and firmly exerted the supervisory function of the OAG over the political and bureaucratic branches in a series of public scandals.[104] Zamir's activist policies won strong support on the part of other OAG seniors (such

e.g. E. Porsher, "Now It Is Official: Chief Justice Beinish," *Ma'ariv-NRG* September 7, 2006, available at www.nrg.co.il/online/1/ART1/475/873.html, last accessed July 16, 2013; "Shetreet: Beinish for Chief Justice," *Arutz 7*, August 24, 2006, available at www.inn.co.il/News/News.aspx/153961, last accessed July 16, 2013.

102 See the discussion in Chapter 1 Section C.2 and Chapter 4 Section B.2 at p. 128.

103 See e.g. HCJ 802/79 *Samara* v. *The Commander of Juda and Somaria* [1980] IsrSC 34 (4) 1, 3; FH 2/82 *Ressler* v. *Minister of Defence* [1982] IsrSC 36(1) 708; HCJ 179/82 *Ressler* v. *Minister of Defence* [1982] IsrSC 36(1) 421; HCJ 742/84 *Kahana* v. *The Chairman of the Knesset* [1985] IsrSC 39(4) 85, 89; *The "Kach"Party* v. *The Chairman of the Knesset*, above note 11, at 145–146; HCJ 620/85 *Miari* v. *Chairman of the Knesset* [1987] IsrSC 41(4) 169, 186. For the discussion of the decline of legal formalism in the Supreme Court see M. Mautner, *The Decline of Formalism and the Rise of Values in Israeli Law* (Tel Aviv: Ma'agalei Deot 1993).

104 See above note 20. The most notable of these public scandals was *The Shin Bet* affair discussed above note 20.

as Beinish). In view of these general organizational tendencies, Yarek's conservative professional ideology had only limited impact on the overall development of the practices of the HCJD during the 1980s. The decentralized nature of the working practices within the HCJD, as well as the general atmosphere within the OAG at large, limited the influence of his professional view to cases under his direct responsibility, rather than affecting the practices of the HCJD at large.[105]

In sum, Yarek's sophisticated arguments and superb qualities as a barrister could not overcome the court's ambition to turn itself into a significant player within the Israeli polity. Nor did his professional ideology stop the corresponding developments within the HCJD. Nevertheless, his view of HCJD lawyers as serving their client agencies in a manner closer to the traditional model of "the hired gun" is more than mere history within the HCJD. It represents a model that competes with the model of "the rule of law lawyer" (which will be discussed in detail in the following chapters) and it continues to influence the practices of the HCJD to some degree even today.[106]

Yarek retired from the HCJD in 1987 for private practice. He was replaced by Nili Arad, a lawyer in the department who was closely affiliated with the activist tendencies of the OAG leadership. Under her, the HCJD adopted the concept of "the rule of law lawyer" in its fullest sense. Unlike in the case of Yarek, Arad's professional ideology had wider impact on the practices of the HCJD due to a number of reasons: first, her professional ideology corresponded to the tendencies in the OAG and the HCJ at large; second, while Arad's credentials as an HCJ barrister were less eminent than Yarak's, she had prominent managerial abilities, and therefore managed to bring about some institutional changes in accordance with her professional ideology. Most notably, under Arad the HCJD developed informal but systematic practices of involvement in administrative decision-making processes within the various agency clients as well as practices of mediation between the petitioners to the HCJ and the client agencies.[107] Finally, Arad served as head of the HCJD during the late 1980s and the first half of the 1990s. This was a period during which the breakthrough of judicial activism of the HCJ took place.[108] This was also a period in which the HCJD (following the HCJ itself) had to handle thousands of petitions issued by Palestinians during the (first)

[105] See Section D.3 above.
[106] The two competing models of lawyering and the ideological differences among HCJD members are discussed in Chapter 4.
[107] See Chapters 5 and 6. [108] See Chapter 1 Section C.2.

Intifada. The department had to cope with a rapidly growing docket and with more complicated requirements on behalf of the court. Therefore, it had to develop organizational tools to deal with these pressures, and this was done under Arad, in accordance with her own perceptions as to the department's role. [109]

In 1995 Arad was replaced by Uzi Fogelman, who served as head of the HCJD for five years before leaving the OAG (in 2000) for the bench.[110] He was replaced by Osnat Mendel who still serves as head of the HCJD. Both Fogelman and Mendel served in the HCJD throughout most of their professional career and were major players in the development of 'the rule of law lawyering' model throughout the 1990s. As one would expect, the concept of the HCJD's supervisory role was kept intact, and even intensified during their tenure to the extent that it is now regarded as an established tradition both within the OAG and throughout the executive branch at large.[111]

F. Conclusion

There were various legal, institutional, and cultural factors that contributed to the evolution of the current model of lawyering within the HCJD. Some of these factors are related to the change in legal doctrines and the rise of judicial activism in the Supreme Court. In addition, the strong professional, institutional, and social affiliation between the judiciary and the legal bureaucracy in the Ministry of Justice increased the power of the attorney general and the autonomy of the OAG within the Israeli bureaucracy. Therefore, while judicial activism rose during the 1980s, the Supreme Court found the legal bureaucracy of the OAG to be a natural ally in its struggle to enhance its influence on society. Since the HCJ was the principal forum by which judicial activism was exerted, the HCJD members became the players by which the cooperation between the court and the legal bureaucracy was implemented in its most intensified version. The influence exerted by the Supreme Court on the HCJD, and the ambitions of the OAG leaders to

[109] Arad left the HCJD in 1995 for a senior job within the OAG. In 1996 she was appointed as General Manager at the Ministry of Justice. In 2000, she left the ministry for a judicial post as a judge on the National Labor Tribunal.

[110] Fogelman was appointed as a district judge and in 2009 was appointed as a Supreme Court Justice.

[111] See the discussion in Chapter 4. It is worthwhile mentioning that the number of staff in the HCJD has grown rapidly since the beginning of this century. See above note 63 and accompanying text.

fulfill the expectations of the court, contributed to a significant shift in the professional ideology and practices of the HCJD. The outcome of this process was the evolution of the rule of law lawyering model. The parameters of this model and its implications will be the subject of the following parts of this book.

3

Litigating for the government

In the previous chapters I described the rise of judicial activism in Israel during the 1980s, as well as the shift in the HCJD's professional ideology during the same period. I argued that during this period the HCJD abandoned the traditional model of lawyering for the government (a model that prevailed until the late 1970s) and adopted a new one, which I called the "rule of law lawyering" model. Under this model, the HCJD regards itself as not merely the representative of its agencies in court, but rather as a supervisory organ that seeks to promote the general values of the rule of law in the government, values that are manifested by the institution of the HCJ itself. Thus, the HCJD was transformed from an organ whose main objective is to represent the government in court into a supervisory organ that is primarily accountable to the HCJ and serves as its extension or, at least, views its accountability towards the court on the institutional and ideological level as no less important than its professional duty towards its client agencies. In this chapter I deal with the implications of this transformation on the main function of the HCJD, that is on patterns of litigation in the HCJ.

A. Methodological background

In order to test the shift in patterns of litigation during the 1980s, I conducted a quantitative analysis on two groups of HCJ cases – those from the 1970s and the 1990s. This was done since the process of the rise of judicial activism at the HCJ and the shift in the HCJD began in the early 1980s and was completed, to a large extent, towards the end of that decade.[1] Therefore, the impact of the process should be well reflected in a representative sample of cases disposed of by the HCJ *before* and *after* that

[1] See Chapter 1 Section C and Chapter 2 Section E.3 above. It is worth mentioning that the changes in the *constitutional* framework (also known as "The Constitutional Revolution") took place during the 1990s after the enactment of the new Basic Laws in 1992 (See Chapter 1

shift. This longitudinal analysis was complemented by comparing two groups of cases disposed of during the 1990s: petitions issued to the HCJ against the *central government* of Israel, and petitions issued during the same period against *local municipalities*. The idea underlying this analysis is that municipalities are the only (quantitatively significant) group of public agencies that are *not* represented before the HCJ by lawyers of the HCJD.[2] Therefore, comparing patterns of litigation in such cases may point directly to the impact of the institutional and ideological characteristics of the HCJD and complement the longitudinal analysis by serving as a control group.

B. The longitudinal analysis: 1990s v. 1970s

1. *Research hypotheses*

1) In accordance with the reforms in judicial review in the HCJ during the 1980s, *the overall rate of success* of petitions during the 1990s was significantly higher than in the 1970s;
2) Due to the mounting caseload pressure and the shifts in patterns of litigation, *the relative number of cases settled* by the HCJD (*overall rate of settlements*) rose significantly after the 1980s;
3) Due to the mounting caseload pressure and the shifts in patterns of litigation, *the relative number of conditional orders* decreased significantly after the 1980s.[3]

2. *Database and methods*

In order to study the quantitative impact of the rise of judicial activism in the HCJ, I sampled court files from two periods: 1970–1979 and

Section A.1 above). While the Constitutional Revolution could potentially have impact on outcomes of litigation throughout the 1990s we found no evidence of such influence in our database and therefore we do not discuss this issue here. See Y. Dotan, "Judicial Activism and Government Practices in Litigation in the Israeli High Court of Justice 1970–2000", Paper presented at the Law and Society Association Annual Meeting, San Francisco, June 2–5, 2011 (file with the author). And cf. K. Weinshall-Margel, "Attitudinal and Neo-Institutional Models of Supreme Court Decision Making: An Empirical and Comparative Perspective from Israel," 8 *J. Empirical Legal Stud.* 556 (2011) (suggesting that the Constitutional Revolution did have some impact on judicial behavior with regards to *constitutional cases* in the field of freedom of religion).

[2] See Chapter 2 Section D.1.

[3] See Chapter 1 Section B.2 and Section C.3 below.

1990–1998.[4] Our database contains a sample of *actual court files* (located in the HCJ archives) rather than using electronic databases. I did not base our sample on cases filed in electronic databases for two principal reasons: first, the existing electronic databases for the Israeli Supreme Court do not contain full information on cases disposed of by the court before 1985;[5] second, and most importantly, our analysis requires full information not only on cases disposed of by the HCJ by *final court decision*, but also cases that were *disposed of by out-of-court settlements.* As previous research has demonstrated, the study of out-of-court settlements is essential for the study of outcomes in litigation at the HCJ.[6] This is even more important for the purpose of the current study, which focuses directly on practices and strategies of the HCJD throughout litigation. Since electronic databases do not contain full information about out-of-court settlements, I had to study actual court files.

For each year in the research period, about 10 percent of all files were sampled (i.e. around 50–70 cases for each year during the 1970s and around 100–140 cases for each year during the 1990s). Each file was coded with reference to a large number of factors including the petitioner's status (individual, corporation, interest group, etc.), their ethnic and civil affiliation (Jewish, Arab-Israeli, Palestinian from the Occupied Territories, etc.), legal representation of both parties, the subject matter of the petition, the duration of the litigation, legal arguments raised by the parties, judicial writs issued throughout the litigation, including conditional orders interim injunctions, etc., and the position taken by the state (if involved as a "third party" or *amicus* in the litigation). I also codified the outcomes of the litigation. The codification of outcomes referred to outcomes both in final judicial decisions (i.e. whether judicial writs on behalf of all, or some, of the petitioners were issued) and in out-of-court settlements. This means that in cases of settlement, I studied and codified *the content* of the settlement between the parties. I also codified writs for expenses, if issued by the court as the result of the litigation.[7]

[4] 1999 was not sampled, for technical reasons.

[5] The Supreme Court site contains a database for cases disposed by the court since 1977, but this database includes only partial collection of decisions, and the search-engine in this site is very limited. There are also two popular sites run by commercial contractors: Nevo and Takdin. None of them, however, contains all the decisions disposed by out-of-court settlements.

[6] Y. Dotan, "Judicial Rhetoric, Government Lawyers and Human Rights: The Case of the Israeli High Court of Justice during the Intifada," 33 *Law & Soc'y Rev.* 319 (1999).

[7] Our database also includes codification of the Supreme Court justices that disposed each case. We did not, however, conduct attitudinal analysis within this research (cf. e.g. J. A.

3. *Outcomes*

Table 3.1 summarizes the characteristics of the sample of petitions that were submitted (See Appendix 1 for variable descriptions).

As we can see from Table 3.1, the majority of the petitions in the sample were submitted in the 1990s. About 70 percent of the petitions were issued against respondents that were organs of the state (including government agencies, the military, and ancillary units – all represented by the HCJD).[8] As to the subject matter: the vast majority of petitions in our sample (77.2 percent) dealt with "civil" matters (i.e. petitions regarding regular administrative matters such as licensing, bids, state subsidies, zoning and planning, etc., see Appendix 1). We can also see that some notable changes took place regarding the composition of the cases issued to the HCJ. For example, there was an important change in the ethnic identity of the petitioners. While in the 1970s almost 90 percent of the petitions were issued by Jews, the relative portion of Jewish petitioners dropped to 62 percent and the relative number of petitions issued by Arab citizens of Israel (Arab-Israeli) and by Palestinian residents of the

Segal and H. J. Spaeth, *The Supreme Court and the Attitudinal Model Revisited* (Cambridge University Press, 2002)) for a number of reasons: first, unlike in the United States, judicial appointments in Israel are not made directly by the political branches and the political affiliation of the judges is difficult to identify (see Chapter 1 Section A.3). Secondly, the Israeli Supreme Court normally seats in panels of three that dispose thousands of cases each year. This means that normally only one judge writes the decision for the panel (see Y. Shachar, R. Haris and M. Gross, "Anatomy of Discourse and Division in the Supreme Court: Quantitative Analysis," 20 *Iunei Mishpat* 749 (1997)) while most other justices on the court do not take part in the case. Lastly, the attitudinal approach has been proved largely inapt to explain decisions of the Israeli Supreme Court, even in cases of high political profile (see M. Hofnung and K. Weinshall-Margel, "Judicial Setbacks, Material Gains: Terror Litigation at the Israeli High Court of Justice," 7 *J. Empirical Legal Stud.* 664, 686 (2010)), with some narrow exceptions with regard to decisions in the field of religion and state (see K. Weinshall-Margel, "Attitudinal and Neo-Institutional Models of Supreme Court Decision-Making: An Empirical and Comparative Perspective from Israel," 8 *J. Empirical Legal Stud.* 556 (2011)). Since our study refers to a large number of "ordinary" cases, most of which were disposed without *any* official decision by the court, attitudinal analysis seems irrelevant.

[8] The figure of 71 percent in the table refers to petitions in which the government is *the primary* respondent. The HCJD, however, is involved in many petitions that are issued against other respondents either since some governmental units appear as additional respondents in such petitions or since the court invites the OAG to present its position regarding the petition. Therefore, the overall number of cases in which the HCJD is involved is higher than the figure in Table 3.1.

Table 3.1 *Descriptive statistics of variables*

Variable	*N*	%	1970s (*N=626*)	1990s (*N=1064*)
Petitioner, by institution (X^2=40.96, *df*=3 *p*<*0.001*)				
Private	1306	79	84.1%	75.9%
Public	14	0.8	0.3%	1.2%
Institution/corporation	229	13.8	14%	13.8%
State/a /elected officials	105	6.3	1.6%	9.2%
Petitioner, by ethnicity (X^2=101.78, *df*=2 *p*<0.000)				
Jew	920	72.2	88.5%	62.4%
Arab-Israeli	178	14	6.1%	18.7%
Palestinian	176	13.8	5.4%	18.9%
Petitioner's lawyer (X^2=105.30, *df*=2 *p*<0.001)				
Private	1082	65.5	60.8%	68.2%
Organization	126	7.6	1%	11.5%
Self-representation	444	26.9	38.2%	20.2%
Respondent (X^2=15.19, *df*=3 *p*<0.01)				
State	1198	71	73%	69.8%
Corporation or Tribunal	234	13.9	9.8%	16.3%
Private	38	2.3	2.6%	2.1%
Local Authority	217	12.9	14.6%	11.8%
Subject of petition (X^2=233.06, *df*=3 *p*<0.00)				
Civil	1304	77.2	63.7%	66.8%
Prisoners and detainees	194	11.5	25.2%	3.4%
Occupied Territories/ security related	75	4.4	5.8%	21.9%
Constitution	117	6.9	5.3%	7.9%
Conditional order (X^2=49.74, *df*=1 *p*<0.00)				
Issued	457	27.1	37.1%	21.3%
Not issued	1229	72.9	62.9%	78.7%

Source: HCJ files.

Territories (Palestinians) rose accordingly.[9] Correspondingly, there have been important changes in the subject matter of the petitions. In particular, during the 1970s every fourth petition to the HCJ was issued by a prisoner. This category dropped dramatically to around 3 percent during the 1990s.[10] Correspondingly, the relative proportion of petitions issued with regard to security matters related to the Occupied Territories rose dramatically from around 6 percent to almost 22 percent of all petitions. This change in the subject matter of petitions is far from surprising. As previous research on the HCJ suggests, during the 1980s (and even more so toward the end of that decade) security-related events (in particular the eruption of the first *Intifada* in the Territories) brought about a sharp rise in petitions issued by Palestinians to the HCJ.[11] To sum up the main shifts in the composition of HCJ litigation during the 1980s, one might say that, while the relative portion of the main "regular" administrative ("civil") petitions remained steady, the second-largest category of petitions issued by (mostly unrepresented) prisoners (see below) was supplemented by a growing category of petitions issued by Palestinians (chiefly represented by interest groups). Correspondingly, the relative number of petitions in which interest groups were involved rose from almost none (1 percent) in the 1970s to 11.5 percent during the 1990s. As we shall see, this shift in the composition of petitions to the HCJ had a great influence on the outcomes of our analysis. Table 3.1 also demonstrates that the relative number of cases in which the HCJ issued conditional orders dropped sharply during the 1990s – from around 37 percent to around 21 percent of all petitions (the meaning of this finding is discussed below).

[9] The study distinguishes between litigation initiated by Arab-Israeli (i.e. citizens of Israel of Arab decent) and Palestinian residents of the Occupied Territories. The distinction between these two groups of cases in the current study suffers, however, from some inaccuracies and cannot, at the current stage, serve as a basis to draw direct conclusions with regard to the outcomes of litigation of these two groups. One major source for this inaccuracy is the fact that in various cases the *official* petitioner (which is the subject of our codification) may belong to one group (e.g. Arab-Israeli) but the actual subject matter of the petition is related to the Territories. This is, for example, the case in a petition issued by an Arab-Israeli who wishes to obtain a family unification certificate for purposes of marriage with a non-citizen resident of the Territories. Accordingly, I am cautious to draw any direct conclusions from the current study with regard to outcomes in litigation of these two groups.

[10] This change was the result of a statutory change in 1980 that bestowed the jurisdiction to dispose prisoners' petitions in the District Courts (see Procedures Regulations (Prisoners Petitions) 1980).

[11] See Dotan, above note 6; R. Shamir, "'Landmark Cases' and the Reproduction of Legitimacy: The Case of Israel's High Court of Justice," 24 *Law & Soc'y Rev.* 781 (1990).

1) Success in litigation

To what extent did rising judicial activism during the 1980s influence the readiness of the court to interfere and strike down administrative decisions in the course of deciding petitions to the HCJ? The relative rates of success of petitions to the HCJ are presented in Figure 3.1.

Figure 3.1 seems to provide clear support for the hypothesis that during the 1990s the HCJ struck down official decisions at a much higher rate than in the 1970s. The overall rate of success of decisions, according to our findings, rose from 25.5 percent in the 1970s to almost 41.8 percent during the 1990s.[12] The sharp rise in the success rate of petitioners does not necessarily point to a change in the *court's* policies. Rather, it can be influenced by other factors such as the shifts in the petitions' subject matter, the ethnic composition of the petitioner's population, and changes related to the representation of both petitioners and respondents in litigation. In order to test the strength of the relative explanations for the rise in the success rate, I conducted a multivariable analysis. However, before showing the results of this analysis, it is worth looking at the results of the bivariate analyses that provide an understanding of the characteristics of petitions that ended in success for the petitioner, as opposed to those that did not.

As we can see from Table 3.2, there are a number of variables related to the composition of the petitions that may well account for the rise in the success rates of petitions during the 1990s. Among other things, the table shows that the most successful institutional category of petitions were those *issued* by the state (or by state officials).[13] The relative number of petitions issued by the state rose sharply during the 1990s (see Table 3.1 above). Likewise, in terms of legal representation, the most successful representation for petitioners was provided by organizations (a category that also rose sharply in number during the 1990s, see

[12] When we take the prisoner petitions out of the analysis (see above note 10) the overall success rate of petitions in the 1970s is 32 percent and in the 1990s 42.1 percent. The regression in Table 3.3 below stays stable even when conducting the analysis without petitions that were submitted by prisoners.

[13] The high success rate of the government is hardly surprising and corresponds with many studies in various jurisdictions. See generally H. M. Kritzer, "The Government Gorilla: Why Does Government Come Out Ahead in Appellate Courts?," in H. M. Kritzer and S. Silbey (eds.), *In Litigation: Do the "Haves" Still Come Out Ahead?* (Stanford University Press, 2003), 342 and see Introduction above note 3. Moreover, the government was also found to be far more successful in both civil and criminal appeals in the Supreme Court, see T. Eisenberg, T. Fisher and I. Rosen-Zvi, "Israel's Supreme Court Appellate Jurisdiction: An Empirical Study," 96 *Cornell L. Rev.* 693, 717–799 (2011).

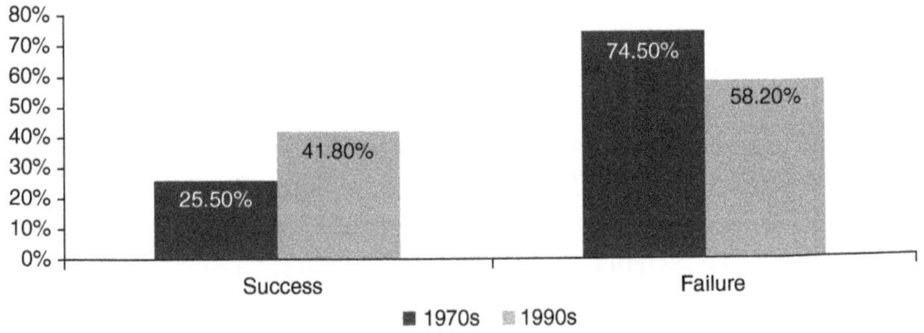

Figure 3.1 Outcome distribution in the 1970s and 1990s
Source: HCJ files.

Table 3.1 above). Correspondingly, Table 3.2 shows that petitioners that were self-represented were markedly less successful in litigation (with an overall rate-of-success of 13.1 percent). Once again, this category of self-representation was almost twice as large in the 1970s (38.2 percent) than in the 1990s (20.2 percent). Lastly, Table 3.2 shows that the least successful petitions were those issued in the field of prison conditions (10.3 percent) while the most successful category of petitions were those dealing with the Occupied Territories (rate-of-success of 55.6 percent). The above-described changes in the size of each group within the population of petitions throughout the 1980s could obviously account for the rise in the overall success rates of petitions. In order to evaluate the relative influence of each of these factors, a logistic regression was conducted.

The outcomes as presented in Table 3.3 shed more light on the explanation for the rise in rate-of-success of petitions to the HCJ during the research period. The first notable finding is that the odds for success for petitions issued during the 1990s were significantly higher than those submitted in the 1970s (odds ratio 0.52). This corroborates our first hypothesis that the shifts in judicial policies in the HCJ during the 1980s influenced the outcomes of litigation.

Table 3.3 also illustrates that there are various other factors related to the composition of the case that bear significant influence on success rates in litigation. First, the institutional composition of the petitioners had a significant influence on their prospects for success. The odds for success of petitions issued by the state (or state officials) are almost twice that of petitions submitted by private persons (odds ratio of 1.86). Secondly, the odds for success of petitioners represented by organizations were over two-and-a-half times higher than petitioners represented

Table 3.2 *Summary of data on success rates (bivariate analysis)*

Variable	Success for the petitioner	Failure for the petitioner	*N*
Year X^2=40.04, *df*=1 *p*<0.001			
1970s	25.5%	74.5%	546
1990s	41.8%	58.2%	933
Petitioner, by institution X^2=23.25, *df*=3 *p*<0.001			
Private	32.5%	67.5%	1146
Public organization	38.5%	61.5%	13
Institution/corporation	42.1%	57.9%	197
State/authority/elected officials	54.9%	45.1%	91
Petitioner, by ethnicity X^2=46.51, *df*=2 *p*<0.001			
Jew	27.5%	72.5%	799
Arab-Israeli	48.1%	51.9%	158
Palestinian	49.7%	50.3%	159
Petitioner's lawyer X^2=136.89, *df*=2 *p*<0.001			
Private	41.7%	58.3%	962
Organization	64.3%	35.7%	115
Self-representation	13.1%	86.9%	367
Respondent X^2=2.31, *df*=3 *p*>0.05			
State	35.4%	64.6%	1058
Corporation or tribunal	33.5%	66.5%	206
Private	36.4%	63.6%	33
Local authority	40.6%	59.4%	180
Subject of petition X^2=93.34, *df*=3 *p*<0.001			
Civil	34.1%	65.9%	1142
Prisoners and detainees	10.3%	89.7%	165
Occupied Territories/security related	55.6%	44.4%	66
Constitution	45.3%	54.7%	106
Conditional order X^2=77.34, *df*=1 *p*<0.001			
Issued	53.5%	46.5%	409
Not issued	29%	71%	1068

Source: HCJ files.

by private lawyers (odds ratio 2.62). Personal characteristics of the petitioner also affected the likelihood for success in the petition. When the petitioner was an Arab-Israeli, the odds for success were almost twice as high (odds ratio 1.85) than for Jewish petitioners, and when the petitioner was a Palestinian, the odds for success rose by 60% (odds ratio 1.62). The

Table 3.3 *Logistic regression coefficients for predicting success in litigation*

Variable	*B*	*Standard Error*	Exp *(B)* odds ratio
Constant	-0.96***		
Year (0=1990s)			
1970s	-0.65	0.14	0.52***
Petitioner, by institution (0=Private)			
Public	0.04	0.59	1.04
Institution/corporation	0.26	0.17	1.30
State/authority/elected officials	0.62	0.25	1.86*
Petitioner, by ethnicity (0=Jew)			
Arab-Israeli	0.61	0.19	1.85**
Palestinian	0.48	0.21	1.62*
Petitioner's lawyer (0=Private)			
Organization	0.96	0.23	2.62***
Respondent (0=State)			
Corporation or tribunal	-0.04	0.18	0.96
Private	0.03	0.39	1.03
Local authority	-0.07	0.18	0.93
Subject of petition (0=Civil)			
Prisoners and detainees	-0.93	0.29	0.39**
Occupied Territories/security related	0.35	0.28	1.41
Constitution	0.11	0.23	1.12
Conditional order (0=Not issued)			
Issued	1.22	0.14	3.37***
Dependent variable – outcome of petition (0=failure; 1=success) N=1477 Chi-square = 214.86*** Cox & Snell R^2= 0.13 / Nagelkerke R^2= 0.19			

* = p<0.05, ** = p<0.01, *** = p<0.001
Source: HCJ files.

subject matter of the petition also affected the odds for success, at least to the extent that petitions dealing with prison conditions had much lower odds for success than petitions in regular "civil" matters (odds ratio 0.39). Lastly, and unsurprisingly, for cases in which the HCJ decided to issue conditional orders during the litigation the odds were much higher than when conditional orders were not issued (odds ratio 3.37, see below).

2) Court Decisions and out-of-court settlements

In the second hypothesis, I assumed that the sharp rise in the HCJ caseload during the 1980s and the 1990s, as well as the changes in patterns of litigation, brought about an increase in the relative number of cases that were disposed of by out-of-court settlements. The relevant findings are summarized in Table 3.4 and Figure 3.2.

As we can see from Table 3.4 and Figure 3.2, there was a sharp change in the relative number of out-of-court settlement during the 1980s. While during the 1970s almost two-thirds (64.3 percent) of the petitions to the HCJ were disposed of by final court decisions, the relative number of such cases dropped sharply after the 1980s, and the relative rate of out-of-court settlements rose sharply from 35.7 percent to almost six out of every ten cases (58.3 percent).[14]

The analysis of the rate of settlements during the research period also sheds new light on the data for success rates presented above (see Figure 3.1). Figure 3.3 points to the division of outcomes in the HCJ while referring simultaneously to both success and settlement rates.

As we can see from Figure 3.3 the steep rise in success rates of petitioners to the HCJ during the 1990s did not result from more court decisions that had struck down executive decisions. In fact, the relative number of interventions in final court decisions during the 1990s was even slightly *lower* than in the 1970s (4.1 percent in the 1990s compared to 5.1 percent during the 1970s). Petitioners to the HCJ were more successful during the 1990s due to one major reason: the relative number of cases in which the respondent agencies in the HCJ agreed to settle out-of-court rose sharply and in fact almost doubled during the 1990s (relatively to the 1970s) from around 20 percent to almost 38 percent during the 1990s.

Since the formation of out-of-court settlements is so crucial for the outcomes of litigation in the HCJ, it is important to study the variables that influence the rate of settlement. This was done by a logistic regression, in order to estimate the likelihood of a petition's being disposed of by the

14 When examining the differences in settlement rates between the 1970s and 1990s without prisoner petitions we see that in the 1970s 42.4 percent of petitions ended in settlement, while in the 1990s almost 58.3 percent ended in settlement. The regression in Table 3.5 below stays stable even when prisoner petitions are excluded.

Table 3.4 *Summary of data on settlement rates (bivariate analysis)*

Variable	Trial	Settlement	*N*
Year X^2=70.32, *df*=1 $p<0.001$			
1970s	64.3%	35.7%	546
1990s	41.7%	58.3%	933
Petitioner, by institution X^2=4.42, *df*=3 $p>0.05$			
Private	51.8%	48.2%	1146
Public	53.8%	46.2%	13
Institution/corporation	44.2%	55.8%	197
State/authority/elected officials	47.3%	52.7%	91
Petitioner, by ethnicity X^2=43.12, *df*=2 $p<0.001$			
Jew	57.2%	42.8%	799
Arab-Israeli	32.9%	67.1%	158
Palestinian	38.4%	61.6%	159
Petitioner's lawyer X^2=101.86, *df*=2 $p<0.001$			
Private	42.9%	57.1%	962
Organization	30.4%	69.6%	115
Self-representation	71.1%	28.9%	367
Respondent X^2=7.06, *df*=3 $p>0.05$			
State	50.4%	49.6%	1058
Corporation and tribunal	53.9%	46.1%	206
Private	57.6%	42.4%	33
Local authority	41.7%	58.3%	180
Subject of petition X^2=79.54, *df*=3 $p<0.00$			
Civil	49.6%	50.4%	1142
Prisoners and detainees	77%	23%	165
Occupied Territories/security related	32.1%	67.9%	66
Constitution	52.8%	47.2%	106
Conditional order X^2=4.21, *df*=1 $p<0.05$			
Issued	45.7%	54.3%	409
Not issued	51.7%	48.3%	1068

Source: HCJ files.

court in comparison to its ending in a settlement based on the variables examined. Table 3.5 presents the results of this regression.

Table 3.5 indicates the variables that influenced the likelihood for out-of-court settlement during the research period. As the table shows, the odds for petitions submitted during the 1970s to end court decision are

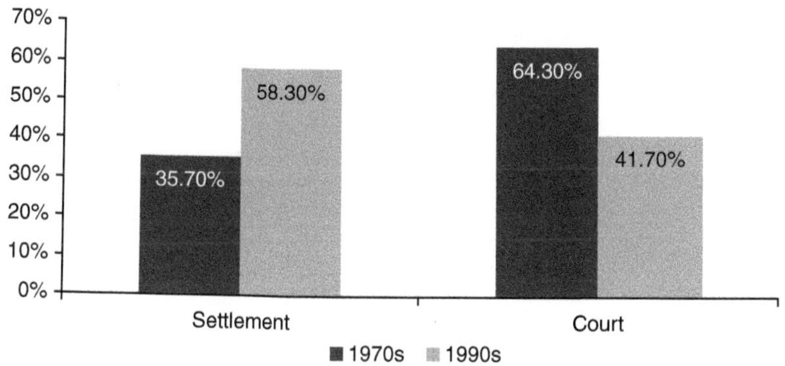

Figure 3.2 Settlement rates 1970s and 1990s
Source: HCJ files.

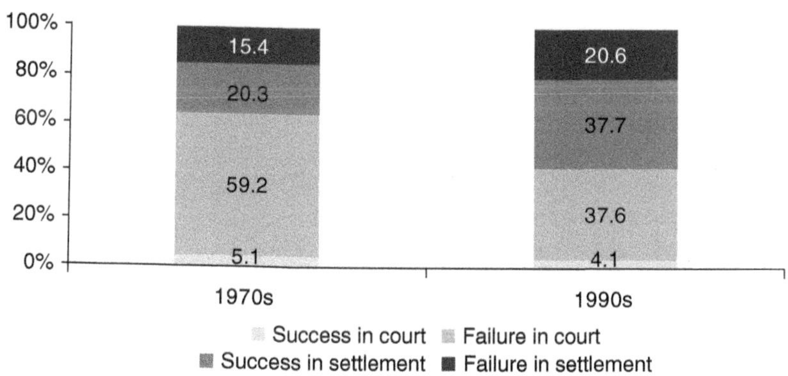

Figure 3.3 Success rates and settlement rates: 1970s and 1990s
Note: We define "success" in court decisions to include decisions disposed by final court decisions in which petitioners achieved everything or part of what they asked for in the original petition. Success in out-of-court settlement includes cases in which the petitioners achieved everything they asked for in the original petitions (i.e. the respondents backed off before the final judicial decision) or part of what they asked for as the result of the settlements. Failure in settlement means that the petitioners decided to drop the petition before a judicial decision was made. Around 12 percent of the cases included in our sample could not be classified as either success or failure, such as in the case of petitions that were dismissed as moot, or cases in which the outcome of litigation could not be verified from the file. Those cases were dropped from our sample (see Appendix 1).
Source: HCJ files.

Table 3.5 *Logistic regression coefficients for predicting the likelihood for disposition of the case by court decision*

Variable	*B*	*Standard Error*	Exp *(B)* odds ratio
Constant	-0.11		
Year (0=1990s)			
1970s	0.74	0.13	2.11***
Petitioner, by institution (0=Private)			
Public	0.26	0.57	1.29
Institution/corporation	-0.23	0.17	0.80
State/authority/elected officials	0.10	0.24	1.11
Petitioner, by ethnicity (0=Jew)			
Arab-Israeli	-0.65	0.19	0.52*
Palestinian	-0.27	0.20	0.76
Petitioner's lawyer (0=Private)			
Organization	-0.45	0.23	0.64
Respondent (0=State)			
Corporation or tribunal	0.21	0.16	1.23
Private	0.25	0.37	1.29
Local authority	-0.26	0.17	0.77
Subject of petition (0=Civil)			
Prisoners and detainees	0.78	0.22	2.18***
Occupied Territories/security related	-0.31	0.28	0.73
Constitution	0.25	0.22	1.28
Conditional order (0=Not issued)			
Issued	-0.34	0.13	0.71*
Dependent variable – type of proceeding (0=settlement; 1=court) N=1477 Chi-square = 136.34*** Cox & Snell R^2= 0.09 / Nagelkerke R^2= 0.19			

* = $p<0.05$, ** = $p<0.01$, *** = $p<0.001$
Source: HCJ files.

twice that of those submitted during the 1990s (odds ratio 2.11). In addition, the odds that petitions dealing with the conditions of prisoners and detainees would end in court were more than twice that of ending in a settlement (odds ratio 2.18). On the other hand, the odds that petitions issued by Arab-Israelis would end in settlements are higher in comparison to petitions issued by Jewish petitioners (odds ratio 0.52), and so were petitions that were represented by organizations (odds ratio 0.64; the significance level being 0.053). Finally, for cases in which the HCJ decided to issue conditional orders during the litigation, the odds that they would end in settlement were much higher than in court (odds ratio 0.71).

3) Conditional orders in litigation

The last part of our longitudinal analysis deals with the procedural structure of the litigation before the HCJ, and in particular with the decision of the court to issue conditional orders.

The procedure regarding petitions to the HCJ can be roughly divided into two main stages. The first stage is *preliminary*. The main objective of the petitioner at this stage is to convince the court to issue a conditional order (order *nisi*) that would open the door to a *full hearing* at the second stage. The procedure at the preliminary stage is brief. The respondent is only required to answer the petition by submitting a short document called a "respondent notice" that need not be supported by affidavits: the hearing before the court is very brief and does not involve a thorough examination of the facts of the case. Only after the court issues a conditional order does the main stage of the litigation ensue. This stage includes a more comprehensive inquiry on behalf of the court into the facts and legal questions, and it is based on affidavits and full arguments (both oral and written) by the parties.[15] Therefore, the decision to issue a conditional order bears significant importance for the procedural settings of the litigation and, presumably, for its outcome. Accordingly, I assumed that the mounting caseload in the HCJ after the 1980s and the shifts in litigation patterns would bring about a decrease in the relative number of cases in which a conditional order was issued (hypothesis 3 above).

As Figure 3.4 illustrates, the relative number of cases in which the HCJ issued conditional orders dropped sharply during the 1990s relatively to the 1970s – from 37.1 percent to only 21.2 percent during the 1990s – thus

[15] See also Chapter 1 Section B.2.

Table 3.6 *Logistic regression coefficients for predicting the issuance of conditional orders during litigation*

Variable	*B*	*Standard Error*	Exp *(B)* odds ratio
Constant	-1.62***		
Year (0=1990s)			
1970s	1.20	0.13	3.33***
Petitioner, by institution (0=Private)			
Public	-0.14	0.68	0.87
Institution/corporation	0.94	0.16	2.57***
State/authority/elected officials	0.86	0.23	2.37***
Petitioner, by ethnicity (0=Jew)			
Arab-Israeli	-0.34	0.22	0.71
Palestinian	-0.10	0.24	0.90
Petitioner's lawyer (0=Private)			
Organization	0.38	0.25	1.47
Respondent (0=State)			
Corporation or tribunal	-0.20	0.18	0.82
Private	0.41	0.36	1.51
Local authority	0.69	0.17	1.99***
Subject of petition (0=Civil)			
Prisoners and detainees	-2.15	0.32	0.12***
Occupied Territories/security related	-0.55	0.35	0.58
Constitution	0.58	0.22	1.79**
Dependent variable – Conditional order issued (0=not-issued; 1=issued) N=1686 Chi-square = 254.17*** Cox & Snell R^2= 0.14 / Nagelkerke R^2= 0.20			

* = p<0.05, ** = p<0.01, *** = p<0.001
Source: HCJ files.

corroborating hypothesis 3.[16] The full description of the findings is presented in Table 3.6.

[16] When taking prisoner petitions out of the analysis conditional orders are issued in 10.5 percent more cases (47.6 percent) in the 1970s and 0.5 percent more in the 1990s (21.7 percent). The regression in Table 3.6 below stays stable.

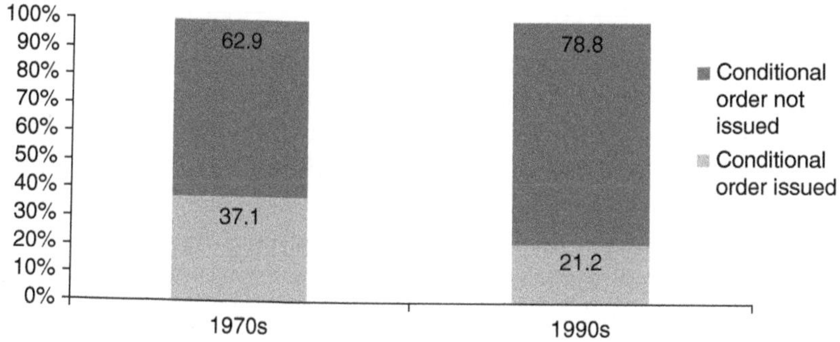

Figure 3.4 Conditional orders issued in the 1970s and 1990s
Source: HCJ files.

As we can see from Table 3.6, *the odds of conditional orders being issued for petitions submitted during the 1970s* were over three times that of petitions submitted in the 1990s (odds ratio 3.33). Likewise, the odds for petitions issued by institutionalized petitioners and by state authorities to be disposed of after conditional orders were issued were more than twice that of petitions submitted privately (odds ratio of 2.57 and 2.37 correspondingly). Other factors that influenced the tendency to issue conditional orders were the petitions' subject matter (the odds that conditional orders would be issued for petitions in constitutional matters were almost twice that of civil matters (odds ratio 1.79), while the odds that conditional orders would be issued for petitions dealing with prisoners' rights were much lower than for civil matters (odds ratio 0.12)). Finally, Table 3.6 indicates the fact that the odds that petitions issued against local municipalities would be disposed of through conditional orders were much higher than for petitions submitted against the state (odds ratio 1.99; I discuss the matter in detail in the next section).

The analysis regarding the issuance of conditional orders sheds more light on the changes in the nature of litigation before the HCJ and is important for understanding the practices and functions of the government lawyers in litigation – as the next section explains.

C. Comparing state and local municipality litigation

1. *Background*

As the previous sections have demonstrated, there were considerable changes in the way the HCJ disposed of petitions after the 1980s: the overall success rate rose, and so did the relative number of cases settled out-of-court while, on the other hand, there was a considerable drop in the relative number of cases in which conditional orders were issued. To what extent, however, can these changes in the practices of litigation be ascribed to changes in the ideology and practices of the HCJD? Arguably, changes in court practices and outcomes of litigation can alternatively be related to changes in the practices of *the court* itself, not only to changes in the practices and ideology of government lawyers. After all, the underlying assumption of the whole discussion here is that judicial ideology and practices changed markedly throughout the 1980s with the rise of judicial activism at the HCJ and the amounting caseload pressure. How, if at all, can we separate the impact of the changes in the legal apparatus of the government from other processes – particularly in the court itself?

In order to answer this question I complemented the longitudinal analysis by an additional comparative analysis between cases litigated by state lawyers (at the HCJD) and cases litigated by local municipalities. A considerable number of petitions to the HCJ during the research period were issued against local municipalities. Unlike most other agencies whose actions are reviewed by the HCJ, municipalities are not represented by the HCJD. Rather, municipalities are represented by their own lawyers (that is, either by lawyers who are the employees of the legal department of the relevant municipality or by *private* lawyers hired by the municipality specifically for the purpose of representing it in the litigation). Therefore, not only do municipalities form the most (quantitatively) significant group of respondent agencies in the HCJ that are not represented by the HCJD, but also *the structure* of their representation is completely different than in the case of the HCJD. This means that the most important institutional characteristics entailed by the *centralized model of representation* that exists in the HCJD do not exist in the case of municipalities.[17] Accordingly, the social and cultural factors that characterized the HCJD do not exist in the case of lawyers representing municipalities.[18] Thus, petitions issued against local municipalities during the 1990s seem to form a useful control group for the purposes of our study.

2. *Methodology*

1) Hypotheses

1) The overall *success rate* of petitions against local municipalities is expected to be higher than in petitions against the state;

[17] See Chapter 2 Section D.1.

[18] See Chapter 2 Sections D.2 and D.3 and see interview with RR (an HCJ Justice).

2) Due to the differences in practices of litigation the *tendency* of the state to *settle out-of-court* during the 1990s would be higher than municipalities;
3) The relative number of cases in which *conditional orders* are issued is expected to be higher in petitions against municipalities than in petitions issued against the state.

2) Data

In order to deepen the understanding regarding petitions issued against local municipalities, I enlarged the sample of petitions filed against local municipalities during the 1990s.[19] For this purpose all petitions that were submitted between January and March, and between July and September of even years were sampled. Thus, for every even year throughout the 1990s (1990, 1992, 1994, 1996, 1998), six months of petitions were examined; the sample was comprised of 551 petitions. Since our purpose is to compare variables related to litigation by state lawyers and lawyers representing municipalities, petitions in which the state took part as one of the respondents were omitted from this sample. This left us with 298 petitions that were issued solely against and defended by local authorities during the 1990s. This group of cases was compared with 641 cases (from our original database) in which the sole respondent was the state (i.e., cases in which all the respondents were represented by the HCJD) (see Appendix 2 for variables description).

From Table 3.7 we see that the majority of petitions in this sample were submitted against the state (68.3 percent). In around 36 percent of the petitions conditional orders were issued. The majority of petitions were civil related (87.6 percent). With regards to the petitioners' characteristics, we see that two-thirds of the petitions were issued by Jews while the rest were issued by Arab-Israelis and Palestinians. Also, over two-thirds of the petitions were submitted by private individuals. In addition, the majority of the petitions were represented by private lawyers (73.3 percent). We can also see that in the majority of cases (64.1 percent) a conditional order was not issued by the court during litigation.

[19] In my original database 217 petitions (i.e. around 13 percent of all petitions in the database) were issued against local authorities, of which 125 were disposed of during the 1990s (see Table 3.1). However, not all the petitions in this group could serve for the purpose of our analysis since in some of these cases the respondents included *both* local authorities and the state as respondent and had to be omitted here. In any case, in order to achieve outcomes that were statistically significant the database had to be enlarged accordingly.

Table 3.7 *Petitions against the state and local municipalities – descriptive statistics of variables*

Variable	*N*	Percentage
Respondent		
State	641	68.3
Local authority	298	31.7
Petitioner, by institution		
Private	616	67.9
Public	9	1
Institution/corporation	157	17.3
State/authority/elected officials	125	13.8
Petitioner, by ethnicity		
Jew	409	66
Arab-Israeli	131	21.1
Palestinian	80	12.9
Petitioner's lawyer		
Private	688	73.3
Organization	112	11.9
Self-representation	126	13.4
Conditional order issued		
Yes	337	35.9
No	602	64.1
Subject of petition		
Civil	823	87.6
Non-civil	116	12.4

Source: HCJ files.

3. *Findings*

1) Success in litigation

When examining success and failure rates for petitions submitted against the state and local authorities, I found that petitions against the state ended in success for the petitioner in 41.5 percent of the petitions, while the petitioners succeeded in 54.2 percent of petitions against local authorities (see Figure 3.5). This means that petitions *against* local authorities during the 1990s enjoyed a much higher rate of success in litigation than petitions against the state. The difference in success rates was also found to be statistically significant, as Table 3.8 shows.

Table 3.8 *Logistic regression coefficients for predicting success in litigation*

Variable	*B*	*Standard Error*	Exp (*B*) odds ratio
Constant	-0.58*		
Respondent (0=State)			
Local authority	0.43	0.19	1.54*
Subject of petition (0=Civil)			
Non-civil petitions	-0.05	0.24	0.95
Conditional order (0=No)			
Conditional order issued	-0.17	0.18	0.84
Petitioner ethnicity (0=Jew)			
Arab-Israeli	0.81	0.22	2.24***
Palestinian	0.92	0.28	2.52**
Petitioner institution (0=Private)			
Organization/institution	0.34	0.21	1.41
Public	0.19	0.76	1.22
State/authority/public official	0.96	0.24	2.62***
Petitioner's lawyer (0=Private)			
Organization	0.65	0.24	1.92**
Self-representation	-0.99	0.28	0.37***
Dependent variable – outcome of petition (0= failure; 1=success) N=828 Chi-square = 76.99*** Cox & Snell R^2= 0.09 / Nagelkerke R^2= 0.12			

* = $p<0.05$, ** = $p<0.01$, *** = $p<0.001$
Note: When looking at the ability of the independent variables to predict the outcome of the petition, we see that while for the null model the overall percentage of prediction was 54.5 percent; the overall percent of cases that are correctly predicted by the full model rose to 63.6 percent; thus the variables improved the prediction by 9.1 percent.
Source: HCJ files.

As the table illustrates, the odds for success in litigation according to our database was influenced by various factors such as ethnicity (non-Jewish petitioners were found to have significantly higher success prospects than Jewish petitioners) and the representation of the petitioner (organized representation was found to have positive impact on chances for success

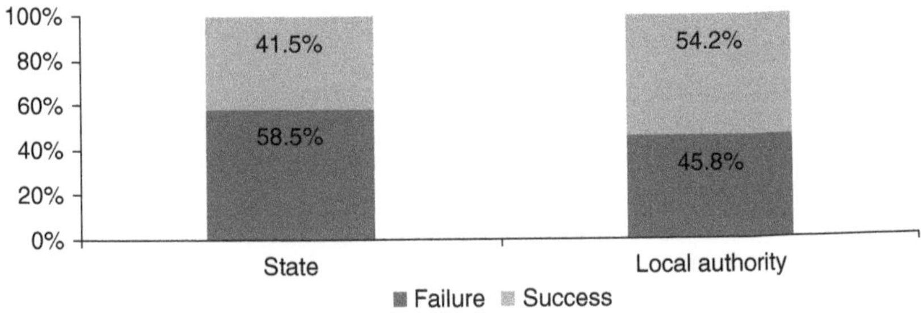

Figure 3.5 Success rates of petitions submitted against the state and municipalities during the 1990s
Source: HCJ files.

(odds ratio 1.92), while self-representation was found to significantly reduce chances for success in litigation (odds ratio 0.37). For the purpose of the current analysis, however, Table 3.8 points to the fact that the likelihood of petitions against local municipalities to succeed in litigation is 1.5 times *higher* than petitions against the state (odds ratio 1.54 $p<0.01$) – thus corroborating hypothesis 1.

2) Judicial decisions and settlements

The second question I investigate asks whether litigation ended in final judicial orders or in out-of-court settlements. When we break down the success and failure rates and examine the type of proceeding as well, we see interesting results. Figure 3.6 illustrates the differences between petitions submitted against the state and those submitted against local authorities in this regard.

As we can see from the diagram, the differences between success rates of petitioners against the state and against municipalities are explained mainly by outcomes in out-of-court settlements. Success rates in court decisions of petitioners against local municipalities are only somewhat higher than those who petitioned against state agencies (4.2 percent vis-à-vis 3.4 percent), although the rate of *failure* in court was much higher for petitioners against the state (38 percent vis-à-vis 25.2 percent). The differences in success rates in settlements are, however, much larger. In 50 percent of the cases against municipalities, petitioners won their case without the final judicial disposition, while the success rate against the state in out-of-court settlement was only 38 percent. The total rate of settlement is presented in Figure 3.7.

Figure 3.7 points to the fact that – contrary to our second hypothesis – local municipalities settled in (relatively) *more* cases than state agencies

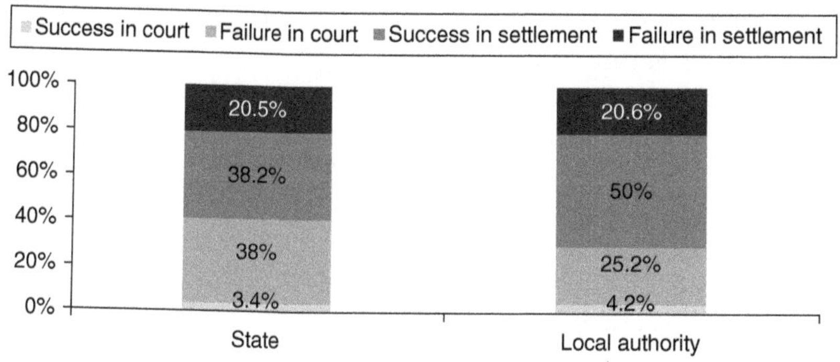

Figure 3.6 Success and failure in court and through settlements for petitions submitted against the state and against municipalities
Source: HCJ files.

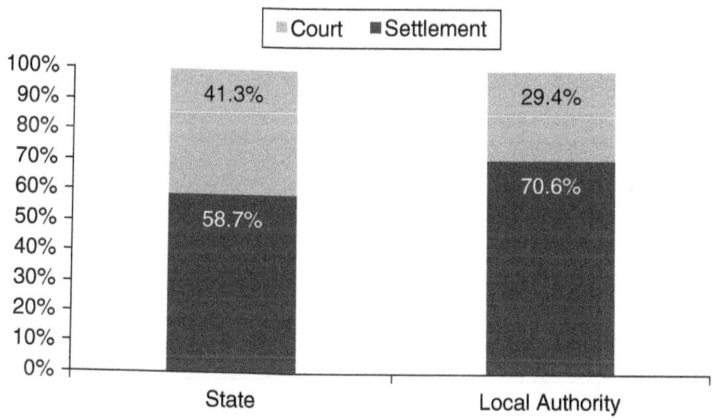

Figure 3.7 Rate of settlements: state and municipalities
Source: HCJ files.

during the 1990s. Indeed, state agencies settled almost 59 percent of all petitions, but the settlement rate of local municipalities was even higher and reached 70.6 percent of all cases. It should also be noted that the vast majority (over 70 percent) of cases settled by municipalities were settled *negatively* from the respondents' point of view, i.e. they were settlements that yielded (at least partial) success for the petitioners (see Figure 3.6 above). These differences in settlement rates are statistically significant ($\chi^2 = 10.91$, $df=1, p<0.01$) as presented in Table 3.9.

Table 3.9 describes the variables that affect the type of proceedings conducted (the likelihood for disposition of the case by court decision). As

Table 3.9 *Logistic regression coefficients for predicting the likelihood for disposition of the case by court decision*

Variable	*B*	*Standard Error*	Exp (*B*) odds ratio
Constant	-0.22		
Respondent (0=State)			
Local authority	-0.61	0.19	0.54**
Subject of petition (0=Civil)			
Non-civil petitions	-0.09	0.23	0.91
Conditional order (0=No)			
Conditional order issued	0.31	0.18	1.37
Petitioner ethnicity (0=Jew)			
Arab-Israeli	-0.83	0.24	0.44**
Palestinian	-0.36	0.28	0.70
Petitioner institution (0=Private)			
Organization/institution	-0.12	0.21	0.89
Public	0.21	0.73	1.23
State/authority/public official	-0.13	0.24	0.88
Petitioner's Llawyer (0=Private)			
Organization	-0.36	0.25	0.70
Self-representation	0.68	0.23	1.97**
Dependent variable – type of proceeding (0= settlement; 1=court)			
N=828			
Chi-square = 43.74***			
Cox & Snell R^2= 0.05 /			
Nagelkerke R^2= 0.07			

* = p<0.05, ** = p<0.01, *** = p<0.001

Note: When looking at the ability of the independent variables to predict the issuing of a conditional order, we see that while for the null model the overall percentage of prediction was 62.4 percent, the overall percentage of cases that are correctly predicted by the full model rose to 63.4 percent; thus, the variables improved the prediction by 1 percent.

Source: HCJ files.

we can see from the table there are a number of variables that increase the odds for the disposition of the case by a final court decision, including the ethnicity of the petitioners (the chance that petitions issued by Arab-Israeli would be settled are twice that of petitions issued by Jews), while the odds for petitions issued without legal representation to be disposed of by court decision were almost twice that of petitions represented by private lawyers (odds ratio 1.97). However, the odds that petitions issued against local municipalities would be settled are almost twice that of petitions issued against the HCJD's clients (odds ratio 0.54). Thus, on the face of the matter, our second hypothesis above is *not* corroborated by the findings.

3) Conditional orders

We saw that local municipalities represented by their own lawyers lost (relatively) many more cases in the HCJ during the 1990s than did state agencies that were represented by the HCJD, since local municipalities *settled* (relatively) more cases out-of-court than state agencies. Why did local municipalities do so? That is: why did they agree to *give up* their initial position in litigation and settle out-of-court? Part of the answer to this question seems to follow from the data in Figure 3.6 above. We can see that local municipalities *won* far *fewer* cases than state agencies in final court decisions (25.2 percent vis-à-vis 38 percent). Since local municipalities expected to have a much lower success rate in final court decisions, it may not be surprising that they also tended to settle out-of-court in order to avoid court defeat. The other, more complex, part of the answer to that question can be derived from looking into the practices of the HCJ with regard to conditional orders during litigation.

As explained above, the HCJ's decision to issue a conditional order is a crucial step that opens the door to a full hearing of the case within which the respondent agency is required to provide detailed arguments accompanied by affidavits.[20] In other words, the issuance of the conditional order is, in essence, a clear signal by the court that it is *not* going to end the litigation by dismissing the petition after the preliminary hearing but rather that it views the petition as raising serious issues that merit the court's full attention through a full hearing.

With this background in mind, we now take a look at data relating to the issuance of conditional orders in petitions against the state and local municipalities.

Figure 3.8 illustrates the huge difference in patterns of litigation between state and local municipalities. It points to the fact that, while in litigation

[20] See Section B.3.3 above.

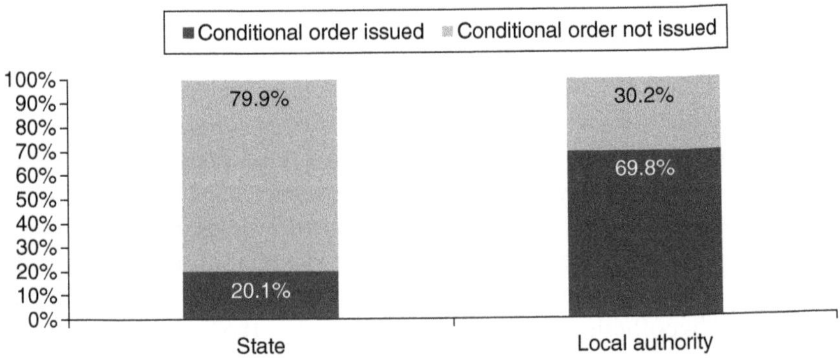

Figure 3.8 Conditional orders issued against the state and municipalities
Source: HCJ files.

against state agencies represented by the HCJD, the HCJ issued conditional orders in only around 20 percent of the cases, in petitions against local municipalities, conditional orders were issued in around 70 percent of all petitions during the 1990s. Not surprisingly, the differences in the rate of conditional orders are statistically significant, as Table 3.10 illustrates.

As the table demonstrates, there are a number of coefficients that increase the odds for the issuance of conditional orders during litigation – such as the ethnicity of the petitioner (odds ratio 0.42 for Arab-Israelis in comparison to Jews) and legal representation (odds ratio 2.24 for representation by public organization, while on the other hand, self-representation decreases the odds for conditional orders by almost 60 percent). *The strongest coefficient that increases the odds for the issuing of a conditional order in our analysis is, by far, the respondent's affiliation*. According to our finding, the odds for the issuance of a conditional order against local authorities are markedly higher than petitions against state agencies (odds ratio 7.64).

Thus, the above analysis of the issuance of conditional orders complements the answer to the question as to why local municipalities settle in litigation before the HCJ more often than state agencies. To put it simply, *municipalities settle cases because they have to*. They settle cases, normally, after a conditional order has been issued against them, which means that the court provides them with *a clear signal* that they will face defeat if they do not settle the case.[21] The reasons behind the HCJD decisions to

[21] The issuance of a conditional order is in itself a statistically strong predictor for failure of the respondent in court. As Table 3.3 shows, the issuance of a conditional order increases the likelihood for the petitioner's success by over 340 percent, see Table 3.3 and accompanying text.

Table 3.10 *Logistic regression coefficients for predicting the issuing of a conditional order*

Variable	*B*	*Standard Error*	Exp (*B*) odds ratio
Constant	-0.90***		
Respondent (0=State)			
Local authority	2.03	0.18	7.64***
Subject of petition (0=Civil)			
Non-civil petitions	-0.29	0.25	0.74
Petitioner ethnicity (0=Jew)			
Arab-Israeli	-0.86	0.27	0.42**
Palestinian	-0.50	0.33	0.61
Petitioner institution (0=Private)			
Organization/institution	0.21	0.22	1.23
Public	-1.42	1.12	0.24
State/authority/public official	-0.33	0.24	0.72
Petitioner's lawyer (0=Private)			
Organization	0.81	0.25	2.24**
Self-representation	-0.89	0.32	0.41**
Dependent variable – issuing of conditional order (0= not issued; 1= issued)			
N=939			
Chi-square = 256.19***			
Cox & Snell R^2= 0.24 /			
Nagelkerke R^2= 0.33			

* = p<0.05, ** = p<0.01, *** = p<0.001

Note: When looking at the ability of the independent variables to predict the issuing of a conditional order, we see that while for the null model the overall percentage of prediction was 64.1 percent, the overall percentage of cases that are correctly predicted by the full model rose to 75.6 percent; thus, the variables improved the prediction by 11.5 percent.

Source: HCJ files.

settle are much less conspicuous and call for a far more complex analysis. As our analysis suggests, conditional orders against state agencies are given only in around 20 percent of all cases (see Figure 3.8), while the HCJD settles almost 60 percent of all cases (Figure 3.7). Moreover, state agencies represented by the HCJD enjoy a very high success rate in final judicial disposition, as they lost only around 4 percent of all cases by court decision.[22]

D. Conclusion

Significant changes in patterns of litigation in the HCJ took place during the 1980s. Comparative quantitative analysis between cases disposed of by the court during the 1970s and the 1990s demonstrates than the rate of success of petitions during the 1990s was significantly higher than in the 1970s. The rise in success rates of petitions, however, was not the result of changes in the outcomes of cases disposed of by final judicial decisions of the HCJ. Rather, it was the result of the sharp rise in the relative rate of the cases settled in favor of the petitioners.

The hypotheses underlying our research suggested that the changes in patterns and outcomes of litigation were not only the subject of changes in the *Court's* policies but also related to changes within the apparatus that represents the state in litigation. In order to test this we conducted an additional quantitative analysis to compare petitions issued during the 1990s against state agencies and petitions issued in the same period against local municipalities. The idea underlying this analysis was that, unlike state agencies that are represented exclusively by the HCJD, municipalities are represented by their own lawyers. Thus, shifts within the central legal bureaucracy are not expected to influence litigation against local municipalities.

We found that there were indeed important differences between patterns and outcomes of litigation between state agencies and local authorities during the 1990s. While the tendency of municipalities to settle petitions issued against them was not lower (and in fact was even higher) than state agencies, there was a remarkable difference in the *stage* of litigation within which the settlement took place. We found that the likelihood that the court issue a *conditional order* against local municipalities was almost eight times higher than with regard to state agencies (odds ratio 7.64). This means that in contrast to state agencies, which tended to settle in the early stages of the litigation, municipalities tended to settle only in the face of a clear signal of a likely adverse court decision.

[22] See figure 3.2 and 3.6 above. In fact, even these figures regarding the failure rates of the HCJD (or success rates of petitioners) by final judicial decisions are somewhat inflated, because they include not only cases in which petitioners had *absolute* victory in court but also those in which the petitioners achieved a *partial* victory by court order (that is, they achieved part of what they asked for by court order but not everything).

These findings pose even more intriguing questions with regard to the ideology, practices, and decisional mechanisms that explain decision-making by state agencies and their representatives during litigation. To answer these questions we need to complement our quantitative analysis by a qualitative analysis regarding practices of litigation in the HCJD. This is done in the following chapters.

Appendix 1 – Variables in the longitude analysis

Dependent variables

The study examined three dependent variables – the outcome of the petition, the type of proceeding conducted, and the issuance of conditional orders.

The *first* outcome variable for this analysis was built as a dichotomous variable with two categories – success and failure. Success and failure were defined in relation to the petitioner's claim: thus success was when the case ended in favor of the petitioner, and failure was when it ended in favor of the respondent. The original variable included five categories: success in the decision held in court (when the petition was either fully or partially accepted); failure in the decision held in court (the petition was turned down either after a conditional order was issued or without a conditional order); success in the settlement (when a settlement was achieved or when the respondent backed down); failure in the settlement (when the petitioner backed down from his petition), and other outcomes. Success in court and settlement were united into one category, and failure in both court and settlement were united into another category. All other cases were omitted from the analysis.

The *second* dependent variable was the type of proceeding conducted. This variable is also a dichotomous variable composed of two categories – cases that ended in court and those that ended in a settlement out-of-court. This variable was built on the same original variable discussed above; however the categories were grouped differently. All cases that were discussed in court, whether ending in success or failure for the petitioner, were grouped into one category. The same was done for all cases that ended in settlement. The fifth category was yet again excluded from the analysis.

It should be noted that since the database is based on actual court files we were able to study the *actual* outcome of the litigation rather than the *formal* outcome. This is relevant particularly to the distinction between out-of-court settlements and court decisions. In many cases the parties reach an out-of-court settlement and then the court is asked to formally approve the settlement by official decision (consent decree). In some cases the parties agree that the court would dismiss the petition by formal decision after the petition achieved part or all of what it sought. All these cases were coded in our database as settlements and according to the actual achievement of the petitioner.

The *third* variable, the conditional order, is also a dichotomous variable composed of petitions in which the judges issued a conditional order and those in which conditional orders were not issued.

Independent variables

The *first* independent variable was the year of the petition. Due to the interest of this study to examine differences between petitions submitted in the 1970s in comparison to the 1990s, the interval variable of year of petition was reduced into a dichotomous variable, grouping all petitions that were submitted in the 1970s into one group and all petitions submitted in the 1990s into another group (0=1990s; 1=1970s).

The *second* variable examined was petitioner ethnicity. This variable is a multi-nominal variable including three categories – Jewish petitioner, Arab-Israeli petitioner, and Palestinian petitioner. The Arab-Israeli petitioner included all private Arab petitioners and local Arab authorities. The Palestinian petitioner's group included Palestinians who live in the Occupied Territories and in East Jerusalem (but see above note 9).

The *third* independent variable was petitioner affiliation. This variable is also a multi-nominal variable with four categories – private, public, institution or corporation, and state, authority or elected official petitioners. The private petitioner included all private petitioners – Jewish, Arab-Israeli, and Palestinian petitioners; the public petitioner included political and public-action organizations (NGOs); the institute–corporation variable refers to all corporations including cooperative societies, institutes, corporations, economic associations and other economic groups; the last group – state, authority, and elected officials – includes all Jewish and Arab local authorities, state-owned corporations, local and religious council members and Knesset members.

The petitioner's lawyer is the *fourth* independent variable. This variable was divided into three categories: a private lawyer, an organization (a public organization or the legal advisor of the organization); and self-representation. Petitions in which the state attorney was the lawyer were omitted. We also omitted a small number of petitions which, on their face, lack any basis for true legal reference (usually petitions that are issued by mentally disordered persons) which are summarily dismissed by one judge even before the preliminary hearing (futile petitions).

The respondent was the *fifth* independent variable. This variable was categorized into four groups: the state (including petitions against the state, the army, and other security forces); corporations and tribunals (including government and statutory corporations, civil, religious, military and labor courts, administrative tribunals, religious councils, and public institutions); private (including business corporations, private parties, interest groups, institutions, cooperative unions, and voluntary associations); and local authorities. All other respondents, including political parties and economic associations, were omitted from the analysis.

The *sixth* independent variable is the conditional order. This variable is a simple binomial one – either a conditional order was issued, or not.

The *seventh* and last independent variable is the subject of the petition. This variable is a multi-nominal variable including four categories: prisoner and detainee petitions; petitions regarding the Occupied Territories and security-related petitions; constitutional petitions; and civil petitions (including issues regarding civil cases, planning and construction issues, disciplinary and bidding cases, administrative issues, staffing issues, and all criminal cases that are not prisoner-related).

Appendix 2 – Variables in the local municipality study

Dependent variables

The study examined three dependent variables: the outcome of the petition, the type of proceeding conducted and the issuing of conditional orders (for details see Appendix 1 above).

Independent variables

The first independent variable is the respondent. This variable was categorized into two groups: the state (including petitions against the state, the army, and other security forces) and local authorities (municipalities). Petitions in which the respondents were *both* the state and municipalities were omitted.

The other independent variables in this analysis were petitioner ethnicity; petitioner institutional affiliation; the petitioner's lawyer; the subject matter of the petition; and the issuance of a conditional order (see Appendix 1).

4

The dilemma of serving two masters

In the previous Chapter I demonstrated the implications of the changes in the ideology and practices of the HCJD on patterns of litigation. The rise of the model of lawyering for the rule of law inevitably gave rise to professional and ethical dilemmas between the lawyers' duties to their client agencies and their commitment to broader ideas of the public interest. In the current chapter I discuss these dilemmas. I begin with a theoretical analysis based on three hypothetical test cases that illustrate these dilemmas. Then I examine these test cases from the point of view of various theories on government lawyers' professional, ethical, and constitutional commitments. The theoretical overview is followed by a detailed empirical description of the views and practices espoused by the HCJD. That is, I demonstrate how the attitude of the HCJD towards this central dilemma changed throughout the 1980s. I then examine possible justifications for the existing model of lawyering in the HCJD from a normative point of view. In the last section I investigate the extent to which the professional ideology of individual lawyers influences actual practices and outcomes in litigation, and do so by using a quantitative analysis of outcomes in litigation in HCJ files.

A. Theoretical Overview

1. *Three "hard cases"*

Let us consider the following three hypothetical cases:[1]

Case A (information disclosure): A government lawyer represents the Ministry of Transport in a petition against a decision to refuse an

[1] Cf. C. J. Lanctot, "The Duty of Zealous Advocacy and the Ethics of the Federal Government Lawyer: The Three Hardest Questions," 64 *S. Cal. L. Rev.* 951, 951–952 (1991). The three cases presented here are not wholly identical to those presented by Lanctot, and their facts are adjusted to the setting of HCJ litigation in Israel.

operating license to a public carrier. During her preparations for trial, the lawyer learns that there were significant flaws in the decision-making process. She also knows, however, that, due to the procedural limitations of the judicial review process, the chances that the other party would obtain knowledge of these flaws are negligible. Should the lawyer come forward and *disclose information* about those flaws in her brief to the court?

Case B (procedural defenses): Let us assume now that those serious flaws in the decision-making process are evident, and might well have brought about judicial intervention to strike down the administrative decision. The petition, however, was submitted beyond the time-limits set by the procedural regulations of the reviewing court. Should the government lawyer raise the preliminary *procedural defense* in order to fail the petition or should she waive her right to do so?

Case C (frivolous positions): A government lawyer represents the Ministry of Education in a case questioning the legality of governmental appropriation to a private school that espouses discrimination on the basis of gender. A few months before the petition was issued, the Supreme Court ruled unanimously that the appropriation of public funds to a private school – under similar circumstances – was unconstitutional. Should the lawyer take the case to the court and defend it?

Had we discussed these three cases from the point of view of lawyering in the *private* sector, none of them would have raised any serious ethical, moral, or practical dilemma. As a private attorney representing (say) a private corporation in litigation, no ethical obligation whatsoever devolves on the lawyer in *Case A* to expose in court damaging information revealed to her by her client (in fact, she would have probably violated her duty of confidentiality toward her client had she done so).[2] Likewise, it would be her professional duty to raise any procedural defense at her disposal in order to bring about the dismissal of the petition. There is also hardly a question that (as, for example, the representative of the private

[2] For a general discussion of confidentiality duties of government lawyers in the United States, see K. Clark, "Government Lawyers and Confidentiality Norms," 85 *Wash. U.L. Rev* 1033 (2007). For a discussion of confidentiality duties of lawyers in the UK see A. Boon and J. Levin, *The Ethics and Conduct of Lawyers in England and Wales* (Oxford: Hart, 2008), 219 *et. seq*. For similar duty in Israel see The Lawyers Bar Law 1961 section 90 (providing confidentiality to any exchanges between a lawyer and a client within the ambit of professional service and prohibiting the lawyer from exposing them); The Lawyers Bar Rules (professional ethics) 1986 section 19 (prohibiting a lawyer from uncovering any information provided by a client).

school in *Case C*) it was her right (if not her duty) to forcefully argue the case (at her client's request) even though she believes that her chances to succeed in court are nominal.[3]

The discussion's point of origin is, however, that government lawyers are presumed to differ from private lawyers. Therefore, questions that receive straightforward answers in the case of private lawyers may receive very different ones in the case of government lawyers or, at the very least, even if we end up with the same answers, they cannot be given *straightforwardly* and without a careful examination of the complicated considerations involved.

2. *Methodology: Identifying the "client" or identifying the commitments?*

A common methodology for dealing with dilemmas regarding government lawyers is to identify the lawyer's client.[4] The point is, of course, that in the case of a government lawyer identifying the client is not always a simple task.[5] One possibility is that the "client" is the government *agency* who is represented by the lawyer in the *specific case* (such as the Ministry of Transportation in *Case A* above).[6] Another view is that the client is *the*

[3] See L. L. Fuller, The Adversary System in *Forum Lectures*, Series 3, 1 (Washington D.C.: Voice of America, 1961), 2 ("… it [is] perfectly proper for a lawyer to undertake in a criminal case the defense of a man whom he knows to be guilty."). For the situation under the ethical codes in the United States see e.g. Lanctot, above note 1, at 962–964; Note, "Rethinking the Professional Responsibilities of Federal Agency Lawyers," 115 *Harv. L. Rev.* 1170, 1174 (2002) (hereinafter: Note–Harvard 2002). For the duty of zealous advocacy in the UK see Boon and Levin, above note 2, at 29 *et. seq.* For the law in Israel see section 54 of The Lawyers Bar Law 1961 ("… A lawyer shall act for the benefit of the client with loyalty and devotion, and shall help the court to do justice."). See also Limor Zer-Gutman, "The Lawyer's Duty not to Mislead the Court," 24 *Iunei Mishpat* 413 (2000) (Hebrew).

[4] See e.g. H. W. Perry, Jr., "United States Attorneys – Whom Shall They Serve?," 61 *Law & Contemp. Probs.* 129 (1998); E. E. Ugarte, "The Government Lawyer and the Common Good," 40 *S. Tex. L. Rev.* 269, 270–271 (1999); R. M. Salokar, "Politics, Law, and the Office of the Solicitor General," in C. W. Clayton (ed.), *Government Lawyers: The Federal Legal Bureaucracy and Presidential Politics* (University Press of Kansas, 1995) (hereinafter: *Clayton–Government Lawyers)* 59, 76–77; N. V. Baker, "The Attorney General as a Legal Policy-Maker: Conflicting Loyalties," in *Clayton–Government Lawyers*, at 31, 33–34;

[5] For discussions of the various possibilities in this respect, see e.g. Clark, above note 2, at 1049–1050; Note, "Government Counsel and their Obligations," 121 *Harv. L. Rev.* 1409, 1414–1415 (2008) (hereinafter: Note–Harvard 2008); R. C. Solomon, "Wearing Many Hats: Confidentiality and Conflicts of Interests Issues for the California Public Lawyer," 25 *Sw. U.L. Rev.* 265, 272 (1996).

[6] See e.g. Lanctot, above note 1; G. P. Miller, "Government Lawyers' Ethics in a System of Checks and Balances," 54 *U. Chi. L. Rev.* 1293 (1987); M. S. Paulsen, "Who 'Owns' the Goverent's Attorney-Client Privilege?," 83 *Minn. L. Rev.* 473, 487–488 (1998).

government as a whole, embodied in the head of the executive branch or the agency to which the lawyer belongs.[7] Yet a third approach would submit that the government lawyer represents "*the public at large*" or "*the public interest.*"[8]

The methodology of identifying the client of the government lawyer seems, however, to suffer from some deficiencies. It is often difficult to identify the exact client, since government lawyers are often presumed to owe duties to multiple entities within the government (and, sometimes, outside it). Therefore, on a practical level, such an approach does not provide a simple and effective solution to dilemmas of the sort presented above.[9] In addition, this approach is based on the assumption that the dilemmas of government lawyers should be dealt with in the narrow context of the ethics of the legal profession. Arguably, however, the dilemmas of government lawyers have broader implications for the way governments create and enforce policies, for relationships between the executive and the judiciary, and for the commitment of government agencies

[7] See e.g. R. P. Lawry, "Who is the Client of the Federal Government Lawyer? An Analysis of the Wrong Question," 37 *Fed. B.J.* 61, 66 (1978) ("The client of the federal government lawyer is the federal government."); see also J. R. Harvey III, "Note, Loyalty in Government Litigation: Department of Justice Representation of Agency Clients," 37 *Wm. & Mary L. Rev.* 1569, 1575–1576, 1594 (1996) (noting that "the Solicitor General['s] … client is most often the government as a whole, or the executive branch in particular, rather than an individual agency"); W. R. Dailey, "Who Is the Attorney General's Client?," 87 *Notre Dame L. Rev.* 1113, 1115–1116, 1128 (2012) (arguing that while the attorney general's client is the American People, the President is the People's chief spokesman). In the United States this approach is often identified with the concept of "unitary executive," see N. Devins, "Unitariness and Independence: Solicitor General Control over Independent Agency Litigation," 82 *Cal. L. Rev.* 255 (1994). In Israel, much like in the federal system in the United States, government agencies are not represented in courts by their own "house" lawyers but by a special agency that specializes in litigation (i.e. the Department of Justice in the United States and the OAG in Israel), see Chapter 2 Section B, pp. 57–59 and Section 0.1 at 71–72. This means that the "client" may be the attorney general or the head of the executive, i.e. the prime minister. It should also be noted that the attorney general in Israel is not appointed by political preferences of the government and thus enjoys a relatively higher degree of independence vis-à-vis the government than in the United States (see Chapter 2 Section B, p. 54).

[8] See e.g. S. K. Berenson, "Public Lawyers, Private Values: Can, Should, and Will Government Lawyers Serve the Public Interest?," 41 *B.C.L. Rev.* 789 (2000); S. K. Berenson, "The Duty Defined: Specific Obligations that Follow from Civil Government Lawyers' General Duty to Serve the Public Interest," 42 *Brandeis L.J.* 13 (2003); B. A. Green, "Must Government Lawyers 'Seek Justice' in Civil Litigation?" 9 *Widener J. Pub. L.* 235, 235–237 (2000); Ugarte, above note 4, at 274. For several manifestations of this approach in judicial decisions in the United States, see Clark, above note 2, at 1050 and note 69.

[9] See Lawry, above note 7; Clark, above note 2, at 1056; Note–Harvard 2008, above note 5, at 1413.

towards the public at large. Therefore, when discussing that commitment, one should also bring to the table various considerations of constitutional law and public policy.

Accordingly, it seems more useful to discuss the commitment of government lawyers by contrasting two principal models of lawyering: The first is the "*regular*" (adversarial) lawyering model under which the lawyer is primarily (and perhaps ultimately) committed to the interests of her immediate client in the litigation (also known as "the single-client model").[10] The second is the "*public interest*" lawyering model under which the lawyer is committed to a wider set of concerns.[11]

In any case, it should be noted that the implications of choosing each of these alternatives for the commitments of the lawyer in each of the three hypothetical cases are significant. In *Case A*, if the lawyer owes fiduciary duty to the public at large and not merely to its client agency, she may be under a duty to disclose information regarding the agency's wrongdoing and to assist the court in reaching a decision on the basis of the maximum information.[12] Likewise, in *Case B*, the general public interest may require that illegal administrative decisions should not persist, and therefore, forgoing the procedural defense could be considered the proper avenue for promoting the public good.[13] While in *Case C*, adopting the view that the lawyer represents the interest of the executive at large or the "public interest" may lead to the conclusion that the lawyer should refrain from going to court to argue a frivolous case, since this would be regarded as an improper waste of government resources.[14] Moreover, providing zealous

[10] See Miller, above note 6.

[11] Cf. Note–Harvard 2008, above note 5, at 1413. See also P. J. Utz, "Two Models of Prosecutorial Professionalism," in W. F. McDonald (ed.), *The Prosecutor* (Beverly Hills, CA: Sage, 1979), 99 (distinguishing between "adversary" and "magisterial" models of prosecutorial practices and arguing that the latter is characterized by strong commitment to the public interest). Admittedly, the use of these two models does not exhaust all the various ramifications of the above-presented dilemmas, nor do I purport to resolve all complicated questions regarding government lawyers in general by using them. And, in fact, the particular model I discuss below with regard to the HCJD (the lawyering for the rule of law model) is a robust version of the "public interest" model.

[12] See generally Note–Harvard 2008, above note 5 (suggesting government lawyers should serve as gatekeepers); Clark, above note 2 (suggesting that government lawyers owe special duties of disclosure of information despite ethical duties of confidentiality).

[13] See e.g. Schnapper, "Legal Ethics and the Government Lawyer," 32 *Rec. Ass'n. B. City N.Y* 649, 658 (1977) (suggesting that every government lawyer has responsibility to scrutinize "the validity of the conduct or contention he or she is asked to defend." And see Note, "Developments in the Law: Conflicts of Interest in the Legal Profession," 94 *Harv. L. Rev.* 1244, 1413, 1421 (1981).

[14] See D. L. Horowitz, *The Jurocracy* (Washington, D.C., Lexington Books, 1977), 47–48.

advocacy for frivolous cases may end up by eroding the government representative's credibility in the eyes of the judges, and thus compromise the government's overall stature in litigation. Thus, if the client is "the government as a whole," the lawyer should refrain from adopting such a course of action.[15]

Ultimately, there is one persisting question that these lawyers must answer: "Do I have to act *like any other (private) lawyer* – or does the fact that I represent the government require me to *go beyond* the 'lawyering' perspective and consider *wider ('public') interests*?" In the following section I describe the ways in which lawyers in the HCJD answer this question.

B. Empirical overview: The dilemma within the HCJD

Interviews with veterans who served in the HCJD during the 1960s and 1970s suggest that the members of the department never considered themselves as mere "hired guns" who strove to win the case for the government in court at all costs and regardless of any further consideration. The notion that as the representatives of the State of Israel before the High Court of Justice they are "officers of the court" committed to promoting the "public interest" has always been part of the heritage of the OAG office, and the department was no exception.[16] The practical implications of this notion, however, seem to be rather limited during that period. The department always espoused a practice of *full disclosure* of all information at their disposal in court, and regardless of the question of whether such evidence would have been exposed had they chosen to do otherwise. *Procedural defenses*, on the other hand, were presented by the HCJD's members in court on a regular basis (and regardless of the merits of the petition at stake). Cases in which lawyers clashed with client agencies over the question of whether to defend the agency's (seemingly frivolous) positions in court were rare. And, even in those cases, the HCJD's objections were directed more to the concern that the litigation would end up with a precedent damaging the government's overall position, or that the department's professional credibility in court would be compromised, than with any broader sense of ideological commitment to "the public interest."[17]

[15] See *ibid.*, at 45–46 and 64–65; M. Herz and N. Devins, "The Consequences of DOJ Control of Litigation on Agencies' Programs," 52 *Admin. L. Rev.* 1345 (2000).

[16] See Chapter 2 Section B.

[17] Interview with MA and IO (HCJD – 1960s); Interview with NM (HCJD – 1970s) and Cf. Horowitz, above note 14.

On occasion, lawyers felt that their personal morals prevented them from defending a certain agency decision. The consequence was either a process of "negotiation" with the client, with mutual attempts to persuade the other party to accommodate its position or, in rare cases, an appeal to the higher echelons of the OAG to sort out the problem (sometimes by assigning another lawyer to argue the case).[18] If one has to encapsulate the various pieces of information and different personal views presented in these interviews into one picture relevant to the conceptual framework discussed here, the bottom line seems to point to a very "restrained" model of "public interest" advocacy at that time.

The practices and ideology of the HCJD began to shift in the early 1980s with the rise of judicial activism in the HCJ.[19] The changing of the guard in the Supreme Court (most notably with the appointment of Justice Aharon Barak) was followed by rapid developments in public law. At the procedural level, the court eliminated central access doctrines such as standing and justiciability, and significantly curtailed (or softened) other procedural barriers, such as time limitations.[20] At the substantive level it rapidly widened the scope of judicial review. Most importantly for our purpose, it reversed the old doctrine that practically exempted decisions by the attorney general (and OAG) from judicial review and ruled that all prosecutorial (and other) decisions by the attorney general would be fully subjected to review in court.[21]

The changing of the guard in court was accompanied by a similar process in the OAG itself. In 1978 after Barak was appointed to the Supreme Court, Yitzhak Zamir, a colleague of Barak at the Faculty of Law at the Hebrew University (and a close friend) took office as attorney general.[22] Dorit Beinisch, one of Barak's closest allies at the OAG, took office as head of the HCJD.[23] The dramatic expansion of judicial review exerted significant pressures on the HCJD. From Barak's point of view, judicial review was not merely a process in which the court disposes "cases and controversies" between two opposing parties – a private individual and

[18] Interview with MA; Interview with NM; Interview with IO; Interview with LN; Interview with MA. Cf. Horowitz, above note 14, at 45–46.

[19] See Chapter 2 Section E.3.

[20] See Chapter 1 Section C.2, p. 36; HCJ 170/87 *Asulin* v. *Mayor of Kiryat Gat* [1988] IsrSC 42(1) 678.

[21] See Chapter 1 Section C.2, p. 38.

[22] See Chapter 2 Section E.3, p. 82.

[23] See Chapter 2. Beinisch was later appointed as a deputy attorney general (a position from which she retained considerable influence on the HCJD, see Interview with NM (March 7, 1997). Both Zamir and Beinisch were appointed to the Supreme Court after the completion of their service at the OAG.

government agency.[24] Judicial review was rather an opportunity for the court to review the legality and "reasonableness" of government policies. This shift in the court's policies called for a far wider role for the government representatives. In order to exert its full leverage over the administration, the court needed *active assistance* from the HCJD. Assistance meant, for example: providing the court with full and reliable facts that would facilitate expedient disposition of the case; helping the court to ease its rapidly growing docket pressures[25] by *screening out* cases that could be effectively settled without trial;[26] and sorting out effective administrative solutions to ensure *enforcement* of major policy reforms ensuing from litigation.[27] All these missions could hardly be carried out by government lawyers who view themselves (even remotely) as "hired guns" for their client agencies.

The changes in the HCJD's practices and ideological perceptions did not occur overnight and were accompanied by some resistance and internal opposition.[28] By the start of the 1990s, however, the HCJD was already fully espousing a very different model of lawyering, a model that I call "the rule of law" model of lawyering. In terms of defining their professional commitment, this model is reflected in the following statement of the current Head of the HCJD:

> Sometimes [our] practice creates tension with the relevant official who expects that the lawyer will represent him only. Our view, however, is that the state is a multi-organ entity. In the end of the day, the public interest is one [of those organs] … the representation is not of a specific agency but of the state as a whole. Thus, the represented interest is not only of the agency against which the petition is issued but of the whole entity called "the public interest".[29]

Moreover, under this model, government lawyers are not merely vaguely committed to interests wider than those of the client agency in the specific case. Rather, they are expected *to facilitate the process of judicial review over their client's decision* – as one of their principal professional duties.

[24] Cf. Article III to the US Constitution; *Allen* v. *Wright*, 468 US 737 (1984).
[25] See Chapter 1 Section B.1. [26] See Chapter 3 Section B.3.2.
[27] See Chapter 5. [28] See Chapter 2 Section E.3 p. 82–84.
[29] See O. Mendel,"On the Job of the Lawyer at the High Court of Justice Department," 2 *Ma'asei Mishpat* 53, 63 (2009) (Hebrew). See also I. Zamir [former Attorney General], "The Lawyer in the Public Service," in Y. Dotan and A. Bendor (eds.), *Zamir Book: On Law, Government and Society* (Jerusalem, 1995) (Hebrew), 53, 62 (the public lawyer owes duty to "the general public" that is distinct from his duty to his immediate clients).

How does this model work in practice? Let us now demonstrate some of its parameters by using the three "hard case" examples cited above.

1. *Disclosing information*

I noted earlier that for HCJD members, withholding information from the court had never been an option (regardless of the question of whether the other party could gain access to such information).[30] One obvious reason for government lawyers to provide the court with the fullest factual setting of the case is that by doing otherwise they risk losing their credibility and damaging their professional reputation in the eyes of the judges. Given the court's high expectations from the lawyers under the "rule of law" model, the fact that the HCJD is a small group of elite lawyers who appear before the justices on a daily basis, and that the career structure of HCJD members means that they often ultimately join the bench,[31] it is not difficult to understand why any option other than a full, thorough, and reliable disclosure of all the facts is completely off the table. In the words of one lawyer I interviewed: "It is a million times more important for me to retain the Court's trust in me than to win a certain case."[32]

Given the ambitious role adopted by the HCJD on the factual level, the question arises whether *the client agency* would be willing to expose all information to the representing lawyer. Members of the department insist, however, that they not only provide the court with all the information *they receive*, but also *make sure* that this information is complete and accurate by *investigating* their clients in any case of uncertainty or omission. As one lawyer observed:

> We don't put up with the role of "a pipeline" [of information]. We … check the facts thoroughly … There is no case in which I think that [the agency] isn't revealing the facts, and I continue. I stop. There is no case in which I suspect that I'm not revealing the whole story to the Court … I check the file, I question the client … all [agency] members involved … I don't purport to say I know everything in every case but I think I can fairly say

30 See Section B, p. 124 above. 31 Chapter 2 Section D.2, p. 75.

32 Interview with TL (Senior HCJD member). See Y. Dotan, "Judicial Rhetoric, Government Lawyers and Human Rights: The Case of the Israeli High Court of Justice during the *Intifada*," 33 *Law & Soc'y Rev.* 319, 340 (1999). See also interview with AN (HCJD member): "It is certainly not my goal to win as many cases as I can … my goal is … I don't know … to bring the state to act properly …".

that generally the real factual setting, as seen from the point of view of the agency, is presented in court.[33]

2. *Procedural defenses*

I noted earlier that during the 1980s the HCJ severely curtailed and softened most access doctrines in judicial review. Under the new doctrine of *standing*, cases could be brought to judicial review even when the individual petitioner had not sustained "personal injury" but was merely a "public petitioner" bringing some general government policy or abstract constitutional question to judicial review.[34] Likewise, the court softened the rules concerning time limitations, and discarded strict formal procedural rules of governmental immunity from judicial review.[35] Obviously, the shift in the court's doctrine had a major impact on the ability of the HCJD to make use of procedural defenses in court. The question was not whether the lawyers *wanted* to use such weapons, but whether they *could* do so under the new judicial policies. As one lawyer observed:

> In one [major constitutional] case I could argue that the case became moot ... I didn't want to raise the argument ... It was crystal clear to me that the Court would have no interest to deal with it ... I didn't argue it in my brief. I just avoided it. But on the day of the oral hearing for interim injunction, the Treasury [i.e. the client agency], "stood on their hind legs" and insisted that I raise the argument. I said: OK. I'll raise it, just so you know that if they rule against us [on the interim injunction] I exhausted all options. And indeed, I started arguing this and immediately Justice Barak expressed his discontent [and I backed off] ... [36]

All this is not to say that after the 1980s the HCJD stopped raising in court procedural defenses or arguments based on access doctrines. But the decision to raise such arguments involved less of a dilemma since the lawyers knew that the fate of the case could hardly be decided solely on

[33] Interview with INZ (senior HCJD member). See also the discussion of the practices of the HCJD regarding factual investigation within client agencies in Chapter 5 Section B. See Also Y. Roitman, "The Public Lawyer and the Protection of Human Rights" (Lecture, 2004) ("Many times the cross examination, which does not exist in HCJ formal procedures [see Chapter 1, Section B.2] is conducted by the HCJD lawyer. The public lawyer conducts thorough investigation into the relevant facts that there is no other way to have access to such facts.").

[34] See Chapter 1 Section C.2, p. 37. [35] See above note 20 and accompanying text.

[36] Interview with TL (HCJD senior). See also Mendel, above note 29, at 66 (stressing that public lawyers should not always raise procedural defenses even if they can do so from a purely formal point of view).

formal procedural grounds. Moreover, given the new doctrines of judicial review, the decision to raise such arguments, based on old precedents was, in many cases, equivalent to the adoption of a frivolous legal position (see below). Still, the HCJD members insist that even today when they have a practical choice as to whether to raise procedural defenses or not their decision is influenced by conceptions of professional morality.[37]

3. *Defending frivolous positions*

Issues regarding disclosure of information and raising procedural defenses seem to be quite settled under current legal doctrine and professional practice. However, the question as to when and to what extent the HCJD should defend in court positions that it considers frivolous appears unresolved and is the source of many disagreements within the department. Two important factors contribute to this state of affairs.

The first major factor is the considerable *powers* that the attorney general holds vis-à-vis the government with regard to both the question of asserting the right interpretation of the law and the issue of representation in court. Under the presiding legal doctrine – shaped by the HCJ during the 1990s – the attorney general is authorized to read the law and interpret it, and his reading is *binding* on all government agencies (unless and until the Supreme Court itself overrules him).[38] The attorney general also holds (with the OAG)– under current doctrine – a full *monopoly* in representing all government agencies before the court. Thus, under the court's ruling, the attorney general may refuse to defend a given government case in court, and should he do so, the government is not entitled to representation by any other lawyer.[39]

Obviously, this state of affairs leaves government agencies in a rather awkward position when facing the HCJD. On the one hand, the agency is *a captive client.*[40] Yet on the other, as a client, it is subject to its lawyer's decision whether and under what conditions they are to bring its case to court. It should be noted that the power of the attorney general to refuse representation has been used only on rare and exceptional occasions,[41] and the lawyers of the HCJD are well aware of the repercussions of such a refusal. However, the very existence of this power seems to serve

[37] See Roitman, above note 33. [38] Chapter 2 Section B, p. 55.
[39] Chapter 2 Section B, p. 58. For cases in which the Solicitor General in the United States refused to represent, see L. Caplan *The Tenth Justice: The Solicitor General and the Rule of Law* (New York: Knopf, 1987), 34 *et. seq.*; Note–Harvard 2002, above note 3, at 1190.
[40] Cf. Horowitz, above note 14, at 5. [41] Chapter 2 Section B, p. 58–59.

as a framework for the give-and-take process that often occurs between the agency and the representative lawyer over which strategy should be applied to deal with the case. As one lawyer observed:

> We are not a bunch of "prima donnas" who don't defend hard cases or take to court only cases we think are likely to succeed. We appear in a large variety of cases that involve politics, with many constraints. There are circumstances in which even if you think the chances are slim the client is entitled to representation ... If, according to our legal analysis, the minister's position can be defended as a valid position, then ... even if we aren't enthusiastic about it, we'll defend. If, on the other hand, we are convinced that his position won't stand review, I think it is our job to say so, and *we say so loud and clear*. Whenever the disagreement is with the ministerial level, and it does not end up with some agreement between us, then we refer it to the attorney general to hear all parties and reach the *final* decision.[42]

Besides confronting the client agencies before trial, the HCJD has other means *during trial* to bring the client to accept their position regarding the case at stake. One such tactic is to expose its doubts regarding the client's position in court. As one lawyer said:

> I never raise arguments [and openly say] that I think are wrong ... there are tactics ... I speak "in the name of," I speak *not on my behalf* but on [their] behalf ... I say "*the minister argues*" ... There are certain ways by which the lawyer *distances* herself from an argument she doesn't really believe in ... I think the Court understands this ...[43]

The second major factor that contributes to uncertainty regarding the position the HCJD should take regarding "frivolous" positions relates to developments in the legal doctrine. While judicial review before the 1980s was based mainly on formal doctrines of legality, during the 1980s the court rapidly developed new doctrines such as *reasonableness* and *proportionality*.[44] Unlike its American counterpart, the Israeli Supreme Court did not adopt a bright-line doctrine of deference to administrative discretion, but instead grounds its review on the elusive concept of reasonableness, which opens the way to *ad hoc* analysis of each and every decision.[45] Decisions on legality are based on

[42] Interview with INZ (HCJD senior, emphasis added). See also Mendel, above note 29, at 53, 55–56 and 63.

[43] Interview with TL (HCJD senior, emphasis added) and cf. Note–Harvard 2002, above note 3, at 1189–1190. For a similar technique used by Solicitor General Thomas Thacher in the United States see Caplan, above note 39, at 9.

[44] Chapter 1 Section C.2, p. 37–38.

[45] While in principle the Israeli Supreme Court espouses a doctrine of deference with regard to administrative actions, the scope of review depends on the circumstances of

legal expertise. In contrast, decisions regarding the "reasonableness" of administrative actions are largely susceptible to the subjective assessment of the beholder.

The court's intensive use of these doctrines had two important implications for relationships between the HCJD and its clients. First, the "legal" analysis of the case became far more dependent on the assessment of the individual lawyer who handles the case, an assessment that could not escape being influenced (at least to some extent) by the lawyer's personal opinion of the merits and wisdom of the policy at stake. Secondly, the use of such doctrines significantly hampered the ability of all parties to foresee the outcome of the litigation. It thus enabled the lawyers, and to some extent encouraged them, to expand the "safety margins" they use in their evaluations of the chances in court. HCJD lawyers who come across decisions that appear questionable can safely inform their clients that they "expect trouble" if the litigation proceeds, thereby exerting pressure on the clients to settle the case out-of-court.[46]

In addition, the HCJD is – in any case – under severe pressure by the court to settle cases out of court. From the court's point of view out-of-court settlements carry many advantages.[47] Among other things, *settlements enable the court to informally expand its influence over governmental decision-making* precisely due to the use of the "soft" doctrines of review discussed here. That is, by using the mechanism of settlements by the HCJD, under the encouragement of the court, and by resorting to the indeterminate concept of "reasonableness," the justices could bring about change in administrative policies, *even if such policies would have ultimately stood judicial review had they been litigated "all the way" by the HCJD.* As one member of the HCJD observed:

> You need, on the one hand, to represent the client … who has legitimate expectations to be represented. But, on the other hand, the court expects you to be "an officer of the court" … You have to maneuver between the client who is entitled to have his position presented legitimately, as long as it is not illegal or patently unreasonable, and the court that sometimes has

the specific case and there is no principle equivalent to the bright-line rule of the *Chevron* Doctrine as in the United States (see *Chevron U.S.A. Inc.* v. *Natural Resources Defense Council Inc.*, 467 US 837 (1984)). On the relationship between the *Chevron* Doctrine and the relationship between the Solicitor General and administrative agencies in the United States see e.g. R. L. Pacelle, Jr, *Between Law and Politics: The Solicitor General and the Structuring of Race, Gender and Reproductive Rights Litigation* (Texas A&M University Press, 2003), 19.

46 See Mendel, above note 29, at 59–60 (stressing that the development of the new "soft" doctrines of judicial review made the job of the HCJD members much more complicated).

47 See Chapter 5 Section A.2.

> *pragmatic proposals* which are even correct on the merits, *without necessarily meaning that the current administrative position is illegal.* The court has a proposal which they think is *more appropriate* and they *expect you* [i.e. the lawyer] to [accept it]
>
> Q: Does this mean that you accept the court's offer even when you know that the court, should it need to rule on the matter, would not intervene?
>
> A: Yes, definitely.[48]

As another lawyer commented: "There are many cases in which the court offers a settlement and it is pretty clear that should we say 'no,' they will decide the case in our favor." [49]

And another lawyer recalled:

> I had once a big argument with someone on a professional question. I told him regarding a certain case: "This is the lowest threshold I am willing to defend such cases in the future. If you go lower than that – I won't defend". He answered: "Why do you need to set up a threshold? As long as this is going to stand the HCJ's review – it should be OK with you". I told him: in certain scenarios "standing review" is a very laconic thing. But I think it is *improper* to *bring this* to court and therefore *we should save the court the need to deal with issues that they may have no choice but to affirm.*[50]

If one wants to sum up the "raison d'être" of the positions and practices that the HCJD espouses with regard to the dilemmas of government lawyers, it is fair to say that following the activist revolution of the 1980s, the HCJD responded to the new "rules of the game" set by the HCJ. The way in which the lawyers function according to the "rule of law" model is pretty much the way the HCJ *expects* them to function. The HCJD's members see themselves as committed to the "public interest," but the notion of the public interest is largely *shaped and manifested* by the court and by the ideal of *serving the court.*

In the words of a senior member in the department: "We are in fact – I don't want to say, 'dancing to the court's tune' because this may carry negative connotations – but we operate within a framework whose boundaries and rules are set by the court."[51]

48 Interview with INZ (HCJD senior, emphasis added); interview with AN (HCJD member); interview with TN (HCJD member).
49 Interview with TN (HCJD member).
50 Interview with ES (HCJD member, emphasis added).
51 Interview with INZ (HCJD senior).

C. Analysis

In the opening section of this chapter I suggested that we discuss the dilemma of government lawyers by referring to two competing models: the "regular – adversarial" model of lawyering and the "public interest" model.[52] As the previous discussion demonstrates, it is evident that the HCJD adopted a quite robust version of the "public interest" model (lawyering for the rule of law). It is now time to evaluate the pros and cons of this model from the policy point of view. A number of arguments against the public interest model have been raised in academic scholarship. I shall now examine these arguments with reference to the case of the HCJD.

1. *Democracy and legality*

One argument against the public interest model is that it is undemocratic. Under the doctrine of separation of powers, administrative policies should be shaped by the administrative agencies to which the law and the constitution assign powers to create and shape policies that promote the public good, and who are accountable to the public. In this line of thinking, government lawyers are not authorized to adopt and promote a concept of the public good different than that of their clients and if they do so, they exceed their statutory powers and defy their constitutional mandate.[53]

Leaving aside the question as to what extent administrative agencies are "democratically accountable" to the public,[54] it seems that the above argument begs the main question regarding the legitimacy of the public interest model. It is true that government agencies are awarded by law the power to formulate policies in their field. It is also true, however, that government lawyers (the HCJD included) are assigned by law the power

[52] See Section A.2 above.

[53] See Miller, above note 6, at 1295 ("Nothing systemic empowers government lawyers to substitute their individual conceptions of the good for the priorities and objectives established through these governmental processes."); Lanctot, above note 1, at 994; Note–Harvard 2002, above note 3, at 1174–1175.

[54] In the United States the debate on democratic accountability of the administrative agencies revolves around the question of the status of the "independent" agencies, and the "public interest" model is identified with the concept of "unitary administration," see note 7 above and accompanying text. In Israel, the vast majority of agencies represented by the HCJD form part of the central government and there is no question of their "independence" vis-à-vis the government (see Chapter 2 Section B). Moreover, in a parliamentary system such as Israel, the government itself is not directly elected but depends on the support of the parliament (Knesset).

to represent the government in litigation. The main question is therefore *how* those powers of representation should be exercised, and how we should *interpret* the mandate given to the HCJD to represent its client. The answer to the question lies not within some abstract formulation of democracy but by referring to policy considerations that deal directly with the model of representation.

2. *Zealous adversarial advocacy*

The main argument against the public interest model is based on the adversarial conception of litigation. Government lawyers should not promote any interests in litigation besides those of their immediate client agencies, because doing otherwise would violate the fundamental principles of adversarial advocacy.[55] As one critic of the "public interest" model stated: "The central principle that purportedly underlies the adversary system is that 'justice' can best be achieved by the battle of two zealous advocates before a neutral decision maker. Allowing a government lawyer to sit in judgment of the justice of a client's cause would be inconsistent with the fundamental principles underlying the adversary system."[56]

The principal flaw of this argument, however, lies with the assumption that the process of judicial review should be regarded as following the traditional characteristics of adversarial litigation. There are a number of reasons to doubt the proposition that judicial review fits into the adversarial framework. First, the adversarial model assumes that the main *objective* of the litigation is to decide the concrete controversy between the parties. It also assumes that the interests involved with such a decision are limited to those of the immediate parties.[57] In judicial review it is very difficult to maintain that the court should limit its attention solely to the narrow interests of the direct parties involved. Take, for example, a litigation in which a major piece of legislation (such as the healthcare reform statute in the United States)[58] is brought before the Supreme Court for review. The legislation at stake may have a major impact on millions of

[55] See e.g. Lanctot, above note 1, at 959–960. [56] *Ibid.*, at 985.

[57] See e.g. J. Tidmarsh and R. H. Trangsrud, *Complex Litigation and the Adversary System* (Foundation Press, 1998), p. v; R. A. Kagan, *Adversarial Legalism: The American Way of Law* (Harvard University Press, 2001), 9. This is certainly the case with regard to civil law litigation, but arguably less so in the case of criminal law, in which this rationale is weaker.

[58] Patient Protection and Affordable Care Act (PPACA) – Pub. L. No. 111–148, 124 Stat. 119 (2010) and see *State of Florida et al.* v. *Department of Health and Human Services* (2012).

persons whose interests could be directly influenced by the court's decision. Presumably, many different groups will be represented (either as petitioners, respondents, or as *amici curiae*), and indeed such a process is usually a multi-party one. The court must take into consideration a variety of conflicting interests and has to analyze a wide array of considerations.[59] The adversarial framework seems quite unfit to encompass this kind of process, or, at the very least, needs to be adapted to the context of judicial review. Using the mechanism of government lawyers as providers of *assistance* to the court is exactly the kind of adaptation of the litigation process essential to allow the court to sort out the matter.[60]

Unlike the case of a regular adversarial setting (in civil litigation), the objective of such a process is not merely to decide the controversy among the parties, but also *to ascertain the legality of governmental action and to prevent abuses of official powers.*[61] This is certainly the case for judicial review in Israel after the 1980s but also true, I believe, regarding any process of judicial review in a democracy. Accordingly, in judicial review it would be both unrealistic and wrong to regard the judiciary's role as "neutral." The judicial review "game" is not only a game between the parties to the litigation, but also *between the judiciary and the administration*, within which the judiciary assumes an active role in correcting administrative abuses. The framework of the adversarial model should be adopted accordingly. Not surprisingly, in such complex litigation the governmental legal apparatus is often called on to provide assistance to the court in disposing the case.[62]

An additional inadequacy refers to the fact-finding process. The adversarial model assumes that, overall, the best way to reach the true facts in litigation is by zealous competition, in which each party seeks to present facts on its behalf and countervail the opposing party's evidence.[63]

[59] See Tidmarsh and Trangsrud, above note 57, at 1–3.

[60] For a discussion of the function of Solicitor General as *amicus*, see Salokar, above note 4, at 73–75. In Israel the institution of *amicus curiae* was acknowledged by the Supreme Court in 1999 (FH 7929/96 *Kozali* v. *State of Israel* [1999] IsrSC 53(1) 529) but is much less developed than in the United States since the flexible rules of standing enable a wide array of parties to join the proceedings in the Supreme Court, either as petitioners or respondents. Still the number of *amicus* applications approved by the courts has been on the rise during the last decade (see I. Doron *et al.*, "A decade to 'Amicus Curiae': Empirical Analysis of Court Decisions," 34 *Iunei Mishpat* 667 (2011) (Hebrew). See generally, C. J. Ogletree Jr. and Y. Sapir, "Keeping Gideon's Promise: A Comparison of the American and Israeli Public Defender Experience," 29 *N.Y.U. Rev. L. & Soc. Change* 203, 229 *et. seq.* (2004).

[61] See P. M. Wald, "'For the United States': Government Lawyers in Court," 61 *Law & Contemp. Probs.* 107, 114–117 (1998).

[62] See e.g. Caplan, above note 39, at 3, 7, 19–25.

[63] See Fuller, above note 3; Lanctot, above note 1, at 993–994.

The model thus assumes some parity between the opposing parties concerning access to information. None of these assumptions are valid in the case of judicial review. In judicial review the government usually enjoys significant advantages over the petitioner with regard to access to information, since the whole decision-making process is carried out within the government and by its staff. In addition, the government enjoys significant procedural advantages while presenting evidence in court.[64] Not surprisingly, many scholars believe that *it is the role of government lawyers to offset these advantages* by coming forward and providing evidence on illegality in administrative actions, even when such flaws cannot be ascertained through regular adversarial proceedings.[65]

Thus, in fulfilling its supervisory function the court needs *ancillary mechanisms*. Government lawyers that follow the "public interest" model of lawyering may serve as important players within such ancillary mechanisms, as they do in practice in the case of the HCJD.[66]

3. *Decentralization and incoherence in the formation of public policy*

Yet another critique of the "public interest" model is directed against the implied problematic way in which public policy is formed. It is inconceivable, so goes the argument, that each individual lawyer would hold the power to identify the "public interest" in every case brought to court, for this would not only run contrary to agencies' power to form policies but also contradicts the idea of hierarchy and centralization in government.[67]

[64] For the procedural advantages of the Federal Government in US courts see e.g. R. Roots, "Unfair Federal Rules of Procedure: Why Does the Government Get More Time?," 33 *Am. J. Trial Advoc. 493* (2010). Under both UK law and Israeli law, administrative actions enjoy the *presumption of regularity*, which means that the decision is presumed to be legal unless and until the contrary is proved; see, for the UK, H. W. R. Wade and C. F. Forsyth, *Administrative Law*, 10th edn. (Oxford University Press, 2009), 246–248 and for Israel HCJ 7351/95 *Nevuani* v. *Minister for Religious Affairs* [1996] IsrSC 50(4) 89, 128; I. Zamir, "Evidence in the High Court of Justice," 1 *Mishpat Umimshal [Law and Government]* 295 (1993). In the United States, the burden is on the petitioner to prove that the administrative action is "unsupported by substantial evidence" under the Administrative Procedure Act, 5 U.S.C. § 706(2)(E), see P. L. Strauss, T. D. Rakoff and C. R. Farina, *Gellhorn & Byse's Administrative Law: Cases and Materials*, 10 edn. (Foundation Press, 2003), 267–269.

[65] See e.g. Clark, above note 2; Note–Harvard 2008, above note 5; Wald, above note 61, at 117.

[66] I shall discuss these ancillary functions in detail in Chapter 5. See Chapter 5 Section A.4, p. 156 and Section C, p. 169.

[67] See Miller, above note 6, at 1295; J. R. Macey and G. P. Miller, "Reflections on Professional Responsibility in a Regulatory State," 63 *Geo. Wash. L. Rev.* 1105, 1116–1119 (1995)

The force of this critique should not be downplayed in the context of the HCJD, particularly due to the above-discussed implications of the reasonableness doctrine that the HCJ espouses.[68] Yet, it seems that the danger of decentralization and chaos in policy-making should not be overstated either, and for a number of reasons. First, even for the HCJD under the "rule of law" model, confronting the client over issues of policy is still the exception, not the rule. As explained above, in the vast majority of "regular" cases, the lawyers would take the administrative policy choice "as is" and represent it in court.[69] Secondly, it is exactly because cases of disagreement are exceptional that they are never resolved at the level of the individual lawyer. Instead, whenever there is a doubt regarding the legality (or reasonableness) of the administrative position at stake, the matter is instantly brought to the attention of the higher ranks of the HCJD.[70] A process of deliberation between the department and the agency then takes place and, if necessary, the matter is brought to the decision of the attorney general.[71] Lastly, one should consider the position of governmental lawyers in such cases. They need to carefully maneuver between different, and often conflicting, interests and to accommodate pressures from all directions, i.e., the agency, the court, and their superiors within the OAG.[72] Under these circumstances it would seem a gross exaggeration to assert that individual lawyers are "free" to shape governmental policies according to their personal preferences. It appears more realistic to assume that personal ideology or preferences may sometimes influence administrative policies on the margins, rather than shape their very substance.[73]

4. *Separation of powers: Shifting the balance between the judiciary and the executive*

An additional argument against the "public interest" model of lawyering is that it runs against the idea of separation of powers. The model, so it argues, turns government lawyers into gatekeepers on behalf of the judiciary. Accordingly, it is very convenient from the judiciary's point of view

(arguing that in practice the supervision over government lawyers is less effective even in comparison to lawyers in private corporations).

68 Section B.3 above, p. 130–131.

69 See Section B.3 above, and see the discussion in Section D.3 below.

70 See Section B.3 above, and see Interview with KT (HCJD member).

71 See Section B.3 above.

72 See e.g. Horowitz, above note 14, at 10; Salokar, above note 4, at 78–80.

73 This point will be further developed in Section D.3 below.

because it gives the court various advantages: it saves judicial time and eases the caseload whenever government lawyers forgo their positions and settle; it provides the courts with ample access to information with relatively little effort, and so forth.[74] Government lawyers, however, should resist the temptation to answer the judicial calls for cooperation, since otherwise they would violate their duty towards their client agencies.

On the descriptive level it seems that the case of the HCJD perfectly demonstrates the validity of the claim that there is an intimate connection between the model of lawyering and judicial activism. On the normative level, however, it seems that the pros and cons of this phenomenon largely depend on other considerations that have already been discussed above.

More importantly, however, this argument calls attention to the following question: *do government lawyers really have a choice* when required "to cooperate" with courts that espouse activist practices of review? In other words, to what extent does the model of lawyering actually depend on the individual lawyer's professional morality? I shall try to answer this question in the following section.

D. The relationship between professional ideology and outcomes in litigation

1. "High-stature" and pragmatists in the HCJD

Earlier I described the rise of "the rule of law" model of lawyering in the HCJD during the 1980s. The change in the practices and ideology of the HCJD was not absolute, however, and did not occur without resistance. In fact, there were lawyers in the department that openly objected to those changes as challenging their ideological settings, while trying to stick to the older, more conservative vision of their role as government lawyers. In the early 1980s there were two principal figures in the department who represented the opposing concepts of lawyering. Renato Yarek, the head of the department, represented the conservative view. While his predecessor,

[74] See Harvey, above note 7, at 1600 ("The courts prefer the public interest model because it empowers government attorneys to act as gatekeepers who manage the courts' burden. This is a cynical but true statement") and see Judge Patricia Wald, above note 61, *praising* the public interest model for the exact same reasons; cf. M. H. Lemos, "The Solicitor General as Mediator between Court and Agency," 185 *Mich. St. L. Rev.* (2009) (discussing the relationship between judicial activism and deference and the model of centralized representation in litigation). The importance of settlements from the court's point of view is further discussed in Chapter 5 Section A.2.

Dorit Beinisch (who was promoted at the time to senior positions within the OAG and still had a good deal of influence on the department during that period) represented the "public interest" model of lawyering.[75] The divergence did not end with Yarek's retirement, however, but continued in the department throughout the 1990s and even later on.

When I began my service in the HCJD in 1994 I learned that in the HCJD's corridors some lawyers were referred to (by their peers and by themselves) as "*high statures*," that is, as the "militants" who were not willing to succumb to the temptations of the "lawyering for the rule of law" practice. Others were tagged as "*low stature*," that is, as pragmatists that espoused the model more willingly. The fact that this unique terminology (the meaning of which was not transparent to anyone outside the department) developed within the HCJD indicates that HCJD lawyers were well aware of the dilemma inherent to their role and that it occupied their minds at a sufficiently intensive level to create this unique kind of discourse.

The differences between the "high" and "low" stature revolved around the basic questions discussed above: how vigorously should they defend in court frivolous agency positions, how often should they raise procedural defenses, and so forth.[76] As one lawyer observes:

> There is no doubt that in some situations there are those who would defend and those who wouldn't. There are topics that are very [politically] controversial … but there is no statutory provision that dictates a certain reading. In this kind of situation Renato [Yarek] (and his followers) would defend, and others would say: we don't defend … I call it a kind of "high stature." In these cases I think we have no mandate to say "we don't defend" … No one appointed me to the bench, I am a lawyer, not a judge. I can say to the client I estimate the chances (of defeat) 90 percent … [but it's their call, not mine][77]

Another lawyer remarked:

> It is also a matter of personal style and character. There are those who think that when they go to court and receive [from the court] a hint that they don't like it, then they should "pack their things" [i.e. withdraw] and there are those – and I'm one of them – that [say that] if we believe in a certain view … the fact that the judge said something should not [change our course] and we should insist on our position being [fully] tested in court.[78]

[75] See Chapter 2 Section E.3, pp. 82–84. See also interview with MR, January 13, 2000 (identifying Yarek as "more militant" than Beinish).

[76] Issues concerning disclosure of information were much less controversial; see above, p. 124.

[77] Interview with IN (HCJD senior).

[78] Interview with IZ (HCJD senior).

The exact meaning of "high stature" was never defined by the members of the department – even unofficially – and almost everyone seemed to agree that the differences between "high" and "low" statures were a matter of degree. Nevertheless, awareness that these differences existed was conspicuous enough for them to identify some of their peers as typical high statures (HSS) and others as typical low statures (LSS) (there was no consensus among the lawyers with regard to many other members of the department).

2. *Methodology*

The question that I seek to answer is whether professional ideology affects lawyers' decisions and outcomes in litigation. Interviews with the members of the department indeed suggested that professional ideology influenced their strategies and behavior in litigation, so presumably outcomes in litigation were also affected by lawyers' ideology. The question is, however, whether the connection between lawyers' ideology and outcomes goes beyond anecdotal evidence as reflected in interviews, and may be traced in a systematic quantitative analysis. For that purpose I used the internal (unofficial) classification of lawyers in the HCJD (into HSS and LSS) as a proxy to represent professional ideology, while outcomes in litigation were studied on the basis of the quantitative analysis of HCJ files.[79]

The *hypotheses* of the research were the following:

1) *Rates of success are expected to be higher for HSS*. This is because HSS use more freely all kinds of procedural advantages at their disposal (such as access to information and procedural defenses). Likewise, HSS would settle fewer cases than their peers. That is, they'll also take their chances with "hard cases" that their peers would give up at earlier stages of litigation. Since our analysis includes *all* cases disposed by the court, including those settled at earlier stages,[80] the overall success rate of HSS is expected to be higher.
2) *Settlement rates are expected to be lower for HSS* – for the reasons explained above.
3) *Conditional orders rates are expected to be higher for HSS*. This is because conditional orders serve in the HCJ as a signal by the court to the respondent that it regards the chances of petitioners as substantial.[81] Thus, HSS

[79] See Chapter 3. [80] See Chapter 3 Section B.2, p. 89.
[81] See Chapter 3 Section B.1 hypothesis 4.

Table 4.1 *Descriptive statistics of variables*

Variable	*N*	Percentage
Petitioner, by institution		
Private	298	70.8
Institution/corporation/public organization	83	19.7
State/authority/elected officials	40	9.5
Petitioner, by ethnicity		
Jew	147	48
Arab-Israeli	64	20.9
Palestinian	95	31
Petitioner's lawyer		
Private	305	70
Organization	75	17.2
Self-representation	56	12.8
Respondent lawyer stature		
High stature	214	49
Low stature	223	51
Subject of petition		
Civil	250	58
Occupied Territories/security related	140	32.5
Constitution	41	9.5
Conditional order issued		
Yes	98	22.4
No	339	77.6

Note (i): For a description of the variables see Chapter 3 Appendix 1.
Note (ii): Due to the small number of petitions that were submitted by public organizations, these petitions were merged with petitions submitted by institutions and corporations.
Note (iii): Due to the small amount of cases that were prisoner- or detainee-related, these petitions were omitted from the sample.
Source: HCJ files.

would be expected to settle after the issuance of conditional orders, while LSS would tend to settle more often *before* a conditional order is issued.[82]

For the purpose of identifying HSS, I used information gathered during interviews with the HCJD members and by participant observation.[83] As

[82] *Ibid.* [83] See Introduction Section D, p. 13.

noted, not all HCJD members could be classified as either HSS or LSS. For the purpose of the analysis I chose four lawyers for each group. The lawyers in each group were identified by their peers (and by themselves) in interviews as "typical" HSS or LSS and all of them served significant periods in the HCJD during the 1990s and took part in a large number of court cases. Correspondingly, I created a database that contains 431 cases in which those eight lawyers represented government agencies before the HCJ, and studied the outcomes of these cases in litigation.[84] A description of the sample is found in Table 4.1.

3. *Outcomes*

1) Rates of success

The first question we posed is whether lawyers' ideology influences outcomes in litigation. The relative success rates of the HSS and LSS in our sample is presented in Figure 4.1 below.

As Figure 4.1 demonstrates, the differences in success rates of the two groups were small and were not statistically significant. Thus, our findings seem to refute hypothesis 1 above.

2) Rate of settlement

We assumed that HSS should have a lower settlement rate than LSS (hypothesis 2) because their professional ideology would inspire them to avoid settlements in "hard" cases and increase their tendency to litigate such cases "all the way." The outcomes of our quantitative analysis in this respect are presented in Figure 4.2 below.

As we can see from Figure 4.2, the differences between the tendencies of the two groups of lawyers to settle were found to be very small and not statistically significant. This finding is in sharp contrast to the impression one could draw from the interviews with HCJD members (HSS and LSS alike), and it refutes hypothesis 2 above.

3) Conditional orders

In Chapter 3 we found that the HCJ issued conditional orders against local municipalities far more frequently than against state agencies.[85] We ascribed the difference to the different structure of representation

[84] Our database of HCJ files contained 1,064 cases disposed by the court during the 1990s (see Chapter 3 Section B.2). The eight lawyers to whom we refer here represented the State of Israel in around 40 percent of all cases in our database.

[85] Chapter 3 Section C.3.3.

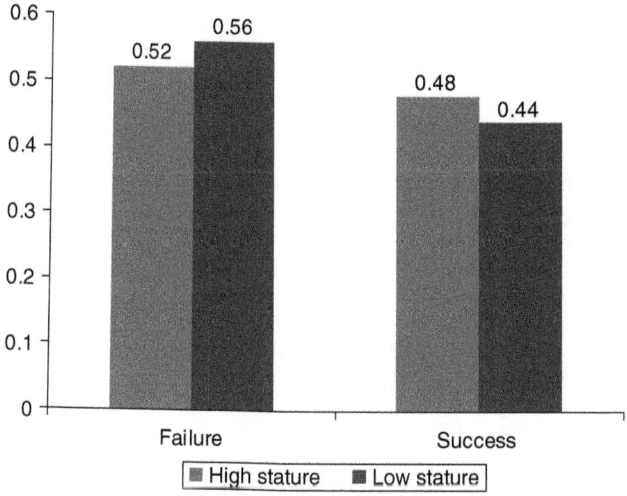

Figure 4.1 Outcome distribution for high and low stature lawyers
Source: HCJ files.

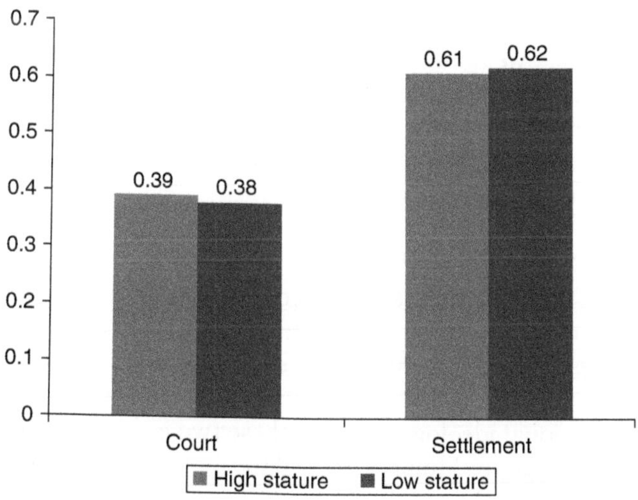

Figure 4.2 Type of proceeding distribution for high and low stature lawyers
Source: HCJ files.

of municipalities. Correspondingly we could reasonably expect that the more militant style of representation by government lawyers identified as HSS would be correlated with a higher rate of conditional orders (hypothesis 3). The outcomes of our analysis appear in Figure 4.3.

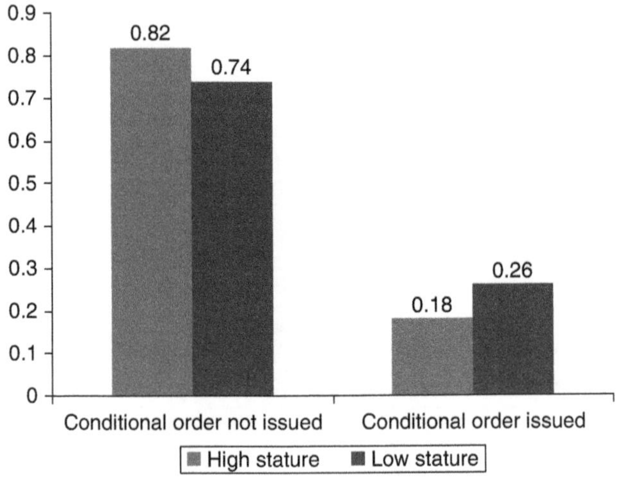

Figure 4.3 Distribution of conditional orders among high and low stature lawyers
Source: HCJ files.

As Figure 4.3 demonstrates, our third hypothesis was not corroborated by the data either. In fact, we found that the relative number of cases in which the HCJ issued conditional orders against HSS was even *lower* than in the case of their peers whom we identified as LSS (though the difference was not found to be statistically significant after we conducted logistic regression of all the variables in our sample).

4) Analysis

Our findings suggest that the professional ideology of individual lawyers – *at least as presented in their rhetoric* – seems to have limited impact on actual day-to-day practices in litigation, and even less so on outcomes in litigation. How can we explain the fact that differences that seem to be so robust in the professional ideology between these two groups of lawyers had hardly any (quantitative) impact in the daily reality of litigation?

One possible explanation is that we should be cautious in using rhetoric (as reflected in interviews etc.) as a baseline for evaluating professional ideology. A more plausible explanation is that the evidence that we gathered with regard to professional ideology is credible, but such ideological differences should be expected to have only a marginal impact on practices in litigation. This is because moral and ethical dilemmas are expected to arise only in "hard cases" that are relatively rare. Thus, while the existence of such dilemmas *is* traceable through the interviews, the overall impact of such cases on the daily routine of the HCJD, as reflected in our quantitative analysis, is *marginal.* In fact, the relative rarity of cases of that kind is reflected in interviews with HCJD members. Almost all lawyers interviewed (HSS and LSS alike) emphasized the fact that their primary task is to represent governmental agencies in court, and that normally, such representation does not give rise to the dilemmas discussed here.[86] While this explanation sounds reasonable, it still leaves some questions unresolved. For example, given the marked differences (between HSS and LSS) in the attitudes towards settlements, one might expect to see some differences in the relative rate of settlements.

More generally, however, our findings seem to point to the relative marginality of professional ideology and personal preferences on lawyers that function within a given institutional setting. Throughout this book I argue that, in essence, the whole apparatus of the HCJD was *responding* to the changes in the legal and political framework as dictated by the Supreme Court during the activist revolution of the 1980s. *Institutional conditions* certainly shaped the response of the HCJD to these changes (which explains the differences between patterns of litigation in the HCJD and local municipalities, as demonstrated in Chapter 3).[87] Our findings suggest, however, that *personal preferences* by HCJD members had little (if any) influence on this process. Indeed, professional ideology might have some influence on lawyers' *attitudes* towards these changes. Some enthusiastically joined that judicially initiated revolution, while others dragged their feet. But the bottom line is that those differences in personal attitude had hardly any impact on the reality of litigation (at least to the extent that such impact can be quantitatively measured). To refer once more to the words of the senior member of the HCJD who has already been quoted above: "The court was calling the tune – and HCJD members had to dance."[88]

E. Conclusion: The causes of the rise of the lawyering for the rule of law model

In a 1979 article Pamela Utz studied the behavior of two district attorney offices in Alameda and San Diego.[89] She found considerable differences between the two. In San Diego, the office adopted a rigid and formal approach that she called the "adversary" model of prosecution. It was characterized by the belief that all felonies should be charged, and that minimal

[86] See e.g. interview with INZ, above note 42.
[87] See Chapter 3 Section C.
[88] See above note 51 and accompanying text.
[89] See Utz, above note 11.

prosecutorial discretion should be utilized with regard to public policy considerations. San Diego prosecutors also viewed plea-bargaining as a threat to the idea of law enforcement and they negotiated settlements only for the sake of maximizing sentences.[90] In Alameda, on the other hand, the district attorney office emphasized the "public interest" as guidance for their action, and demonstrated considerable flexibility in their approach to plea-bargaining. The staff were willing to listen to defense attorneys and to use discretion based on the actual specifics of the defendant's behavior, rather than on formal legal classifications.[91] Utz called this model the "magisterial" model of prosecutorial behavior. She pointed out that the difference in practices between the two offices cannot be related to exogenous factors such as crime rates or the political composition of each district.[92] Rather, she found that the rise of the magisterial model was related to *institutional conditions* and in particular to the flexible and decentralized internal structure of the office, and to the *close relationship between the district attorney's office staff and the judges in the criminal courts*. The high level of professionalism in the court – Utz argued – encouraged the development of a "managerial" style of conflict resolution, which put pressure on the prosecution to develop similar practices.[93]

During the 1980s the HCJD adopted quite a robust version of the "public interest" model, a model that I referred to as the "lawyering for the rule of law model." As in the case of Utz's prosecutors, it seems that the causes for this model's development are primarily institutional. They are related to the drastic changes in the legal setting and the growing affinity between the court and the legal apparatus of the government. Within this setting, personal preferences of individual lawyers and their vision regarding their role as government lawyers seem to have had marginal impact. The dilemma between public interest and "adversarial" lawyering was decisively resolved on the institutional level.

The adoption of the rule of law model is reflected not only in patterns of litigation by the HCJD but also with other functions performed by the department. These functions will be the subject of discussion in the following chapters.

[90] *Ibid.*, at 103–109. [91] *Ibid.*, at 109–114.
[92] *Ibid.*, at 99, 114. [93] *Ibid.*, at 116–118.

5

Sorting things out: government lawyers in transformative litigation

In previous chapters of this book I described the evolution of the "rule of law" model of litigation and its implications on the practices of litigation before the HCJ following the activist revolution of the 1980s. One of the principal features of this model was the rise in the relative number of out-of-court settlements (discussed in Chapter 3). In the current chapter I wish to shed light on some additional functions of the HCJD with respect to the formation of out-of-court settlements. In particular, I wish to demonstrate the connection between the practice of settlements and the processes of *policy change* through litigation. I start by presenting the theoretical background. I discuss the relationship between transformative litigation[1] and out-of-court settlements. I also point to the importance of collaboration on behalf of the administration in the contemplation of judicially initiated institutional reforms. To demonstrate the argument I discuss in some detail a well-known case study of prison reform in the United States that drew much attention from the theoretical literature in this field. The theoretical discussion serves as a background for a detailed discussion of the functions of the HCJD with respect to the formation of out-of-court settlements and other managerial functions of the department. I present two case studies to demonstrate these functions: the case of the Bedouin tribes in southern Israel and the case of human rights litigation regarding the Occupied Territories. I conclude with some general remarks regarding the role of government lawyers in judicial review.

[1] The term "transformative litigation" means litigation aimed at bringing about change in governmental policies. This term is somewhat wider than the term "institutional reform litigation" often used in the literature, since the latter refers to situations in which the litigation refers to some *institution* or administrative structure that the litigation aims to transform. In some cases, however, the policy change at stake is not related to any structural change. For convenience sake I shall use both terms interchangeably.

A. Courts, transformative litigation, and policy-making

In a classical article published in 1976 Abram Chayes presented a new model of litigation which he termed as the "public law" model of adjudication.[2] The traditional conception of "civil adjudication," according to Chayes, featured (1) a bipolar lawsuit, (2) facts that had happened in the past (the "litigation is retrospective"), (3) interdependence of right and remedy (relief "derived more or less logically from the substantive violation"), (4) a self-contained episode, in which "entry of judgment ends the court's involvement," and (5) a "party-initiated and party-controlled" process.[3] *The public law model* of adjudication, on the other hand, is commonly a multi-party litigation aimed at bringing about institutional reform through a continuing process by which the court generates policy changes while using a variety of flexible remedies not necessarily resulting from liability determination.[4] Indeed, Chayes's account of the nature of litigation captured well the phenomenon of a growing number of court cases initiated to bring about institutional reforms. The flow of institutional reform litigation in the United States began in the early 1970s and has persisted since. It has involved thousands of public institutions (at both a state and federal level) and touched upon various areas of governmental activities, including prison reform initiatives, school desegregation plans, city housing plans, child welfare agencies, and mental health facilities.[5]

[2] A. Chayes, "The Role of the Judge in Public Law Litigation," 89 *Harv. L. Rev.* 1281, 1284 (1976). See also O. M. Fiss, "Foreword: The Forms of Justice," 93 *Harv. L. Rev.* 1, 12 (1979).

[3] Chayes, above note 2, at 1282–1283 and see also D. Zaring, "National Rulemaking Through Trial Courts: The Big Case and Institutional Reform," 51 *UCLA L. Rev.* 1015, 1022 (2004).

[4] See Chayes, above note 2, at 1289, 1293–1294; Zaring, above note 3, at 1022.

[5] See Zaring, above note 3, at 1018–1021 and note 14 (citing reports according to which in 2001 hundreds of prisons reported court orders concerning conditions of confinement; indicating that "a wave of consent decrees in the mid-1990s has placed some of the largest public housing authorities in the country under judicial supervision"; and that 45 states are "either facing lawsuits designed to reform public school funding or have changed their funding practices in response to such suits"); W. Parker, "The Future of School Desegregation," 94 *Nw. U. L. Rev.* 1157, 1189–1191 (2000) (noting that 10 percent of all school districts in the south are currently under court supervision). See also D. I. Levine, "The Modification of Equitable Decrees in Institutional Reform Litigation: A Commentary on the Supreme Court's Adoption of the Second Circuit's Flexible Test," 58 *Brook. L. Rev.* 1239 (1993) (noting that "in the nearly forty years that have passed since Brown v. Board of Education was decided, institutional reform litigation has become almost commonplace, especially in federal courts."). The phenomenon of "institutional reform" litigation, however, reached beyond the realm of pubic law and governmental policies into areas such as employment discrimination (see e.g. N. Levit, "Megacases, Diversity, and the Elusive Goal of Workplace Reform," 49 *B.C. L. Rev.* 367 (2008)) and mass tort class actions (see e.g. P. H. Schuck, "The Role of Judges in Settling Complex Cases: The Agent Orange Example," 53 *U. Chi. L. Rev.* 337 (1986)).

The rise of transformative litigation in the United States (and elsewhere[6]) sparked academic discussion regarding normative questions such as the moral and constitutional legitimacy of transformative litigation[7] and its efficacy in initiating social and institutional reforms,[8] as well as its overall social impact.[9] The focus of the current analysis, however, is on the positive aspects of this phenomenon, and specifically on the question as to *how* does the model of transformative litigation work? In other words, given the institutional constraints under which courts operate, how do courts perform their task as creators of institutional reforms?

1. *The institutional constraints of litigation*

Courts normally suffer from serious constraints when they act as policy-makers. One paramount constraint of legal adjudication (at least as conceived by the traditional "civil law" model) is its *formality*. The judicial process is extremely formal, particularly so if one compares it to executive or legislative processes of policy-making. It begins and ends at a given point in time, and in accordance with formal legal moves (the moment of filing the action; the moment of the final court decision).[10] Throughout its duration, the court process is subject to strict, formal, legal rules (such as the rules of procedure) that control almost every aspect of the process, including the way the parties communicate with the decision-maker (the judge),

[6] For the development of special remedies (such as "continuing mandamus") in prison reform litigation in India see *Hussainara Khatoon* v. *State of Bihar* (1980) 1 SCC 98; M. Mate, "Public Interest Litigation & The Transformation of the Supreme Court of India," in D. Kapsizewski, G. Silverstein and R. A. Kagan (eds.), *Consequential Courts: Judicial Roles in Global Perspective* (forthcoming, Cambridge University Press, 2013).

[7] See e.g. L. A. Graglia, *Disaster by Decree: The Supreme Court Decisions on Race and the Schools* (1976); R. Sandler and D. Schoenbrod, *Democracy by Decree: What Happens When Courts Run Government* (Yale University Press, 2003); W. A. Fletcher, "The Discretionary Constitution: Institutional Remedies and Judicial Legitimacy," 91 *Yale L.J.* 635 (1982); P. J. Mishkin, "Federal Courts as State Reformers," 35 *Wash. & Lee L. Rev.* 949 (1978); R. F. Nagel, "Separation of Powers and the Scope of Federal Equitable Remedies," 30 *Stan. L. Rev.* 661 (1978).

[8] See e.g. M. Schlanger, "Civil Rights Injunctions over Time: A Case Study of Jail and Prison Court Orders," 81 *N.Y.U. L. Rev.* 550 (2006).

[9] See e.g. G. N. Rosenberg, *The Hollow Hope: Can Courts Bring About Social Change?* 2nd edn. (University of Chicago Press, 2008); Schlanger, above note 8.

[10] See D. L. Horowitz, *The Courts and Social Policy* (Washington, D.C.: Brookings Institution Press, 1977), 38. Courts also have no control over their dockets and little influence on the timing in which the process begins since, as Horowitz notes "courts must act when litigants call" *ibid.* For the rise of organized litigation in the HCJ see Chapter 1 Section C.2).

the ways by which information is gathered, screened, and presented (rules of evidence), the way in which decisions are made and policy is formulated (legal reasoning and court decisions), and ending by the way in which the policy is to be implemented (court decrees).[11] Another notable constraint of adjudication (from the point of view of policy-making) is its *piecemeal* and *focal* nature. The judicial process is built to deal with the application of general legal rules to a set of specific facts presented and established in court. It is a "case by case" type of decision-making process and, to the extent that such process yields general principles, this is done incrementally by the development of precedents. Courts are ill-equipped to study and contemplate the overall picture, let alone to systematically accumulate information with regard to complex social problems.[12] Courts are even less equipped to foresee the consequences of their decisions, to evaluate the implications of their intervention, or to monitor the accuracy of enforcement of legal remedies over time.[13] As a result, policy-making by the judiciary suffers from a serious problem of *coordination* since separate judicial institutions may be called upon to deal with specific cases that relate to the same social problem but are handled simultaneously by different courts without any coordination (or even without knowing of each others' activity).[14] Likewise, courts lack the managerial ability to ensure coordination between the different players that may be influenced by their decisions or that are called to enforce their orders. Lastly, judicial *remedies* are traditionally extremely limited in their ability to cope with the needs of institutional transformation. They are drafted in the format of judicial writs, i.e. formal, rigid, imperative, legal commands that should presumably correspond with all the requirements of procedural rules, and be simple and definitive. All this makes them highly inapt to cope with complex social problems.

Obviously, with the rise of the public law model of adjudication, courts sought to overcome these constraints in order to be able to serve as effective institutional reformers. They used a variety of means for this purpose.[15] For example, they developed jurisprudence that enabled public action organizations (NGOs) to initiate litigation in order to overcome constraints of passivity;[16] they relaxed to some extent the rules of evidence in order to facilitate

[11] See Horowitz, above note 10, at 34–35; C. S. Diver, "The Judge as Political Powerbroker: Superintending Structural Change in Public Institutions," 65 *Va. L. Rev.* 43, 63 (1979).

[12] Horowitz, above note 10, at 45–49. [13] *Ibid.*, at 51–53.

[14] See *ibid.*, at 40 and cf. Zaring, above note 3, at 1074–1075 (discussing the phenomenon of "horizontal" coordination among trial courts in institutional reform litigation).

[15] For a discussion of the tactics used by the HCJ in this respect see Chapter 1 Section C.3.

[16] See Chapter 1 Section C.2 at 36–39.

the presentation of "social facts";[17] and they refrained from issuing final judicial decisions and stayed the proceedings for long periods of time in order to enable inspection of the enforcement of their decisions in the context of institutional reforms.[18] The bottom line is, however, that the overall ability of courts to overcome these constraints is limited. As Donald Horowitz put it: even if lawyers and courts are aware of these limitations "it does not follow that they can generally do anything much about it."[19] Moreover, to the extent that courts *can* take action to overcome these *inherent* limitations of the adjudicative process, they cannot do so by acting *alone*. Rather, they need *collaboration on behalf of other players* in the adjudicative process.[20]

In the following sections I shall discuss three aspects of transformative litigation: the importance of *settlements*; the importance of *governmental collaboration*; and the need to develop *monitoring mechanisms* ancillary to the reviewing court. All three aspects are interrelated and all are important to the understanding of the role of government lawyers.

I shall first discuss these aspects in the general context of transformative litigation and then move on to the discussion of the role that government lawyers play in this respect.

2. *The importance of settlements*

One distinctive feature of institutional reform litigation is that it is almost always carried out through *consent decrees* or other forms of *settlement*.[21] Out-of-court settlements are extremely common in transformative

[17] See also the discussion below, pp. 166–167. For a skeptical view regarding the ability of courts to effectively develop such fact-finding tools see Horowitz, above note 10, at 49–50.

[18] See Diver, above note 11, at 63–64. For an overview of the history of the development of special remedies in prison reform litigation see Schlanger, above note 8.

[19] Horowitz, above note 10, at 40 (referring to the incremental, precedential character of the judicial process) and see also M. McCann and H. Silverstein, "Rethinking Law's 'Allurements': A Relational Analysis of Social Movement Lawyers in the United States," in A. Sarat and S. A. Scheingold (eds.), *Cause Lawyering: Political Commitments and Professional Responsibilities* (Oxford University Press, 1998), 261.

[20] See M. Schlanger, "Book Review: Beyond the Hero Judge: Institutional Reform Litigation as Litigation," 97 *Mich. L. Rev.* (1999) (suggesting that prison reform litigation cannot be understood without an account of the role of players beyond the court themselves).

[21] The term "out-of-court" settlement is somewhat inaccurate with regard to settlements discussed here since, as we shall see, often settlements are formed with the active involvement of the judges, who use various means to push the parties into settlement and are involved in the content and structure of the settlements as well as in their implementation (see e.g. Schuck, above note 5). Likewise settlements are commonly brought before the court for formal approval in the form of consent decrees (or by other kinds of judicial

litigation.[22] They serve as an essential vehicle that enables courts to transgress the boundaries of the traditional model of litigation and fulfill their role according to the format of the public law model.

Settlements are conducive for transformative litigation for many reasons. First, settlements are not subject to the rigid formal requirements of compulsory legal remedies. They do not require formal findings or legal argument. Thus, they may be very efficient from the point of view of a court that seeks to save time and institutional resources in order to bring about institutional reforms.[23] Secondly, settlements are much more *flexible* than court orders in their terms and contents on the *remedial* level. The rigidity of court orders makes them ill-equipped to function efficiently with regard to institutional reforms. Such reforms may require a complex array of tools including the preparation of detailed plans for structural and functional changes, the formation of ancillary mechanism such as "task forces" to promote reforms, the appointment of experts and commissions, and so forth. All these are moves that are often beyond the scope of official judicial remedies. Likewise, settlements enable the courts to act beyond their formal boundaries of jurisdiction and interfere in matters that may be vital for the success of the reform, but outside the scope of their official powers.[24]

The third virtue of settlements from the point of view of transformative litigation is that they facilitate *collaboration* between state officials, corporate management, and other types of player whose collaboration may be vital for the success of institutional reforms through litigation (see below). As Sandler and Schoenbrod point: "Settlement offers real advantages. Agreeing with plaintiffs' attorneys on a corrective program allows defendant officials *to switch* from the role of lawbreaker to that of reformer. Officials can protect and expand budgets and programs, trump political

writ). For reasons of convenience, I shall use the terms "settlement," "out-of-court settlement," and "consent decree" interchangeably in the course of the discussion.

22 This is also true with regard to class actions issued against corporations and other organizations outside the governmental field, see e.g. Levit, above note 5, at 372–373; E. W. Trapolin, "Sued into Submission: Judicial Creation of Standards in the Manufacture and Distribution of Lawful Products The New Orleans Lawsuit Against Gun Manufacturers," 46 *Loy. L. Rev.* 1275, 1299 (2000) (noting that "ninety-eight percent of all lawsuits settle").

23 Schlanger, above note 20, at 2011–2012 ("Settlement saves the enormous expense and uncertainty of trial and appeal, and it gives the parties augmented control over the specifics of a remedy").

24 See *ibid.*; Diver, above note 11, at 45–46; Levit, above note 5, at 370, 372. See also M. M. Feeley and E. L. Rubin, *Judicial Policy Making and the Modern State: How the Courts Reformed America's Prisons* (Cambridge University Press, 1998), 60 (discussing "suggestions" made by the judge in the course of prison reform litigation).

bodies, gain protection against even more stringent laws and rules, and avoid the risk that the judge might impose a worse remedy."[25]

In other words, in the complex world of bureaucracy and politics that characterizes institutional reform litigation, settlements are often much more conducive in achieving effective collaboration to promote reforms on behalf of government officials than rigid formal court orders. This is particularly the case if the settlement enables some players *within* the bureaucracy to overcome obstacles and opposition to the reform presented by other segments.[26] Of course, in order to ensure that settlement achieves the above objectives the court must, in many cases, exert sufficient pressures on the parties. That is, the court must be involved in "managerial activism" and use all their legal and operational tools to push the parties into settlement.[27]

Lastly, settlements may enjoy a significant advantage over compulsory judicial remedies since they are much less exposed to the possibility of *future changes in the law* (either by statute or by precedent). This is particularly important in the context of institutional reform litigation within which enforcement may take several years.[28] Thus, the flexibility and (relative) informality of settlements not only make them much more efficient from an operational and economic point of view but also provide more stability and durability than compulsory court orders.

3. *The need for governmental collaboration*

One aspect of transformative litigation related to settlements but meriting separate discussion is the fact that successful reform through litigation necessitates collaboration with (at least *some*) players within the government. This point may seem trivial due to the fact that transformative litigation is often carried by settlements (which themselves, by definition, involve bureaucratic collaboration). Nevertheless, the point justifies further elaboration. Of course, settlements can be reached only when the defendants show a willingness to cooperate with reform initiatives. Agencies, however, are not normally expected to be willing to

25 Sandler and Schoenbrod, above note 7, at 122.

26 Schlanger, above note 20, at 2012–2013 and see Section A.3 below.

27 See Schuck, above note 5, at 347–350; Levit, above note 5, at 379–382; Schlanger, above note 20, at 2012–13. Settlements may carry additional "political" benefits from the point of view of courts such as lower exposure to the media in cases in which courts may suffer from damage to their public image due to unpopular decisions, see Y. Dotan, "Judicial Rhetoric, Government Lawyers, and Human Rights: The Case of the Israeli High Court of Justice during the *Intifada*," 33 *Law & Soc'y Rev.* 319, 346–347 (1999).

28 Schlanger, above note 20, at note 62.

change their established policies overnight, just because a lawsuit was filed. Settlement is often the result of a *complex process* of mutual interactions and pressures exerted by all parties to the litigation (including the court) as well as within the relevant government agency or administration. Often there are various different views within the agency (or agencies) with regard to the merits of the lawsuit and the importance of the challenged policies. Sometimes there are forces within the administration that actually support the plaintiff's agenda (even if they are not willing to come forward and openly admit it).[29] For these forces, the issuance of the lawsuit may be a golden opportunity to overcome internal opposition and to bring about reforms.[30] Others may feel less committed to the existing status quo than their peers and thus view the court case as an opportunity to gain political revenue. In any case, a firm and *cohesive* opposition on behalf of *all* relevant governmental players against the judicial challenge may significantly impede institutional reforms or even completely block any chances for change.

The point can be well illustrated by using the case of prison reform litigation in southern states of the United States, as described in the classic book by Malcolm Feeley and Ed Rubin.[31] The lawsuits brought against prison authorities in most states during the 1960s and the 1970s shared many common characteristics. They were all filed in federal court, by lawyer-activists who specialized in prison litigation (and coordinated their efforts) and they were all litigated according to the same legal and constitutional doctrines during (roughly) the same period.[32] Despite these similarities, the pace of reform in different states was very different. In some states, litigation took a relatively short period and the ensuing reform was implemented (relatively) smoothly. In other states, litigation became a long and fierce battle that lasted for over a decade and the process of implementation lasted even more. In Colorado, for example, the two main phases of litigation each lasted a few weeks and the whole process (including the period between the initial settlement – that the state failed to comply with – and the final decision) took a little more than one year. The duration of the reform process, that is, from the date of the

[29] See e.g. O. Mendel, "On the Job of the Lawyer at the High Court of Justice Department," 2 *Ma'asei Mishpat* 53, 62 (2009) (Hebrew) (sometimes petitioners to the HCJ choose to add an additional respondent government agency that they expect to *support* the petition issued against another agency).

[30] See e.g. Schlanger, above note 8, at 562–563 (indicating that "Prison and jail officials were frequently collaborators in the litigation. If they did not precisely invite it, they often did not contest it."); Sandler and Schoenbrod, above note 7 and the citation at pp. 152–153.

[31] See Feeley and Rubin, above note 24. [32] *Ibid.*, at 85–86.

issuance of the initial class-action suit, until the closure of the infamous "Old Max" prison and its replacement by modern correctional facilities, was less than five years.[33] In Texas, on the other hand, the first action was issued in the early seventies, but by the end of that decade the reformists were still involved in fierce and complicated court battles with the Texas Department of Correction (TDC). The implementation of the court orders only began in the mid-eighties and the full implementation of the judicial orders had to wait until the early nineties.[34] The reason for this difference (according to the authors) seems quite straightforward. In Colorado, when the initial suit was issued, the executive branch of the state had already publicly acknowledged the fact that its correctional facilities did not meet federal standards (and in fact, did not comply with its own official standards).[35] Accordingly, the main function of the litigation in Colorado was not to change executive policies but to overcome resistance in the state legislature to finance the reform espoused by the governor.[36] In such a state of affairs, it is unsurprising that the litigation went "relatively smoothly" as the authors describe it,[37] and the reform was carried out quite expediently. In Texas, on the other hand, the prison reform movement had to cope with the stern and persisting opposition of the TDC to any change in its correctional policies, which were widely regarded (in the state and elsewhere) as "efficient, orderly, and inexpensive."[38] Moreover, unlike in the case of Colorado, there were no cracks or "weak points" in any part of the Texan government in this respect. Both the executive branch and the legislature supported the TDC policies.[39] As a result, the reform movement was forced to conduct a long battle – both in the courtroom and subsequently at the implementation level – where they had to cope with the adamant reluctance of the TDC to carry out the reforms (and despite the fact that those reforms were implemented through consent decrees).[40]

33 *Ibid.*, at 100–107. 34 *Ibid.*, at 74, 84 and 92. 35 *Ibid.*, at 100.
36 *Ibid.*, at 102–103. 37 *Ibid.*, at 101. 38 *Ibid.*, at 83. 39 *Ibid.*
40 *Ibid.*, at 89. Even more interesting is the fact that the breakthrough in this battle for reform was a "defection" by one of the TDC's own lawyers, who, at a crucial stage of the litigation, used his personal experience as a guard in the state prison to confirm that the main factual claims of the Special Master (appointed by the court) with regard to the infamous "building tenders" system of the TDC – were in fact true (*ibid.*, at 88). He addressed the state attorney general and members of the Texas Board of Correction with this information, and thus brought about a dramatic shift in the *state* position vis-à-vis the need for fundamental reform. The "dramatic turning point" (as the authors put it, at 88) in this Sisyphean battle for reform was not a court decree, but rather a move *within the government* that signaled the beginning of the collapse of the old regime.

The prison reform case demonstrates the fact that *collaboration on behalf of government officials* is an essential condition for the success of institutional reform litigation. Such collaboration is needed to provide the court with comprehensive and accurate information; to facilitate the terms of the settlement by supplying the needed expertise;[41] to gather political support to achieve the settlement; and to secure financial resources and coordination in order to ensure implementation. Even if not all these functions are carried out by governmental players, most of them, in most cases, are, and in any case, the complicated tasks involved in institutional reform litigation cannot be achieved without, at the very least, their acquiescence.[42]

Given their professional training, their special position in transformative litigation, and their moral and professional commitment to the judicial process, government lawyers are, of course, natural candidates to serve as the "collaborators" in cases of institutional reform litigation.[43] One notable example in this respect is Lincoln Caplan's study[44] on the attorney general role in *Brown* v. *Board of Education*.[45] He argues that it was the attorney general's decision to argue in court that the infamous precedent of *Plessy* v. *Ferguson*[46] should be overturned that paved the way to *Brown* "because it signaled to the Justices that the Executive Branch was ready to enforce a call for desegregation of public schools."[47] As we shall see, similar functions are performed by the government lawyers in Israel who are the subject of the current study.

4. *The need for ancillary institutions*

The last aspect of transformative litigation that should be elaborated upon is the role of officials and institutions that serve as *ancillaries* to the court in transformative litigation. Given their serious institutional constraints, courts often find assistance from other players in the

[41] See e.g. Diver, above note 11, at 52 [defendants are required to submit a comprehensive plan for the eradication of violations].

[42] And cf. Levit, above note 5, at 417 ("Another feature that is emblematic of successful employment discrimination class settlements is corporate commitment to antidiscrimination and cultural diversity in the workplace and a high level of engagement by those responsible for implementation of those policies.").

[43] See Chapter 4.

[44] L. Caplan, *The Tenth Justice: The Solicitor General and the Rule of Law* (New York: Knopf, 1987).

[45] *Brown* v. *Board of Education*, 347 US 483 (1954).

[46] 163 US 537 (1896).

[47] Caplan, above note 44, at 26–27.

litigation.[48] Such players may gather information (such that cannot be efficiently established through adjudicative procedures), provide the court with expert opinion and reports,[49] coordinate efforts regarding the implementation of consent decrees, monitor compliance, or even preside over efforts to overcome political and bureaucratic opposition to the reform. Their participation is essential for the court since by themselves courts are seldom capable of "penetrating the dense fog of bureaucratic structure, resolving conflicts, and forcing compliance – all this within the confines of a traditional role that prizes principled decision-making and strict neutrality."[50]

The mechanisms that perform such tasks in transformative litigation are sometimes formed by external "neutral" players that the court resorts to on the basis of the consent of the parties. Thus, in almost all cases of prison reform litigation the court appointed a "special master" (an individual or a committee) to perform the complex tasks resulting from the consent decree.[51] In other cases the court appointed an expert as a "consultant" in technical or scientific matters.[52] Yet, in some other cases the courts facilitated, in the course of the settlements, special funds to oversight groups and "task forces" established to monitor compliance.[53] Sometimes, however, courts relied on *existing mechanisms within the bureaucracy* which they identified as supportive to reform initiative and capable of carrying the substantial bureaucratic and political efforts required to ensure implementation.[54]

B. The HCJD: Policy-making and other missions

Given the strong professional and social relationships between the HCJD and the Supreme Court – as described in other parts of this book[55] – it would hardly come as a surprise that the HCJD played a pivotal role within the rising regime of judicial activism of the HCJ since the 1990s.

[48] Therefore, the study of institutional reform litigation must always refer to the role of such ancillary players, see Schlanger, above note 20, at 1999–2000.

[49] See e.g. Schuck, above note 5, at 344–345 (discussing the appointment of a consultant by the judge to develop a settlement strategy and plans in the Agent Orange mass toxic collective action litigation).

[50] Diver, above note 11, at 53.

[51] *Ibid.*, at 52; Levit, above note 5, at 381.

[52] See e.g. Schuck, above note 5, at 344.

[53] See Levit, above note 5, at 370.

[54] See e.g. Feeley and Rubin, above note 24, at 60–61 (discussing the case of prison reform in Arkansas in which the commissioner of correction presided over institutional reform under the supervision of the court).

[55] See Chapter 2 Section D.

I argued above that courts can hardly bring about transformation in state institutions without the creation of some ancillary mechanisms that would enable the court to overcome their severe institutional limitations.[56] The HCJD was in an ideal position to provide the court with all elements necessary for institutional reform litigation: they could facilitate settlements (as described at length in Chapter 3), they could ensure governmental collaboration with the court's transformative initiatives, and they could provide the institutional infrastructure needed to transform the court's decisions into effective policy-making processes within the Israeli administration.

In the following sections I shall present two typical case studies to demonstrate the way in which the HCJD performed these functions. I shall then discuss some general characteristics of the HCJD functions in this respect.

1. *The case of the Bedouin in "non-recognized" villages in southern Israel*

The Bedouin are tribes that have lived nomadic lives for centuries throughout the Middle East. Prior to the establishment of Israel an estimated 65,000 to 90,000 Bedouin lived in the Negev Desert in the southern part of the country. According to a government source in 1998 some 110,000 Bedouin still resided in that area.[57] During the 1950s and 1960s large segments of the Bedouin gradually began to change their lifestyle and to establish semi-permanent villages on lands where they traditionally grazed their herds. The Bedouin, however, never formally established their legal rights with regard to these lands in accordance with the Ottoman and British land regulations that existed prior to the establishment of Israel. Therefore, their rights were never officially recognized by the government. Moreover, Israeli law after the establishment instituted a land regime that not only disregarded land rights

[56] The "support structure" needed to bring about social transformation through litigation includes also organizations outside the state, such as NGOs and groups in civil society that can provide the infrastructure needed in this respect (see e.g. C. R. Epp, *The Rights Revolution* (University of Chicago Press, 1998)). See the discussion in Chapter 1 Section B3, C2 and Figure 1.3.

[57] Y. Ben-David, "The Bedouin in Israel," Israeli Ministry of Foreign Affairs (July 1999, retrieved August 26, 2012), available at www.mfa.gov.il/mfa/mfa-archive/1999/pages/the%20bedouin%20in%20israel.aspx (last accessed July 18, 2013). According to other sources the number of the Bedouin in the Negev reaches 160,000. See: ACRI, *Negev Bedouins and Unrecognized Villages* (2012) (available at www.acri.org.il/en/category/arab-citizens-of-israel/negev-bedouins-and-unrecognized-villages/, last accessed July 18, 2013).

of the Bedouin but also introduced various formal obstacles that made it often impossible for them to establish such rights on the basis of possession or antiquity.[58] As a result, about 50 percent of the Bedouin population in the Negev still live in establishments considered "illegal" or "unrecognized." This means that they have no property rights over the lands in these villages and also that under zoning and planning laws any construction in these areas is either banned or strictly limited. As such, many Bedouin dwellings are frequently subject to the possibility of demolition by the authorities.[59]

One of the consequences of this state of affairs is that the Bedouin population in the unrecognized villages do not enjoy basic infrastructure such as roads, connection to the electricity grid, a permanent water supply, or sewerage. In addition, many basic services such as education and healthcare are either not supplied in the villages (and therefore, their inhabitants are forced to travel long distances to receive them) or are supplied in facilities that do not meet even the minimal standard accepted in other parts of Israel (such as schools not connected to the electricity grid).[60] The lack of infrastructure and other services, combined with the

[58] R. Shamir, "Suspended in Space: Bedouins under the Law of Israel," 30 *Law & Soc'y Rev.* 231, 235–238 (1996); A. Kedar, "The Legal Transformation of Ethnic Geography: Israeli Law and the Palestinian Landholder 1948–1967," 33 *N.Y.U. J. Int'l L. & Pol.* 923 (2001); Avinoam Meir, *As Nomadism Ends: The Israeli Bedouin of the Negev* (Boulder, CO: Westview Press, 1997), 90–92; I. Rosen-Zvi, *Taking Space Seriously: Law, Space and Society in Contemporary Israel* (Aldershot: Ashgate, 2004), 43 *et. seq.*

[59] See e.g. M. Rotem, H. Noach and N. Al-Ukbi, *The Arab-Bedouin in the Negev-Naqab Desert in Israel: Response to the Report of the State of Israel on Implementing the Covenant on Economic, Social and Cultural Rights (ICESCR)* (Shadow Report Submitted by: The Negev Coexistence Forum for Civil Equality, 2010), 3 (available in English at http://dukium.org/user_uploads/pdfs/Dukium_Final_Shadow_report_1Nov10.pdf (last accessed July 18, 2013)(hereinafter: Coexistence Report 2010). Other parts of the Bedouin population in the Negev reside in towns established by the government or in villages that were officially recognized (see Ben-David, above note 57). The Israeli government has made attempts throughout the years to solve the problem by presenting plans to reinstate part of the population in new permanent establishments and to legalize some villages (the most recent and comprehensive one was the establishment of a special governmental commission in 2007 – The Commission to Propose a Policy for Arranging Bedouin Settlement in the Negev, presided by Justice Eliezer Goldberg, a former Justice of the Supreme Court). Political opposition (including the resistance of most Bedouin organizations) as well as budgetary and bureaucratic obstacles still account for the lack of any effective policy to cope with the problem. See the Goldberg Commission statement at http://moch.gov.il/SiteCollectionDocuments/odot/doch_goldberg/Dvar_Shofet_Goldberg_ENG.pdf) (last accessed July 18, 2013).

[60] See Coexistence Report 2010, above note 59. See also ACRI (Association for Civil Rights in Israel) Report, *Negev Bedouin: Info Sheet* (February 5, 2009), available in English at www.acri.org.il/en/2009/02/05/negev-bedouin/ (last accessed July 18, 2013).

overall neglect of the Bedouin, makes this population one of the most poor and deprived segments of Israeli society. The government, on its side, reasoned its omission to provide services to those villages on the fact that they were illegal and hence any construction (of roads etc.) was banned. It also maintained that the provision of such services to the villages would discourage the Bedouin from moving from these villages to permanent residences in towns that had been specially planned for the Bedouin diasporas.

While the Bedouin had made some attempts to assert their land rights and to challenge plans to move or reinstate them as early as the 1960 and 1970s,[61] the first organized petitions with regard to the provision of basic services to the unrecognized villages were only issued to the HCJ in the late 1990s. Since then, dozens of petitions have been issued. These petitions deal with almost any aspect of lives in the villages beginning with road construction, the provision of water, electricity, healthcare, education and other social services, as well as many other issues.[62]

The petitions brought the dilemma of the unrecognized villages to the doorstep of the court with all its intensity. On the one hand, given the appalling conditions in the unrecognized villages, the court could hardly remain indifferent without calling into question its fundamental commitment to human rights. On the other hand, given the apparent illegality of those villages (at least from a formal legal point of view) and the enormous complexities involved, any judicial intervention risked serious repercussions with regard to the overall plans of the state to deal with the problem. The HCJ needed, therefore, to develop a doctrine that would bring about some reform in the life conditions of the petitioners without permanently compromising efforts to develop a comprehensive solution to the unrecognized villages problem. In addition, the court was well aware of its limited institutional capacity to deal with complex issues such as road development and the development of healthcare programs.

The court chose to cope with the problem by adopting a dual strategy. The first prong of this strategy were clear expressions of the court's dissatisfaction with the existing state of affairs and its unequivocal commitment to legal intervention that would correct the most immediate cases of hardship. An example of this is a petition issued in 1998 that dealt with the fact that Bedouin schools in the Negev were not connected to the national

[61] See e.g. CA 518/61 *The State of Israel* v. *Badaran* [1962] IsrSC 16(3) 1717, 1720; CA 274/62 *The State of Israel* v. *Ali Suead* [1962] IsrSC 16(3) 1946 (both decisions referring to lands in northern Israel). For a general description of the law see Kedar, above note 58.

[62] See below text and notes 66–71.

electricity grid. In 1998 the court, in a short but decisive interim decision, said the following:

> The current situation by which the *Bedouin* schools subject to this petition are not connected to electricity 50 years after the establishment of the State is patently inconceivable and serves as a disgrace to the State of Israel. This state of affairs cannot go on. [63]

Another decision that expresses the same determination is a case in which the petitioners sought the state to build a bridge over a stream that flooded the only road that children from unrecognized villages could use on their way to the local school and created a serious risk to the children's lives.[64] In one of its most remarkable decisions ever, the court issued an interim injunction, ordering construction of a bridge despite the fact that the zoning and planning regulations forbade any construction in that area at the time. The court used its special constitutional "prerogative" powers for that purpose, indicating that the life-threatening situation in this case justified such an exceptional move.[65]

The second prong of the court's strategy was used to cope with the more general, systematic issues of Bedouin discrimination and neglect. In a series of cases that dealt with all aspects of public services (or the lack of them) the court used the "managerial" strategy of exerting constant pressure on the government to initiate and carry out policy reforms. Among the issues at stake were the provision of healthcare services,[66] mother–child station services,[67] electricity connection for healthcare clinics,[68] the

[63] HCJ 4671/98 *Abu Fariach* v. *Bedouin Education Authority* [1998] IsrSC (interim decision, August 10, 1998). As a result the schools were hooked up to the electricity grid a few months after that decision, see HCJ 4671/98 *Abu Fariach* v. *Bedouin Education Authority* [1999] IsrSC (January 17, 1999).

[64] HCJ 3511/02 *Negev Coexistence Forum* v. *The Ministry of Infrastructure* [2003] IsrSC 57(2) 102, available in English at http://elyon1.court.gov.il/files_eng/02/110/035/F11/02035110.f11.pdf, last accessed July 18, 2013.

[65] *Ibid.* The exceptional nature of the decision sparked academic debate, see e.g. A. Reichman, "A Very Narrow Bridge: Constitution, Justice, Equity and Remedy," 37 *Mishpatim* 701 (2007) (Hebrew).

[66] See e.g. HCJ 4540/00 *Abu Apash* v. *Minister of Health* [2005] IsrSC (May 14, 2006) (health services).

[67] See e.g. HCJ 10054/09 *Vadad* v. *Ministry of Health* [2012] IsrSC (March 6, 2012). In Israel the government provides special services of healthcare and aid to new-born babies at special clinics ("Tipat-Halav"). See also Coexistence Report 2010, above note 59, at 26.

[68] HCJ 6602/07 *El Una – Arab Municipality for the Unrecognized Bedouin Villages* v. *Minister of Health* [2009] IsrSC (June 25, 2009) (electricity connection to healthcare clinics). See also HCJ 7604/08 *Physicians for Human Rights* v. *Ministry of Health* [2009] IsrSC (June 15, 2009) (electricity connection to severely sick persons homes);

construction of roads to schools and other public facilities in the unrecognized villages,[69] the provision of welfare and education services,[70] and so forth.[71] In these cases the petitions were typically left pending for several years while the court addressed the respondents and required that they settled the case by forming comprehensive plans for policy reforms that would eventually be brought before the court for approval.[72]

The complexity of the task to bring about policy reforms for the unrecognized villages derived not only from the legal difficulties, and from the lack of bureaucratic motivation, but also from the fact that there was no agency in charge of the unrecognized villages and no coordinated policy by the different ministries. In other words, there was a bureaucratic *vacuum* that someone needed to fill in order to move the wheels of reform. The HCJD lawyers who were in charge of these petitions were the obvious candidates to serve this function. As one of the lawyers who was in charge of a number of Bedouin cases says:

> [During the hearing in Court] the Court said: 'if you admit that there is a problem, why don't you solve it?' But it was impossible to solve it on the spot ... because *there is no one in charge*, no ministry is responsible for this ... each agency sees only their own petty business ... In order to facilitate practical solutions you need to *bring together* many different players. You need to *unify budgets* of many agencies. You need to *coordinate their action into a coherent course*. This is not a simple task, since each agency has their own mandate, and if something is beyond their official mandate,

HCJ 8062/05 *El Atrash* v. *Minister of Health* [2005] IsrSC (November 23, 2005) (same). See also Coexistence Report 2010, above note 59, at 29.

69 HCJ 6773/05 *Gaboa* v. *Ministry of Education* [2012] IsrSC (April 24, 2012, unpublished); HCJ 9208/06 *El Atrash* v. *Municipality of Abu Basma* [2009] IsrSC (May 25, 2009); HCJ 182/09 *Arab Education Forum* v. *Ministry of Education* [2009] IsrSC (October 20, 2009); HCJ 10030/05 *El Amur* v. *Minister of Education* [2006] IsrSC (April 26, 2006) (transport for kindergarten students).

70 HCJ 5108/04 *Abu Goda* v. *Minister of Education* [2004] IsrSC (September 9, 2004) (childcare facilities); HCJ 6671/03 *Abu Ganem* v. *Ministry of Education* [2005] IsrSC (January 24, 2005) (special education and educational supervision).

71 See also e.g. HCJ 2887/04 *Abu Madigam* v. *Israel Land Administration* [2007] IsrSC 62(2) 57, available in English at http://elyon1.court.gov.il/files_eng/04/870/028/h05/04028870.h05.pdf (last accessed July 18, 2013) (petitions against the state's practice of spraying Bedouin crops grown illegally in order to destroy them); HCJ 7245/10 *Adalla* v. *Ministry of Welfare* [2011] IsrSC (February 21, 2011) (petition challenging a statute that made the payment of social security benefits conditional upon the participation of children in the national immunization program); HCJ 8300/02 *Nasser* v. *The Government of Israel* [2012] IsrSC (May 22, 2012) (equality in tax benefit to residents of peripheral areas).

72 See e.g. cases cited in notes 66 and 69.

> they don't have anyone to deal with it ... and this is where we in the HCJD step in. Our job is, in essence, *unification and coordination* ...[73]

The same lawyer adds:

> What was our role? It started with some meetings in which we said [to the government officials]: "look, if you don't take things into your hands so everyone would file a petition and say 'I want this road near my house' ... and you will lose control and be dragged after the petitioners" ... So it started by us saying: *you need to appoint a specialist for road planning* that would study the whole area ... and all the needs ... someone that would say what requires reconstruction or rebuilding ... you need first [to get] the full evidentiary picture ... if you say it is impossible to construct a road to every village, tell us what you think *can* be done ... we kept track of how the experts were working on all that, and how the finance people were proceeding ... when we came to the treasury it was already a saga of dozens of meetings (I think that I personally was eight times or so in the prime minister's office for this) ... we convened with the [would be] director of the Bedouin agency *even before the agency was officially appointed* ... it was that kind of a job ...[74]

Even with the HCJD's intensive involvement the road to reform was far from short or easy. In many cases even after the government agreed (and officially committed to the court) to construct roads or to build a clinic it took many years and additional court orders to bring about the completion of the task and the court had to be constantly involved.[75] The HCJD for its part used the court supervision as leverage to push forward, as the HCJD member in charge describes:

> I knew that it was right from our point of view, from the public interest point of view and for the sake of the case at stake, *to tell the Court* that we are doing some comprehensive planning. I admit that it was right from *my point of view* to say this *in order to "lock in" the agencies and commit them to doing so*. They had already committed in principle ... but I knew they needed additional push to do what they knew they needed to do ...

[73] Interview with LR (HCJD member) (emphasis added).

[74] Interview with LR (HCJD member) (emphasis added); interview with ARD (HCJD member).

[75] See e.g. *Gaboa* v. *Ministry of Education*, above note 69. While the petition was issued in 2005 and the court dismissed it on the basis of a settlement brought to its approval, in 2011 the court had to re-address the matter in the course of a petition for contempt. The court rebuked the respondents for dragging their feet and ordered them to issue an updated settlement in January 2012 (see decision November 15, 2011). In April 2012 the construction of the road was still not completed and the case was still pending (see decision April 24, 2012). And see H. Shadmi, "The Government to Set Up Clinics for Bedouin: We Shall Build One Clinic," *Ha'aretz* March 21, 2003 (describing the slow pace of the implementation of the court order to build medical clinics for the *Bedouin*).

> Once I tell the Court "we are preparing a plan" next time the Court will ask me to update them … and the respondents know this … so we declare that we are preparing a plan … and it took three or four years but something came out of it …[76]

In the end, after more than a decade and a half of constant litigation it seems that the level of services provided to the unrecognized villages is beginning to change. The government significantly increased the budgets directed to the Bedouin sector and it appointed a special agency (The Agency for the Registration of Bedouin Lands in the Negev)to deal with the issue of Bedouin land claims.[77] It also announced a comprehensive five-year plan to build roads to public facilities and improved the level of services provided to the unrecognized villages. While these changes are far from being sufficient to eradicate the severe inequality that the Bedouin suffer, the HCJD members clearly regard themselves as deserving some credit for those (albeit limited) achievements.[78]

2. *Human rights in the Occupied Territories*

After Israel took control of the West Bank and Gaza Strip in 1967 those Territories were subjected to military occupation by Israeli Defense Forces (IDF).[79] The occupation always involved serious infringements of the human rights of the Palestinian population in the Territories, which included, among other things, limitations on the freedom of movement of Palestinians, infringements on fundamental political rights such as speech and procession, as well as frequent cases of expropriation of lands for military (or other) purposes. The severity of these infringements fluctuated throughout the years in accordance with the security conditions

[76] Interview with LR (September 12, 2011) (emphasis added).

[77] For a critical assessment of this move see Coexistence Report 2010, above note 59, at 17–18.

[78] In an interview the HCJD member said: "In 2009 … the government approved a five year plan in which it would build many roads to many Bedouin public facilities … we were very proud of it …" (interview with LR (HCJD member)).

[79] In 2005 Israeli troops withdrew from the Gaza Strip in the course of the Disengagement Plan, and thus the military occupation of that area ended. The Disengagement, however, failed to bring peace to the area since Gaza is currently controlled by the Muslim Hamas Movement which initiates various hostile attacks on Israeli neighborhoods. Israeli military activities accompanied by human rights concerns continue, and so does the intensive judicial scrutiny over these activities, see e.g. www.btselem.org/topic/gaza_strip (last accessed July 18, 2013) and HCJ 201/09 *Physicians for Human Rights* v. *Prime-minister of Israel* [2009] IsrSC, available in English at http://elyon1.court.gov.il/files_eng/09/010/002/n07/09002010.n07.pdf (last accessed July 18, 2013) (human rights conditions during Israel's military operation Cast Lead).

but always remained substantial. It was particularly intensive in periods of mass riots, such as during the first Palestinian *Intifada* (between 1988 and 1992) or in periods of massive terror waves against Israeli troops and civilians, such as during the second *Intifada* (between 2000 and 2003).[80] During these periods the IDF conducted massive detentions of thousands of Palestinians suspected of being involved in the hostilities, imposed a curfew on several Palestinian communities, demolished houses in which suspected terrorists resided, and used several other harsh military means that severely infringed the human rights of Palestinians.[81]

One of the most idiosyncratic features of the Israeli occupation in the Territories is that it was subject to constant and intensive scrutiny by the Israeli judiciary. As early as 1972 the HCJ ruled that it had full jurisdiction to review actions of the IDF (or any other Israeli agency including the secret services) in the Territories and that such actions would be subject to both the principles of customary public international law and to the general principles of Israeli administrative law as applied to any government agency in Israel.[82] Since then, the court has disposed of several thousands of petitions issued by Palestinians with regard to almost all aspects of Israel's military and civil activities in the Territories. Accordingly, petitions relating to the Territories have occupied a substantial portion of the court's docket over the years.[83]

The intensive involvement of the HCJ in the military activities in the Territories has put a heavy burden on the HCJD. The department is required

[80] Z. Schiff and E. Ya'ari, *Intifada: The Palestinian Uprising – Israel's Third Front* (New York: Simon and Schuster, 1990); U. Amit-Kohn, R. Jarach, C. B. Glick and N. Biton, *Israel, The 'Intifada' and the Rule of Law* (Israeli Ministry of Defense Publications, 1993); B'Tselem, *10 Years to the Second Intifada* (press release, September 27, 2010) available in English at www.btselem.org/press_releases/20100927 last accessed July 18, 2013).

[81] See e.g. A. Straschnov, *Justice Under Fire* (Tel Aviv: Yedioth Aharonot, 1994), 62–73 (during the first *Intifada* 14,000 administrative detentions were made, all under special emergency legislation issued by the military regulations that were put in force after the beginning of the uprising). See also references in note 80.

[82] HCJ 302, 306/72 *Hilu* v. *Government of Israel* [1973] IsrSC 27(2) 169; HCJ 393/82 *Jam'iat Iscan Al-Ma'almoun Al-Tha'auniya Al-Mahduda Al-Mauliya* v. *Commander of IDF in the Judea and Samaria Area* [1983] IsrSC 37(4) 785, available in English at www.hamoked.org/items/160_eng.pdf (last accessed July 18, 2013); M. Shamgar, "The Observance of International Law in the Administered Territories," 1 *Israeli Yearbook of Human Rights* 262 (1971); E. Benvenisti, *The International Law of Occupation* 2nd edn. (Oxford University Press, 2012), 203 *et. seq.*

[83] See Dotan, above note 27; R. Shamir, "'Landmark Cases' and the Reproduction of Legitimacy: The Case of Israel's High Court of Justice," 24 *Law & Soc'y Rev.* 781 (1990). In our database at least 14 percent of the petitions were issued by Palestinian residents of the Territories. See Table 3.1 in Chapter 3 (and cf. note 9 *ibid.).*

to handle hundreds of petitions each year that relate to individual grievances of Palestinian petitioners. In addition, in many cases, such individual grievances may raise more complicated issues that require policy-making or institutional reaction. The HCJD is heavily involved in such policy-making processes. Its members often take part in drafting guidelines and regulations directed to the military agencies in the Territories, and conducting reforms in military practices to accommodate the requirements of the court.[84]

One prominent example of the HCJD impact in this field is the case of the location and identification of detainees during the massive waves of administrative detentions during the first and second *intifadas*. In both cases, the beginning of the violence in the Territories was followed by the mass detention by the IDF of thousands of persons. The detentions were made under emergency regulations issued by the military authorities. Due to the security exigencies those detentions were done in many cases without prior notice to the detainee or their family members. The detainees were held in military camps or other facilities that were built hastily to accommodate a large number of detainees, sometimes in poor conditions.[85] Following these waves of detentions, a large number of petitions were issued to the HCJ by the detainees or by family members. Many of these petitions involved procedural rights, such as the fact that in many cases the detainees were unable to contact their families to inform them about the arrest, and the lack of proper appellate procedures.[86] Other petitions were directed against the conditions within the detention facilities.[87] Thus, the HCJD was overloaded with petitions by family members of the detainees who did not receive notice of the detentions and did not have any information about their whereabouts. As one lawyer testifies:

> In the beginning of 2002 and after masses of petitions were issued by … families of people who were detained without the families knowing where

[84] Such activities are often carried out by the HCJD by collaborating with the legal departments of the relevant military agencies and with other departments of the OAG, such as the Department for Legal Advice and Legislation (cf. Chapter 2 Section B). See interview with LNY (HCJD member).

[85] See references in notes 80 and 81.

[86] See e.g. HCJ 253/88 *Sajadia* v. *Minister of Defense* [1988] IsrSC 42(3) 801; HCJ 670/89 *Uda* v. *Commander of IDF in Judea and Samaria Area* [1989] IsrSC 43(4) 515.

[87] See e.g. *Sajadia* v. *Minister of Defense*, above note 86; HCJ 3278/02 *The Center for Defense of the Individual* v. *Commander of IDF in the West Bank* [2002] IsrSC 57(1) 385, available in English at http://elyon1.court.gov.il/files_eng/02/780/032/A06/02032780.a06.pdf (last accessed July 18, 2013); HCJ 5591/02 *Yasin v. Commander of the Kziot Military Camp-Kziot Detention Facility* [2002] IsrSC 57(1) 401, available in English at http://elyon1.court.gov.il/files_eng/02/910/055/A03/02055910.a03.pdf (last accessed July 18, 2013).

> they are ... our first reaction was to start looking for these people, to call all authorities that could possibly hold them and to find out where they are. This wasn't easy and took ample resources. Then, *we initiated a center* to deal with this job. It was required to gather information [and pass it to the families] ...[88]

With regard to prison conditions the HCJD conducted supervision over the conditions in the detention camps by initiating visits by lawyers to oversee the implementation of court orders. In fact, the practice of the HCJD members physically traveling and visiting the relevant arena in the Territories was common not only with regard to prison conditions but also with regard to many other issues such as land expropriations, road blockades, and other measures that infringed on human rights. As one lawyer testifies:

> For myself, in every case [of a petition regarding human rights in the Territories], no matter what the subject matter was, I used to get to the field and see for myself ... every detention facility where there are complaints you need to go and see for yourself, to get the impression and also to improve your argument in court and to try and form a settlement ... also with issues of land confiscation ... almost any such case I would go and visit the field.[89]

Another lawyer adds to this:

> Yes, you go to the field. This is very common. And you take the legal advisors [of the military agency] with you ... This is important because they know more than we do ... It is always better that they are also fully involved in the process. So we go to the field with the legal advisors and we examine the policy on the ground. There, we also do the questioning: why do you do this ... why you do that ... and sometimes you raise a proposal: why not do this instead? They may answer ... it is impossible ... or they may say: we really didn't think about it. Let us think about it ...[90]

The above practice of supervisory visits to the field are yet just one practice that the HCJD conducts for the purpose of *ascertaining the facts* of the case in order to present it in detail to the court. I described in Chapter 4 the way the HCJD lawyers conceive their role in this respect.[91] The subject

[88] Interview with LNY (emphasis added). See also interview with ID (similar practices by the HCJD during the first *Intifada*). The activity of the HCJD in the field is well reflected in court decisions, see e.g. *Uda* v. *Commander of IDF*, above note 86; HCJ 421/88 *Abu Sror* v. *Commander of IDF in the Gaza Strip* [1988] IsrSC (August 14, 1988) (the formation of appellate procedures on detention decisions and prison conditions); HCJ 237/91 *El Baba* v. *Minister of Defense* [1991] IsrSC (January 21, 1991) (providing gas masks to the detainees during the Gulf War).

[89] Interview with HR. [90] Interview with LNY.

[91] See Chapter 4 Section B.1 at p. 127.

of human rights infringements in the Territories may serve to illustrate the point in more detail. As a lawyer in the department testifies:

> I had a case on issue related to the Territories and there was a meeting to which the colonel who was the military commander in charge was invited. And he sits there and I question him like you question a witness in cross-examination in court. Not gently at all. He was offended by this. I tried to be polite, but I asked him tough questions. I said: "I don't believe this; I don't believe that" and he answers, and I confront him provocatively. So he began yelling at me ... [in the end] one of the lawyers [from another department at the OAG] said to me: "This is how it works at the HCJD?" as if he wasn't aware that we represent [the IDF] ... but before we go to court I must somehow get to the bottom of the facts. So I put pressure on them, and they are not my friends for that matter. And there is a price for this. Because now [after the meeting] he will not be my friend ... and he went out of the meeting and said: "Who is this guy? I am the commander in charge here ..." So this is the price ...[92]

As another lawyer adds:

> Because of the idiosyncrasy of the procedure [at HCJ] as the highest instance which is also a trial court, with no hearing of evidence etc., so [we] have a sense of mission ... not only that, but also you pay a personal price if it turns out that there is a fact that you didn't check thoroughly, so it can also be quite an embarrassment for you ... since the Court trusts you as an officer of the Court ... *they expect you to do the cross-examination at your office* ... This is particularly the case with *weak petitioners* such as Palestinians, indigent persons etc.[93]

And then he concludes: "It is evident that they [the court] can't verify the affidavits ... The HCJ is not truly a trial court ... So it ends up with *the HCJD turning to be the trial court themselves ...*"[94]

C. Analysis

The case studies discussed above are just two examples of many instances of policy-making through litigation in the HCJ. The phenomenon of the court leaving a petition pending for several months or years while pushing the administration to conduct policy reforms is so common and widespread that the justices openly discuss it in their decisions. Thus, for

[92] Interview with LNY. [93] Interview with HR (emphasis added).

[94] Interview with HR (emphasis added). For a critical assessment of the role of government lawyers in forming settlements with regard to human rights in the Territories see S.Krebs, "Lifting the Veil of Secrecy: Judicial Review of Administrative Detention in the Israeli Supreme Court," 45 *Vand. J. Transnat'l L.* 639, 689 (2012).

example, in a recent case that discussed regulations regarding the maximum number of passengers allowed to ride buses while standing, Justice Rubinstein said: "Naturally, the role of the Court in this kind of case is, frequently, to *serve as 'a babysitter' of the authorities* ... to follow the enforcement of the law and guarantee human rights".[96]

The justices of the HCJ cannot, however, perform their "babysitting" function by themselves. Hence they resort to the assistance of the HCJD members who preside over this process of policy-making under the auspices of the court. The lawyers in the HCJD on their part are fully aware of their pivotal role within this process. Some of them openly admit that they regard themselves as *policy-makers* no less than lawyers. Thus, one HCJD member says:

> Some people have a more minimalist approach ... [for them] there are those who make the policy and those who represent [in court] ... because this separation ... ensures some supervision [on the administration] which is good ... I admit that if I can, I very much like cases in which I can be part of the policy-making ... this would also improve [my ability] to represent properly ...
>
> Q: But you're supposed to be a litigator not a bureaucrat ...
>
> A: In my mind the HCJD members are *bureaucrats par-excellence* ... our work is not one-dimensional ... it does not stop at representation. It ... includes consulting and taking part in legislation ... Sometimes, we are the persons responsible for the *organizational memory* [of the relevant client agency]
>
> Q: But how can you serve as the "organizational memory" of the agency – [if you don't even work there]?
>
> A: That is true, but this is part of the overall involvement of the court in decision-making ... It may not be the ideal situation but as long as this is the state of affairs, I would rather be in a place I can have influence ...[95]

95 Interview with ARD.

96 See HCJ 1527/06 *The Movement for Fairness in Government* v. *Ministry of Transportation* [2009] IsrSC (June 9, 2009), at para. 12 (emphasis added). See also e.g. HCJ 5587/07 *Uziel* v. *Property Tax Authority* [2007] IsrSC (September 18, 2007); HCJ 1254/10 *Ploni* v. *Immigration Authority* [2012] IsrSC (April 4, 2012); HCJ 5833/08 *Access Israel Organization* v. *Minister of Transportation* [2013] IsrSC (January 1, 2013). It should be noted that not all HCJ justices demonstrate the same level of enthusiasm with their "babysitting" role, see e.g. Deputy Chief Justice Rivlin in *The Movement for Fairness in Government* v. *Ministry of Transportation*, *ibid.* (noting that while he accepts the strategy in the case at hand, it should serve as an exception rather than as the rule). In addition it is common for HCJ to provide "guidelines" to administrative agencies as part of their decision. These guidelines are usually not part of the official binding

The "managerial" functions of the HCJD are at stake not only in important cases that involve major policy-making. Even in cases dealing with individual grievances that reach the court's docket on a daily basis,[97] the court expects the HCJD to perform functions of *assistance* to the court. These functions include first and foremost a thorough investigation into the facts of the case.[98] In addition, the court also expects, in many cases, the lawyer in charge to "take care" of the matter, reaching a solution (by out-of-court settlement), even if the petitioners do not have a winning legal argument at their disposal. Interviews with HCJD members are full of stories in which they were called by the court to provide a "reasonable" or "human" solution to the individual grievance of the prisoner, the immigrant, or the indigenous person who sought the court's protection. This function of "assistance" to the court is particularly conspicuous in those cases where the court calls the HCJD to be involved in litigation which *none of their clients is party to.* As one of the HCJD members testifies:

> There was one zoning case in which the district commission [i.e., my client] had no interest ... but the judge [nevertheless] summoned the district commission. When we appeared he said: "listen, I summoned [the district commission] because I really need the HCJD in the courtroom ...". I wide-opened my eyes and [said] I don't understand why they need us here. Then he said that as HCJD I have "contacts" at the Land Management Agency [LMA, who were also not party to the litigation], so he asked me to go outside [the courtroom] and to check with LMA what their position is about the [possible solution to the] case ...[99]

While the above example may be somewhat exceptional in its extremity, it demonstrates well how the justices view the role of the lawyers in the HCJD. To summarize the point I could site one (retired) HCJ justice, whom I interviewed about how he sees the role of the HCJD. He replied: "They are like our assistants ..."[100]

decision, but, nevertheless they may have some impact on future administrative behavior (see e.g. interview with RN (HCJD member)) but cf. L. Orgad and S. Lavi, "Judicial Guidance: Comments for Legislative Amendment in Supreme Court Decisions," 34 *Iunei Mishpat* 473 (2011) (Hebrew) (arguing that empirically there is little evidence that such judicial recommendations influenced legislative behavior).

97 See e.g. interview with EV (HCJD member) (testifying that in many cases he "takes care" of the petitioner's interest *vis-à-vis* the bureaucracy even after the petition is dismissed. For the discussion of the HCJ as a trial court see Chapter 1 at Section A.2.

98 See discussion at p. 168.

99 Interview with LR (HCJD member) (emphasis added).

100 Interview with LN (HCJ Justice).

D. Conclusion

The special role of the HCJD with regard to policy-making processes is largely the result of the role that the court itself plays within the overall picture of the Israeli administration. A normative assessment of the implications of judicial supervision over bureaucratic decision-making is beyond the scope of this book. It is clear, however, that for the HCJ litigation is considered as a vehicle to exert influence and to constantly supervise decision-making processes within the Israeli administration. Within this process of supervision, the HCJD lawyers play a pivotal role that goes far beyond the traditional role of litigators within an adversarial setting. This point will be further demonstrated in the next chapter, in which I shall discuss the *adjudicative* functions of the HCJD.

6

The government lawyer as adjudicator: "pre-petitions" and the HCJD

In the previous chapter I described the involvement of the HCJD in policy-making and institutional design. Apart from its various practices related to out-of-court settlement, organizational missions, and supervisory functions, there is one additional unusual practice that evolved within the HCJD during the 1990s. That is the function of the HCJD lawyers as the *adjudicators* of petitions that are issued *directly to the HCJD* by various petitioners. The institutional name – adopted by the HCJD itself – for such petitions is *pre-petitions (PPs)*, and they are the subject of the current chapter.

A. Pre-petitions – an overview

1. *What are pre-petitions?*

A PP is a practice by which a petitioner that has a dispute with a government agency addresses the HCJD and requests the department to review their case and intervene to change the original position of the authorized agency in their favor. These petitions, such as a letter from a citizen to the department complaining about some bureaucratic illegality, are of a highly informal nature. In urgent cases, however, PPs are often issued to the HCJD by fax or even in the form of a telephone call. For example, a call by a lawyer from a civil rights organization to the head of the department concerning a dispute about the legality of a demonstration which is about to begin, or a complaint concerning an illegal arrest of an immigrant would be treated as PPs.

It should be emphasized at the outset that PPs are issued *without any petition issued to the court*. This means that the petitioner needs not issue a formal petition to the court for the sake of triggering the mechanism of the HCJD. Moreover, while the practice whereby a party that *intends* to bring a dispute to litigation addresses its opponent by way of *a threat* of litigation is commonplace, the PP phenomenon differs from a pre-trial warning in at least two respects. First, while in many cases the reference by the petitioner to the HCJD is done in the context of an anticipated litigation (should the PP fail), in many other cases the party that addresses the department does it *without any such link to a possibility of court litigation*. In other words, in many cases that reach the HCJD as PPs, court litigation is unlikely to take place even if the department declines to act and *both parties are well aware of this fact*. The low probability of court litigation in such cases may derive from the fact that litigation is impractical (due to the time schedule of the relevant events and the urgent nature of the petition) or due to the fact that the petitioner knows well that their chances of winning the case in litigation are slim. In any case, in reality, the relative number of PPs that turn out to become normal petitions to the HCJ after the HCJD has declined to intervene in favor of the petitioner is low (see below).

The second characteristic that distinguishes PPs from regular pre-litigation threats has to do with the role of the HCJD. The parties who address the HCJD by PPs do not regard them as a regular pre-litigation threat that is directed to "the other party" in litigation. In fact, PPs are normally issued after the petitioner has exhausted all negotiations with the public agency (and with its in-house legal counselors). They do not address the HCJD as someone who *represents* the client agency (and, indeed, at that stage, when no petition to the HCJ is issued, the department does not represent the client agency). Rather, the petitioners address the HCJD in order to require it *to intervene* and change the position of the public agency. This means that the petitioners view the department as a kind of *third party* – albeit not a fully neutral – mediator that is expected to step in and review the case. Indeed, such intervention may be derived due to the possibility of an expected litigation, but, as noted above, this is not always the case. Therefore, the referral is to the HCJD as a supervisory body (if not an arbitrator or an ombudsman), rather than as the lawyer of the other party that it is expected to represent in litigation.

2. *Pre-petitions: procedural and practical aspects*

Despite the fact that no petition to court is filed, and despite the fact that no basis in statute or regulation exists for such procedures, the HCJD treats PPs in much the same manner as a case in which a petition is filed. PPs are usually brought to the head of the department and transferred to one of the staff members to be taken care of as in any other case under the head's responsibility. Occasionally, however, the PP is referred directly to one of the lawyers in the department. This is the case where the PP is related to an issue that has already been subject to prior negotiations between the HCJD and the pertinent petitioner, or even to a previously held litigation. In some cases, the petitioner (particularly when they are an organization, see below) would address directly a lawyer in the department whom they know to be in charge of a certain field or a certain kind of case.

After receiving the PP, the lawyer in charge conducts a factual investigation of the petition with the pertinent agency as well as a legal analysis of the relevant questions of law. Thereafter, the lawyer may do one of the following: first, refer the petitioner back to the authorized agency (or in some cases to another administrative agency) stating that the HCJD declines to handle the petition. The meaning of such a response is that, in fact, the HCJD refuses to employ the PP procedure in this case. Alternatively, the lawyer may notify the petitioner that – after looking into the matter – the HCJD found no basis for the complaint and therefore it declines to take any action. In such a case, the petitioner is left, in essence, with the option of resorting to litigation knowing that the HCJD fully upholds the position of its client agency. Finally, if the lawyer finds the pre-petition to have merits, the HCJD member may contact both parties in order to settle the case. Cases falling in this category may end when the HCJD (or the client agency, under the guidance of the department) notifies the petitioners that they back off from their original position and allow them what they asked for originally. Alternatively, such cases may end, after a process of negotiations between the HCJD, its client agency and the petitioner, with a settlement providing the latter with some kind of outcome that they would find satisfactory enough to refrain from any further action.

B. The research

1. *The development of pre-petitions during the 1990s*

The phenomenon of PPs was not the creation of an official decision of some governmental institution. Rather, it was an informal practice that gradually developed due to docket pressures, the rise of the influence of the HCJ and the HCJD on the Israeli bureaucracy, and other factors that will be discussed below. The informality of this process makes it impossible to point to the exact date when PPs began to be disposed by the HCJD. It is likely that the department was in fact dealing with such petitions long before any of its members came to the notion that the volume of this activity required some level of institutionalization. Thereafter, the HCJD began to keep (some partial) records of this activity.

While it may be the case that the HCJD was dealing (perhaps without being fully aware of the fact) with PPs beforehand, the first real, if scattered, evidence of PP files dates to 1988, and the first attempt to manage a filing procedure for this sort of petition began a year later, in 1989.[1] For 1990, I found dozens of files containing PPs indexed and handled. Despite the highly informal nature of PPs, the department developed during the 1990s procedures to file and index these cases.[2] The result is that the files of the HCJD contain a considerable amount of data concerning PPs.

2. *Database and methods*

Our research into PP files disposed during the 1990s was carried out by randomly sampling one of every five PP files documented by the HCJD, referring to all documented PPs issued and disposed by the department during the years 1990–1997. Overall, our database contains 355 PP files.[3] No doubt the data cannot give a full picture of this activity, for a number of reasons: the highly informal nature of this process; the fact that many disputes are resolved within a few days (or even during the same day, see below); and the overall working pressure on the HCJD staff, all make the filing process incomplete and inaccurate. The information collected through the observation of HCJD practices and in interviews with its staff revealed that there is a considerable number of PPs disposed of

[1] Interview with KS (HCJD member). Indeed, in interviews referring to earlier periods, some members of the department confirmed that they used to handle "requests" on behalf of interested parties regarding administrative decisions (interviews with IZ (senior HCJD member)). They indicated, however, that such incidents were scattered and that there was no attempt to institutionalize these cases in any form. Even the reference to such cases as "pre-petitions" is a relatively new phenomenon that did not exist prior to the late 1980s.

[2] This filing process was done during the 1990s both on a manual and a computerized basis. Whenever a PP reaches the HCJD, the secretary of the head of the department files a computerized form (which is quite similar to the form used for court cases), and after the completion of the process, the relevant documents are put in a file containing all the PPs from the same period of time. The data that will be presented below is based primarily on examination of the manual files of the department. In some cases I complemented the information from the manual files by using the department's computerized database.

[3] The PP files were not located at the HCJD official archive located in the archive of the OAG. Rather, they were concentrated and shelved at the HCJD offices. The PPs were located in dossiers and numbered according to the order by which they were filed in the dossiers. Accordingly, we sampled every file that was marked by numbers ending with either 1 or 5. At some point during 1998 the department changed the filing system and the location of the PPs was changed in a form that precluded us from gathering data for the period after March 1997.

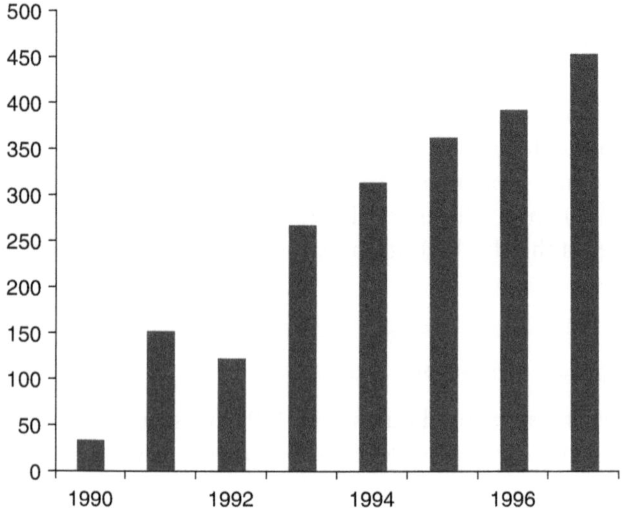

Figure 6.1 Numbers of pre-petitions 1990–1997

without records.[4] Moreover, the files that do exist in the department offices often contain information that is partial, incomplete, and disorganized. Nevertheless, the files are a useful source of information for evaluating some of the implications of this phenomenon as part of the process of litigation in the HCJ. As will be demonstrated below, this general database was complemented throughout the research by examinations of some focused groups of PP files as well as by information gathered through interviews and participant observation.

As we can see from Figure 6.1, the number of PP files in the HCJD rose from a few dozen files in 1990 to almost 400 files during 1996 and above 400 during 1997.[5]

3. *Outcomes of pre-petitions*

As can be seen from Figure 6.2, the data concerning the outcomes of PPs in our database is partial. Although our database contains 355 PP files,

[4] Interviews with ID (HCJD senior) and HR (HCJD member).

[5] The numbers in Figure 6.1 refer only to PP *files*, i.e. to PPs that were filed and indexed by the HCJD. As explained above, the number of PPs was actually much higher since many PPs were disposed by the HCJD without bothering to file and index them. The procedures of filing and indexing PPs were not changed during this period. Therefore, one may assume that the constant rise in numbers of PPs reflected in Figure 6.1 is representative of

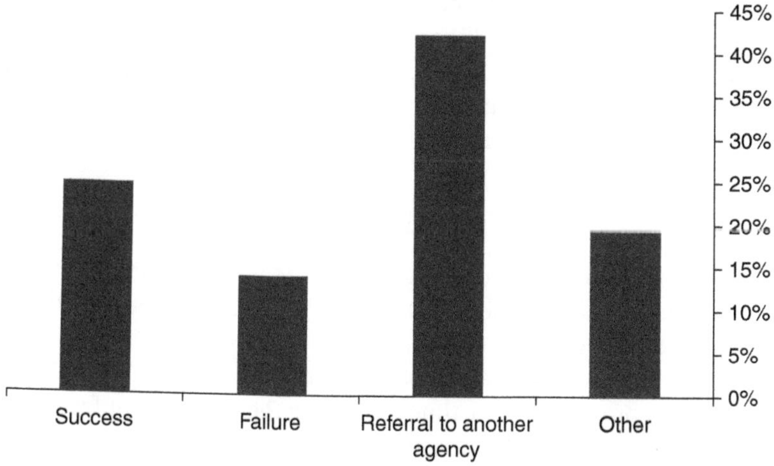

Figure 6.2 Outcomes of pre-petitions 1990–1997
Note: In this diagram: Success – includes full or partial success and settlements; Failure – includes withdrawal of the PP by the petitioner; Other – includes PPs that were found moot or cases still pending.
Source: PP files.

the figure refers to only 187 cases. Due to the informality of the PP procedure and the incomplete practice of filing and indexing, many PP files do not contain information about the outcome of the process. Only in 187 files out of 355 that were included in the database could the outcome of the PP be extracted from the files. Nevertheless, this data gives us a preliminary picture regarding the outcomes of PPs. As Figure 6.2 demonstrates, in roughly 42 percent of the cases disposed by the HCJD (that is, 79 out of 187 cases), the department declined to review the case directly and referred it to another agency. In most cases such a referral means that the HCJD sent the petitioner back to the authorized agency that disposed the case initially (although in some cases the referral may direct the petitioner to a different agency).[6] In 39 percent of the cases, however,

the increase in the general number of PPs throughout this period. The number of files for 1997 is an estimation based on the files issued during the first three months of 1997.

[6] Normally, when the department refers the petitioner back to the original agency the benefits they may gain from the PP are limited to the fact that the department may direct the agency in charge on how to handle the case further on. However, in about twenty cases included in our database (i.e. in around 25 percent of all referrals) we found that the referral to the authorized agency did provide the petitioner with all or part of what they sought in the original PP. In most other cases the final outcome of the referral could not be ascertained from the file.

the HCJD did decide to handle the case, and in almost two-thirds of these cases the outcome was favorable to the petitioner (46 out of 72 cases in columns 1–2 of Figure 6.2). Overall, in almost 25 percent of the cases of which the outcome is ascertainable, the petitioner achieved all or part of what they asked for in their petition.

C. Analysis

On the face of the matter PPs raise some questions as to their legitimacy as a procedure provided by the HCJD. Formally, the department is authorized to represent the government of Israel in a court of law. From the point of view of the HCJD, the procedure of handling PPs can, in many cases, be considered as a pre-trial action aimed at saving the government from the need to be dragged to court. Therefore, the procedure can be regarded as no more than a prudent policy intended to reduce the overloaded docket of both the court and the HCJD. Indeed, in interviews with the HCJD staff, they pointed out that they regard the procedure as a legitimate practice aimed at helping the government to solve disputes at the pre-trial stage.[7]

As a former senior member of the HCJD observes:

> If [as a lawyer of the petitioner] you have a big case, that raises a series of problems, there is no point in resorting to PP. PP is a procedure that is apt for small things, that deal with daily matters. You call [the HCJD] and tell them, what's the point of doing this [i.e. denying my client a certain right]. Why don't you phone the legal department [of the agency] and wrap things up.[8]

While the above statement may serve as an apparent justification for the development of this practice from the point of view of the department, it seems that, in practice, the role of the HCJD members with regard to PPs is much more complex. In processing PPs the HCJD functions, in essence, much more as an arbitrator, an ombudsman, or even as an adjudicative agency, performing functions that go even beyond their supervisory and policy-making role described in the previous chapter. This is because when the HCJD disposes a PP, there are two rival parties (the petitioner and the governmental agency), and the department is in charge of checking *each side's* story, and of forming its position regarding the case. Officially, of course, the department functions as "the government lawyer." In practice, however, government lawyers have to review a petition that is *directed to*

[7] Interview with KS and interview with IN (both HCJD members).

[8] Interview with IZ (senior HCJD).

them, and check whether *they* hold that the petition has merits. Moreover, unlike in the case of litigation in court, the department does not function here in a manner that is *directly* linked to a court case (since, at the stage of a PP there is no court case). In fact, the actions of the HCJD are not always related even to *the possibility* (or the practical chance) of an anticipated litigation (see below). This brings us to a discussion of the reasons for the evolvement of the PP procedure during the 1990s.

The first and obvious factor that contributed to the evolution of PPs was the sharp increase in the caseload of the HCJ and HCJD during the late 1980s and early 1990s.[9] Correspondingly, as the court's ambition to influence administrative and social processes increased, it had to develop new institutional and procedural tools for that purpose. As a result, the court had to delegate many of its functions to the adjacent mechanism of the HCJD. In this respect, the development of the PP practice is a classic – though far-reaching – expression of the general phenomena of delegation of the court functions to the department and the development of informal tools to enable the court to increase its influence on the administration.[10]

The evolution of the practice of PPs was, however, related to another phenomenon that took place in the same period. This is the eruption of the (first) Palestinian *Intifada*. The *Intifada* (and the peace process following it) brought a sharp increase in the number of petitions to the HCJ dealing with allegations of serious violations of human rights.[11] It

[9] See Chapter 1 Section B.1. [10] See Chapter 5.

[11] See generally, Y. Dotan, "Judicial Rhetoric, Government Lawyers and Human Rights: The Case of the Israeli High Court of Justice during the *Intifada*," 33 *Law & Soc'y Rev.* 319, 328 (1999). The end of the *Intifada* and the beginning of the peace process (the Oslo Declaration of Principles on Interim Self-Government Arrangements, September 13, 1993) has not brought an immediate decrease in the number of violations of human rights in the Territories. Paradoxically, it has caused, to some extent, an increase in the number of Palestinian grievances. The use of infringing measures (such as preventive detentions, or deportation orders by the Military Commander) has not stopped, but has since been directed against members of Islamist groups who oppose the peace process. Likewise, restrictions on the freedom of movement of the residents of the Territories were not lessened, and have, in fact, become even more burdensome. See T. Bash and S. Eran, *Bureaucratic Harassment; Abuse and Maltreatment during Operational Activities in The West Bank in the First Year of the Declaration of Principles* (B'Tselem information sheet, September 1994), available in English at www.btselem.org/Download/199409_Bureaucratic_Harrassment_eng.doc (last accessed July 19, 2013); S. Cohen *et al.*, *Impossible Coexistence: Human Rights in Hebron since the Massacre at the Cave of the Patriarchs* (B'Tselem information sheet, September 1995), available in English at www.btselem.org/sites/default/files2/publication/199509_impossible_coexistence_eng.doc (last accessed July 19, 2013); G. E. Bisharat, "Courting Justice? Legitimation in Lawyering under Israeli Occupation," 20 *Law & Soc. Inquiry* 349, 355–356 (1995).

created a serious pressure on the court's docket, which, as previously mentioned, was already under pressure from the continuous increase in the general number of petitions.[12] It also created, however, a significant shift in the *content* of the petitions issued during this period. The court and the judicial system at large (including the Ministry of Justice and the HCJD) faced a huge number of petitions containing allegations of severe infringements of basic liberties. It also faced the fact that many of these petitions dealt with issues that needed an *immediate* response in order to prevent or alleviate violations of human rights. These included, for example, petitions relating to an individual who disappeared from his home during a military operation, and whose family sought to know whether he was detained by the security forces, or a petition on behalf of a detainee denied access to a lawyer, or a petition concerning the closure of roads or areas that would prevent residents from obtaining urgent medical help.[13] These petitions necessitated a response by the judicial system which, in order to be effective, would need to be immediate, organized, and well coordinated with the Military Government itself. In other words, these were petitions that could hardly be dealt with effectively by a formal and cumbersome process in a court of law, particularly when the petitions reached the court in large numbers during a short period of time.[14]

The PP process served as a quick and effective measure to dispose of disputes of the kind described above. Instead of going to court for a relatively slow and cumbersome procedure, the lawyers acting on behalf of the Palestinians gradually accustomed themselves to addressing the HCJD staff directly. Such informal petitions were submitted by mail, or, in more urgent cases, by fax or phone call. The reaction of the department was, in many cases, immediate. In some cases, the relevant detainee was located and details of the place he was held were transferred to his family and his lawyer within a few hours, or the closure of a certain road or village was lifted to enable the population to get medical help or other urgent supplies within half a day.[15]

[12] See Chapter 1 Section B.1 and interviews with KS and IN (HCJD members).

[13] See C. Shalev, *Collective Punishment in the West Bank and the Gaza Strip* (B'Tselem Report, November, 1990), available in English at www.btselem.org/sites/default/files2/publication/199011_collective_punishment_eng.pdf (last accessed July 19, 2013); N. Yashuvi (ed.), *Violations of Human Rights in the Occupied Territories 1990/1991* (B'Tselem Report, 1991), 25–29, 63–76. See also the discussion in Chapter 5 Section B, pp. 164–166.

[14] Cf. the discussion in Chapter 5 Section B, pp. 167–168 of other practices developed during the early 1990s by the HCJD as the result of the *Intifada*.

[15] See Dotan, above note 11, at 353.

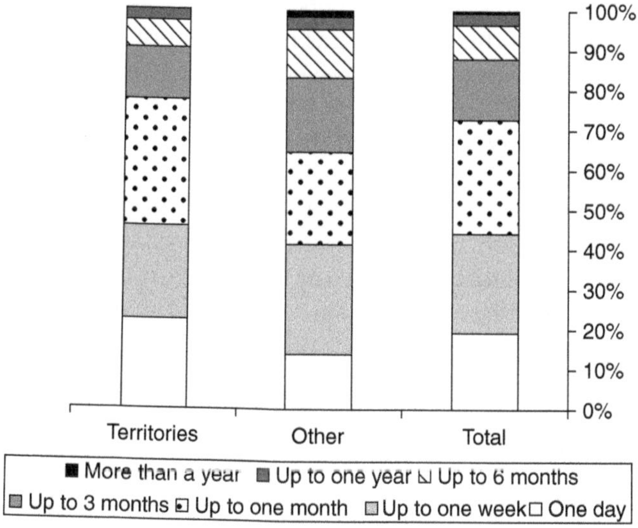

Figure 6.3 Pre-petitions 1990–1997 by processing time
Source: PP files.

The use of PPs as a measure to cope with petitions related to urgent problems in the field of human rights was not limited to petitions issued by Palestinians during the *Intifada*. It was also continued, during the 1990s, in other fields, such as in cases of deportation of illegal immigrants and prison conditions. Nevertheless, residents of the Territories continued to be, by far, the largest group of petitioners using the practice of PPs all through the research period. Overall, out of 355 cases in our sample, 204 (i.e. 57.5 percent) were issued by Palestinians living in the Territories.

The use of PPs as a technique to handle cases that require an instant response from the judicial system can be demonstrated by the fact that almost 20 percent (33 out 172 cases of which the time of the process is known) in our sample were disposed by the HCJD *within one day*, as shown in Figure 6.3. And 62.8 percent of those cases (108 out of 172 PPs) were disposed within two weeks. Once again, the effectiveness – in terms of time of processing – is particularly evident in PPs issued by Palestinian residents of the Territories. Out of 107 such petitions (of which the processing time can be verified from the files) 24 (22.4%) were disposed within one day while 74 (69 percent) were disposed by the HCJD within two weeks (in comparison to 14 percent and 52 percent of other petitions correspondingly).

The main function of the PP procedure was, therefore, to supply an instant and effective solution to urgent cases in which the Israeli bureaucracy denies the petitioner some rights or benefits. This fact also illuminates the function of this procedure as more than just a pre-trial move by the HCJD. This argument, however, requires some further elaboration

As explained below, the *original* reason that led lawyers (in particular lawyers who appear on a regular basis before the HCJ, see below) to address the HCJD before petitioning the court, was to save the parties the need to waste time in litigation. Lawyers who are experienced in litigation before the HCJD began to notice that, in many cases, there is no point in challenging the position of the HCJD in court. This is hardly surprising, considering the extremely low rate of defeats that the HCJD enjoys in litigation before the HCJ and the very high rate of settlements in which the department agrees to allow the petitioner part or all of what they sought originally. In other words, experienced lawyers began to notice (beginning in the late 1980s) that, on the one hand, the HCJD was keen to settle many cases out-of-court, and, on the other hand, that *should* the HCJD decide to litigate the case all the way, the chances that the court would rule against it were extremely low.[16] Therefore, from the point of view of these lawyers, there was (in many cases) little reason to drag their clients through the process of litigation. As one former senior of the HCJD observed:

> If I [as the petitioner lawyer] go to Court, then I get an answer from one of the HCJD lawyers who is in charge. So why shouldn't I phone her instead. After all, *if we go to court, after we do the whole round we shall get to the same point* ... So what is the point in wasting everyone's time?[17]

The fact that PPs, in practice, served to provide solutions for urgent problems, suggests, however, that PPs do more than just bring petitioners to the point they would have reached had they chosen to litigate: it suggests that PPs provide a solution to cases which could not have been effectively disposed by the court *at all* for two main reasons. First, many of these cases deal with urgent problems that require an instant interference on behalf of the judicial system, or else the solution would become moot.

[16] See Chapter 3 Section B.3.2, p. 99 and figure 3.2.

[17] Interview with IZ (senior HCJD). See also interviews with RR (former HCJ judge), IN (HCJD member), and HN (HCJD member). This means, in essence, that in most PP cases that are *dismissed* by the HCJD, the petitioners do not bother to resort to court in order to challenge the department's position. While technically we could not verify in our sample the relative portion of dismissals that do reach the court, it seems that in most cases PPs do not turn into court cases even when dismissed by the department (see also the discussion below in this section).

For example, take the case of a resident of the Territories who seeks to enter Israel in order to get medical treatment in an Israeli hospital, but is prohibited from entering the country on security grounds. In such a case a court interference, that would take at least a number of days, may come much too late (even if this is not an emergency case). Moreover, even if theoretically court interference could solve the problem, the court cannot effectively cope with dozens of such cases per day. Indeed, one may argue that, in fact, the solution for such a situation can only be provided by an efficient bureaucracy, and not by any external intervention by judicial institutions. The fact is, however, that during the *Intifada*, (and also, to a lesser extent, during other periods), the Israeli bureaucracy failed to supply efficient solutions.[18] Therefore, the HCJD, equipped with the prestige and backing of the HCJ, stepped in.[19]

The second reason for the lack of a perceivable court solution for cases that were dealt through PP is even more important for our discussion. Many of the cases that were dealt by the HCJD through PPs were cases in which the petitioner could not go to court since *they had no valid legal case*. Such are cases in which the HCJD is asked to solve a problem with humanitarian aspects, despite the lack of solid legal grounds on the part of the petitioner.[20] In other words, these are cases in which the petitioner (and their lawyer) know quite well that they have little chance to challenge the administrative decision through court litigation. Nevertheless, they address the HCJD by PP, in order to try and convince the lawyer in charge to influence the administrative policy for reasons of good management, or to allow them an exemption as a matter of an *ex gratia* decision. As a lawyer that specializes in human rights litigation observed:

> Another reason to resort to PP and not to court litigation is the fear of the consequences of failure in court. The readiness of the judges to interfere in the discretion of the administration is extremely limited. The HCJD, on the other hand, are in a better position, I think, to say to the decision-makers: you're doing something that is unreasonable and may not stand judicial review. So, you'd better change the policy. Sometimes, since I fear that in full-scale war in court I'd be likely to lose, I have more chances to

[18] The contention as to the failure of the bureaucracy at large and the legal apparatus of the Israeli bureaucracy (i.e., the legal counselors of the relevant agencies) to cope with such a situation was frequently raised in the interviews I conducted, see interviews with RR (former HCJ justice) and with IZ (former senior HCJD member).

[19] In this respect, one may view the PP procedure as part of the general phenomenon of "sorting things out," discussed in Chapter 5.

[20] Interview with IL (human rights lawyer); interview with IN (HCJD member).

change the existing policy through the OAG. This may, of course, be even after a petition is issued, but before the first hearing.

Q: So, you hold that you may get more from the OAG than from the court?

A: Yes, many times I feel that way.[21]

An additional factor that contributed to the development of the PP procedure is the rise of organized litigation in the HCJ during the 1980s and the 1990s. The relationship between these two phenomena merits a detailed discussion in the following section.

D. Pre-petitions and the rise of organized litigation in the HCJ

Pre-petition is an informal procedure that has no basis in statute or in regulation, and – as far as I could check – is not even mentioned in internal codes of the OAG. The procedure does not appear in formal publications of the Ministry of Justice. Therefore, not only was the procedure largely unknown to the general public (at least during the 1990s), but was also unfamiliar to most lawyers, except a small group of lawyers who specialized in HCJ litigation.[22] More specifically, one may say that during the 1990s the procedure was used primarily by organized litigators, i.e., by interest groups such as the Association for Civil Rights in Israel (ACRI) and political lawyers who frequently use HCJ litigation in the field of human rights.[23]

The intensive use of PPs by organized petitioners is generally correlative to the rise of the use of HCJ litigation during the late 1980s and early

[21] Interview with UM (NGO lawyer); interview with IL (NGO lawyer).

[22] The fact that the procedure is not published is explained by HCJD staff by their fear that should the procedure be known to the general public, the department would be flooded with petitions in a manner that would seriously compromise its ability to function. In interview some HCJD members pointed out that they were aware of the fact that the existence of such a procedure that is only known to "in house" players raises serious questions on the constitutional level (see interview with IZ, former HCJD senior). In the late 1990s and early 2000s the existence of the practice was exposed to the legal community by some academic publications, see e.g. Y. Dotan, "Government Lawyers as Adjudicators: *Pre-petitions* in the High Court of Justice Department 1990–1997," 35 *Isr. Law Rev.* 453 (2003); Y. Dotan, "'Pre-petitions' and Constitutional Dilemmas Regarding the Role of Government Lawyers," 7 *Mishpat Umimshal [Law and Government]* 159 (2004) (Hebrew) (see the discussion in Section E below).

[23] For a discussion of political lawyers in the field of human rights litigation in Israel see Y. Dotan, "Public Lawyers and Private Clients: An Empirical Observation on the Relative Success Rates of Cause Lawyers," 21 *Law & Pol'y* 401 (1999).

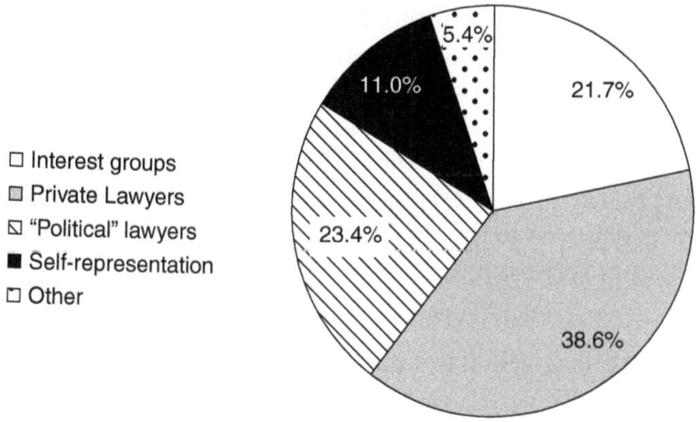

Figure 6.4 Pre-petitions 1990–1997 by organizational affiliation and representation
Source: PP files.

1990s.[24] It should be noted, however, that the use of PPs by interest groups is even more intensive than their relative use of HCJ litigation. This can be demonstrated by Figure 6.4:[25]

As figure 6.4 demonstrates, over a fifth of all PPs in our sample (21 percent) were issued by petitioners represented by interest groups.[26] Nearly another quarter of PPs (23.4 percent) were issued by political lawyers specializing in human rights litigation.[27] This means that around 44 percent

[24] See Chapter 1 Section C.2.

[25] Cases classified under "other" in Figure 6.4 are cases where the PPs dealt with requests from administrative agencies to the HCJD to review a certain procedure or to render an advisory opinion as to the legality of a certain action. Although these cases were classified by the department as PPs, they did not always directly involve interests of individual or groups apart from the relevant agency. In any case, the factor of "representation" of the relevant (potential) petitioner in such cases hardly has any meaning at all.

[26] Out of seventy-seven PPs in which the petitioners were represented by interest groups sixty-three were represented by three organizations that were extensively involved in litigation on behalf of residents of the Territories (ACRI – 25 PPs; Hotline for Victims of Violence – 20; The Society of St. Ives – 18 PPs). This means that over 80 percent of organized activity PPs were linked to civil rights litigation in the context of the Territories. Organized litigation by HCJ petitions at the same period was more diverse. The three groups mentioned here were also, however, among the repeat players in HCJ litigation, see Y. Dotan and M. Hofnung, "Interest Groups in the Israeli High Court of Justice: Measuring Success in Litigation and in Out-of-Court Settlements," 23 *Law & Pol'y* 1, 22 (2001).

[27] In fact, the percentage of PPs issued by NGOs and public lawyers is even higher, and reaches (together) almost 50 percent if we neglect the cases that were classified in Figure 6.4 as "other". Defining political lawyers or identifying a certain lawyer as politically motivated are far from simple tasks. The difficulties in this respect led two leading scholars in the field to conclude that "providing a single, cross-culturally valid definition of the concept [of political lawyers] is impossible." (see A. Sarat and S. Scheingold, "Cause

of PPs in our sample was issued by organized petitioners, who frequently use the HCJ litigation and can be considered as "repeat players."[28] Moreover, as Figure 6.4 demonstrates, the influence of interest groups on PPs is even higher in comparison to their influence on the HCJ docket. The relative proportion of petitions to the HCJ during the first half of the 1990s, while sharply increasing, never exceeded more than 13 percent of the total number of petitions to the HCJ. The percentage of PPs issued by interest groups in our sample is much higher and reaches 21 percent.[29]

E. The aftermath of pre-petitions – the 2000s

The evolvement of the practice of PPs during the late 1980s and the first half of the 1990s was the result of a combination of a number of factors: the outbreak of the *Intifada*, the rise in organized litigation, and the ideological shifts within the HCJD. The PP procedure, however, was purely informal (since it had no basis in any regulations or even in the internal codes of the OAG) and voluntary. It also increased the workload of the HCJD and imposed heavy burdens on the shoulders of its members. It is perhaps not surprising, therefore, that while the procedure "flourished" during the first half of the 1990s, it began to decline towards the end of that decade. In 1995, shortly after the changing of the guard and the replacement of Nili Arad by Uzi Fogelman, the HCJD changed its policies with regard to PPs.[30] Under Nili Arad PPs were first referred to a member of the HCJD that was in charge and they examined the facts vis-à-vis the agency. Under the new procedure, the HCJD significantly reduced the number of PPs it dealt with. In most cases the department declined to deal with the PP and instead referred the

Lawyering and the Reproduction of Professional Authority," in A. Sarat and S. Scheingold (eds.) *Cause Lawyering: Political Commitments and Professional Responsibilities* (Oxford University Press, 1998), 3, at 5. Among the accepted parameters for distinguishing political lawyers from others in the profession are the ambition to use litigation as a tool for social change, the tendency to feel ideologically committed to the cause related to the litigation, and a lack of economic incentives. See also Dotan, above note 23, at 409–413.

28 For a discussion of the concept of "repeat players" in litigation see M. Galanter, "Why the 'Haves' Come Out Ahead: Speculations on the Limits of Legal Change," 9 *Law & Soc'y Rev.* 95 (1974). See also Y. Dotan, "Do the 'Haves' Still Come Out Ahead? Resource Inequalities in Ideological Courts: The Case of the Israeli High Court of Justice," 33 *Law & Soc'y Rev.* 1059 (1999).

29 See Chapter 1 Section C.2 and see also note 27. The relative portion of petitioners represented by NGOs in court in our sample for the 1990s is 11.5 percent see Chapter 3 Section B.3 (Table 3.1 at p. 91).

30 See Chapter 2 at p. 85.

petitioner back to the authorized agency, which was asked by the HCJD to deal with it.[31] The exceptions were mostly files that involved urgent problems that had to be sorted out immediately or those that raised acute humanitarian problems. Accordingly, during the second half of the 1990s the number of PP cases that were actually disposed by the HCJD sharply decreased.[32] Similar practices were continued throughout the 2000s. Still, even now, the HCJD receives a few hundred PPs each year. But most of these are referred immediately to the authorized agencies, without any substantive treatment by the department, and save a minority cases that involve exceptional exigency or special humanitarian issues.[33]

F. Conclusion

The development of the practice of PPs serves as yet another powerful manifestation of the rise of the model of "lawyering for the rule of law" in the HCJD during the 1990s. While dealing with PPs, the lawyers in the department served not only as supervisors of their client agencies but also as arbitrators that disposed "controversies" between the petitioners (mostly represented by organizations or other repeat players) and their own clients. The highly informal nature of this practice, however, rendered it dependent on the policies of the department's heads. Accordingly, while during the first half of the 1990s the practice served as a significant part of the overall activities of the HCJD, its importance has declined in recent years.

[31] Interviews with INZ (HCJD senior).

[32] According to our sample there was no indication that there was a decline in the *general number* of PPs during 1996 or during the first three months of 1997 (see note 5). However, there was a sharp decline in the relative percentage of PPs that were *actually handled* by the HCJD during 1996 to around 30 percent, and the rate of success of petitions during 1996 declined accordingly to around 5 percent (as compared to a general success rate of around 25 percent in our sample, see Figure 6.2 above). During the first three months of 1997 *all* the PPs issued to the HCJD were either referred by the department to other agencies (usually, the agencies authorized to handle the case) or categorized as "other". Therefore, our sample actually supports the information drawn from interviews that the appointment of Fogelman as Head of the HCJD brought about an almost complete termination of the practice of handling PPs that was accepted during the tenure of his predecessor.

[33] Currently, the HCJD conducts computerized filing of PPs. According to the department's records in 2008 it filed 445 PP files; in 2009 – 337 files; in 2010 – 307 files and in 2011 – 245 files. The department could not provide data with regard to the contents or outcomes of those files.

Conclusion

Throughout this book I have described the working practices and functions of lawyers who represent the Israeli government before the Supreme Court. The group I focused on is a relatively small group of elite government lawyers who are certainly distinct in their position and functions from the general population of government lawyers in Israel, let alone from government lawyers at large. Nevertheless, the study of this group of lawyers may contribute to our understanding of the phenomenon of government lawyering, their influence within the governmental bureaucracy, and their relationship with the judiciary.

The evolvement of the "lawyering for the rule of law" model during the 1980s in Israel was closely intertwined with the rise of judicial activism within the High Court of Justice. During this era the court was transformed from a relatively restrained court that viewed its main mission as deciding controversies between individuals and state agencies to a powerful and interventionist institution that views its main role as enforcing the principles of the rule of law over the Israeli executive and political branches. The discussion of the causes of this shift by the court, and the background reasons for the pace and the magnitude of the process, are largely beyond the scope of this book. It is clear, however, that the reforms initiated by the court stirred a process of change within various other institutions (within and without the Israeli bureaucracy). The HCJD was one of the key institutions in this respect.

The current research demonstrates the importance of ancillary institutions in general, and the legal apparatus of the government in particular, within the process of judicial review. Government lawyers are key players essential for any court that seeks to bring about social or institutional transformation. Hence, the process of judicial review cannot be studied by looking at the reviewing court in isolation. Nor does it suffice to look at the process of judicial review as an isolated interaction between the direct parties to specific proceedings. Rather, modern processes of public law litigation involve *institutionalized* players that commonly serve as *intermediaries* between the individual parties and the reviewing court. Such are interest groups and NGOs that often represent individuals who challenge governmental decisions, and such are the government agencies in charge of representing the government in court. The relationship between these institutionalized players, the parties they represent, and the court are complex and the current study, admittedly, sheds light only on some, albeit central, aspects of it.

The rise of judicial activism in Israel during the 1980s and 1990s was largely based on the development of the interrelationships between the court and the HCJD. The court provided the HCJD with ample powers and influence within and without the bureaucracy. It established by judicially-made doctrine the HCJD's monopoly over the representation of all government agencies in litigation and thus bestowed the department with ample power to influence policy-making. The affinity between the court and the department and the credibility that the judges related to their positions and statements in court endowed the department with a high reputation within all governmental and political circles. This reputation was also translated into personal gains for the members of the department in terms of promotion to higher posts within the bureaucracy or to the bench.

The HCJD on its part provided the court with inputs essential to the expansion of judicial power. The department's willingness to carry out complicated fact-finding missions (sometimes in a semi-adjudicatory manner) contributed to an easing of docket pressures and enabled the court to function as an effective trial court, despite its obvious institutional inaptness and procedural limitations. The department's out-of-court settlement practices enabled the court to expand and diversify the array of judicial remedies beyond the constraints of its formal jurisdiction. The practices developed by the HCJD improved the court's ability to supervise decision-making processes within the Israeli administration. They were also vital, from the court's point of view, for the enforcement of the court's decisions, particularly in cases of transformative litigation. The collaboration on the part of the department also enabled the court to lower the visibility of its intervention in governmental decision-making and thus reduce the political cost of such intervention in sensitive political areas.

The development of this close collaboration between the court and the legal apparatus of the government could not be fully explained by looking solely at the reforms in the court's policies. Rather, one should also look at the structural, cultural, and ideological settings within the OAG office and the HCJD. The rise of the model of "lawyering for the rule of law" cannot be related exclusively to the external pressures exerted on the department on the part of the justices who led the activist revolution in the HCJ during the 1980s. Thus, I demonstrated that similar changes did *not* take place as the result of this revolution in other governmental units in charge of legal representation, such as local municipalities. Hence, one has to look to the institutional factors such as the *centralized* structure of representation of government agencies, as well as to the social background of the lawyers in the HCJD and their professional ideology to complete the picture in that respect.

It is difficult to point to one decisive factor that brought about the rise of this robust model of lawyering. It seems that institutional, cultural, and ideological factors all have some role within this complex process. And, indeed, I do not make any strong claim regarding causality in this respect. Rather, it seems that it is the combination of all these factors that contributed to the creation of this model.

Is this model of "lawyering for the rule of law" sustainable over time? The lawyering practices described in this book were developed during the 1980s and the 1990s (along with the rise of judicial activism in the HCJ). The model seems to have remained largely intact during the first decade of the 2000s. Until recently, any critique against the intensiveness of judicial intervention in administrative and political decision-making was directed primarily against the HCJ itself. In recent years, however, it seems that the opponents of judicial activism have acquired a better understanding as to how the process of judicial empowerment works. As a result, direct political pressures on the OAG and the HCJD are much more common and conspicuous than they have been before. Under these circumstances, it remains to be seen for how long government lawyers in Israel will be able to continue to vigorously represent the interests of "the general public" on the account of the immediate demands of their client agencies.

TABLE OF CASES

BIBLIOGRAPHY

Abel, R. L. and Lewis, P. S. C. (eds.), *Lawyers in Society: An Overview* (Berkeley: University of California Press, 1995)

Lawyers in Society: The Common Law World (Berkeley: University of California Press, 1988)

ACRI (Association for Civil Rights in Israel), "Negev Bedouins and Unrecognized Villages" (2010)

ACRI (Association for Civil Rights in Israel) Report, *Negev Bedouin: Info Sheet* (February 5, 2009)

Alon, G. "Ex Chief Justices Support the Seniority Rule," *Ha'aretz*, December 21, 1999

"The Government Rejects the Criticism Made by Religious MKs on Justice Barak," *Ha'aretz* December 12, 1994

Alon, G. and Verter, Y. "The Attorney General Bar-On Resigned," *Ha'aretz*, January 13, 1997

Amit-Kohn, U., Jarach, R., Glick, C. B. and Biton, N. *Israel, The 'Intifada' and the Rule of Law* (Israeli Ministry of Defense Publications, 1993)

Arian, A. *et al.* "Auditing Israeli Democracy: Democratic Values in Practice," (The Israel Democracy Institute, 2010)

Atkins, B. M. "Alternative Model of Appeal Mobilization in Judicial Hierarchies," 37 *Am. J. Pol. Sci.* 780 (1993)

Babcock, B. A. "Defending the Guilty," 32 *Clev. St. L. Rev.* 175 (1983)

Baker, N. V. *Conflicting Loyalties: Law and Politics in the Attorney General's Office 1789–1990* (University Press of Kansas, 1992)

"The Attorney General as a Legal Policy-Maker: Conflicting Loyalties," in C. W. Clayton (ed.), *Government Lawyers: The Federal Legal Bureaucracy and Presidential Politics* (University Press of Kansas, 1995)

Baldwin, R. and McCrudden, C. *Regulation and Public Law* (London: Weidenfeld and Nicolson, 1987)

Barak-Erez, D. "From an Unwritten to a Written Constitution: The Israeli Challenge in American Perspective," 26 *Colum. Hum. Rts. L. Rev.* 309 (1995)

Outlawed Pigs: Law, Religion, and Culture in Israel (University of Wisconsin Press, 2007)

Barzilai, G. "Between the Rule of Law and the Laws of the Ruler: The Supreme Court in Israeli Legal Culture," 49 (152) *Int'l Soc. Sci. J.* 193 (1997)

"Fantasies of Liberalism and Liberal Jurisprudence: State Law and Israeli Arab-Palestinian Community," 34 *Isr. L. Rev.* 425 (2000)

Barzilai, G., Yuchtman-Ya'ar, E. and Segal, Z. —"Supreme Courts and Public Opinion: General Paradigms and the Israeli Case," 4(3) *Law & Courts* 3 (1994)

The Israeli Supreme Court and the Israeli Public (Tel Aviv: Papyrus, 1993)

Bash, T. and Eran, S. *Bureaucratic Harassment; Abuse and Maltreatment during Operational Activities in the West Bank in the First Year of the Declaration of Principles* (B'Tselem information sheet, September 1994)

Bassok, O. "Television Coverage of the Israeli Supreme Court 1968–1992: The Persistence of the Mythical Image," 42 *Isr. L. Rev.* 306 (2009)

Baum, L. *The Supreme Court*, 6th edn. (Washington, D.C.: CQ Press, 1998)

Ben-David, Y. "The Bedouin in Israel," Israeli Ministry of Foreign Affairs (July 1999)

Benvenisti, E. *The International Law of Occupation*, 2nd edn. (Oxford University Press, 2012)

Berenson, S. K. "Public Lawyers, Private Values: Can, Should, and Will Government Lawyers Serve the Public Interest?," 41 *B.C.L. Rev.* 789 (2000)

"The Duty Defined: Specific Obligations that Follow from Civil Government Lawyers' General Duty to Serve the Public Interest," 42 *Brandeis L.J.* 13 (2003)

Bisharat, G. E. "Courting Justice? Legitimation in Lawyering under Israeli Occupation," 20 *Law & Soc. Inquiry* 349 (1995)

Black, R. C. and Owens, R. J *The Solicitor General and the United States Supreme Court* (Cambridge University Press, 2012).

Blumberg, A. S. "The Practice of Law as Confidence Game," in V. Aubert (ed.), *Sociology of Law* (1969)

Bogoch, B. and Holtzman-Gazit, Y. "Mutual Bonds: Media Frames and the Israeli High Court of Justice," 33 *Law & Soc. Inquiry* 53 (2008)

Boon, A. and Levin, J. *The Ethics and Conduct of Lawyers in England and Wales* (Oxford: Hart, 2008)

Bracha, B. "The Protection of Human Rights in *Israel*," *12 Israel Yearbook of Human Rights* 110 (1982)

B'Tselem, "10 Years to the Second Intifada" (press release, September 27, 2010)

Canon, B. C. "Defining the Dimensions of Judicial Activism," 66 *Judicature* 236 (1983)

Caplan, L. *The Tenth Justice: The Solicitor General and the Rule of Law* (New York: Knopf, 1987)

Chayes, A. "The Role of the Judge in Public Law Litigation," 89 *Harv. L. Rev.* 1281 (1976)

Clark, K. "Government Lawyers and Confidentiality Norms," 85 *Wash. U.L. Rev* 1033 (2007)

Clayton, C. W. (ed.) *Government Lawyers: The Federal Legal Bureaucracy and Presidential Policies* (University Press of Kansas, 1995)

The Politics of Justice: The Attorney General and the Making of Legal Policy (New York: M. E. Sharpe, 1992)

Cohen, S. *et al. Impossible Coexistence: Human Rights in Hebron since the Massacre at the Cave of the Patriarchs* (B'Tselem information sheet, September 1995)

Cross, F. B. and Lindquist, S. A. "The Scientific Study of Judicial Activism," 91 *Minn. L. Rev.* 1752 (2007)

Dailey, W. R. "Who is the Attorney General's Client? " 87 *Notre Dame L. Rev.* 1113 (2012)

Davis, M. and Elliston, F. A. (eds.) *Ethics and the Legal Profession* (New York: Prometheus Books, 1986)

De Smith, S. A., Woolf, H., Jowell, J. L. and Le Sueur, A. P. *Judicial Review of Administrative Action*, 5th edn., vol. I (London: Sweet & Maxwell, 1995)

Devins, N. (ed.), "Government Lawyering," 61(1–2) *Law & Contemp. Probs.* 1 (1998)

"Unitariness and Independence: Solicitor General Control over Independent Agency Litigation," 82 *Cal. L. Rev.* 255 (1994)

Diver, C. S. "The Judge as Political Powerbroker: Superintending Structural Change in Public Institutions," 65 *Va. L. Rev.* 43 (1979)

Doron, I. *et al.* "A decade to 'Amicus Curiae': Empirical Analysis of Court Decisions," 34 *Iunei Mishpat [Law Studies]* 667 (2011) (Hebrew)

Dotan, Y. "Cause Lawyers Crossing the Lines: Patterns of Fragmentation and Cooperation between State and Civil Rights Lawyers in Israel," 5 *Int'l J. Legal Prof.* 193 (1998)

"Constitution to Israel? The Constitutional Dialog After the 'Constitutional Revolution'," 28 *Mishpatim [Law]* 149 (1997)

"Does Israel Need A Constitutional Court," 5 *Mishpat Umimshal [Law and Government]* 117 (1999)

"Do the 'Haves' Still Come Out Ahead? Resource Inequalities in Ideological Courts: The Case of the Israeli High Court of Justice," 33 *Law & Soc'y Rev.* 1059 (1999)

"Government Lawyers as Adjudicators: *Pre-petitions* in the High Court of Justice Department 1990–1997," 35 *Isr. Law Rev.* 453 (2003)

"Judicial Activism and Government Practices in Litigation in the Israeli High Court of Justice 1970–2000," Paper presented at the Law and Society Association Annual Meeting, San Francisco June 2–5, 2011

"Judicial Review and Political Accountability: The Case of the High Court of Justice in Israel", 32 *Isr. L. Rev.* 448 (1998)

"Judicial Rhetoric, Government Lawyers and Human Rights: The Case of the Israeli High Court of Justice during the *Intifada*," 33 *Law & Soc'y Rev.* 319 (1999)

"Non-Delegation and the Reformulation of Legality," 42 *Mishpatim [Law]* 397 (2012) (Hebrew)

"'Pre-petitions' and Constitutional Dilemmas Regarding the Role of Government Lawyers," 7 *Mishpat Umimshal [Law and Government]* 159 (2004) (Hebrew)

"Public Lawyers and Private Clients: An Empirical Observation on the Relative Success Rates of Cause Lawyers," 21 *Law & Pol'y* 401 (1999)

"Ripeness and Politics in the High Court of Justice," 20 *Iunei Mishpat [Law Studies]* 93 (1996) (Hebrew)

"Should Prosecutorial Discretion Enjoy Special Treatment in Judicial Review? A Comparative Analysis of the Law in England and Israel," *Pub. L.* 513 (1997)

Dotan, Y. and Hofnung, M. "Interest Groups in the Israeli High Court of Justice: Measuring Success in Litigation and in Out-of-Court Settlements," 23 *Law & Pol'y* 1 (2001)

"Legal Defeats – Political Wins: Why Do Elected Representatives Go to Court?," 38 *Comp. Pol. Stud.* 75 (2005)

Easterbrook, F. H. "Do Liberals and Conservatives Differ in Judicial Activism?," 73 *U. Colo. L. Rev.* 1401 (2002)

Edelman, M. *Courts, Politics and Culture in Israel* (University of Virginia Press, 1994)

"Israel," in C. Neal and T. Vallinder (eds.), *The Global Expansion of Judicial Power* (New York University Press, 1995)

"The Judicial Elite of Israel," 13 *Int'l Pol. Sci. Rev.* 235 (1992)

Edwards, J. Ll. J. *The Attorney General and the Public Interest* (London: Sweet and Maxwell, 1984)

Einstein, J. *Counsel for the United States: U.S. Attorney General in the Political and Legal System* (Maryland: Johns Hopkins University Press, 1978)

Eisenberg, T., Fisher, T. and Rosen-Zvi, I. "Israel's Supreme Court Appellate Jurisdiction: An Empirical Study," 96 *Cornell L. Rev.* 693 (2011)

Epp, C. R. *The Rights Revolution* (University of Chicago Press, 1998)

Epstein, L. and Kobylka, J. F. *The Supreme Court and Legal Change: Abortion and the Death Penalty* (Chapel Hill: North Carolina University Press, 1992)

Etinger, Y. "More than 100,000 ultra-orthodox took part in protest against the rule of law," *Ha'Aretz* June 18, 2010

Feeley, M. M. and Rubin, E. L. *Judicial Policy Making and the Modern State: How the Courts Reformed America's Prisons* (Cambridge University Press, 1998)

Fiss, O. M. "Foreword: The Forms of Justice," 93 *Harv. L. Rev.* 1 (1979)

Fletcher, W. A. "The Discretionary Constitution: Institutional Remedies and Judicial Legitimacy," 91 *Yale L.J.* 635 (1982)

Frankel, M. E. "The Search for Truth: An Umpireal View," 123 *U. Pa. L. Rev.* 1031 (1975)

Freedman, M. H. *Lawyers' Ethics in an Adversary System* (New York: The Bobbs-Merrill Company, Inc., 1975)

Fried, C. "The Lawyer as Friend: The Moral Foundations of the Lawyer-Client Relation," 85 *Yale L.J.* 1060 (1976)

Fuller, L. L. The Adversary System in *Forum Lectures*, Series 3, 1 (Washington, D.C.: Voice of America, 1961)

Fuller, L. and Randall, J. D. "Professional Responsibility: Report of the Joint Conference," 44 *Am. Bar Ass'n. J.* 1159 (1958)

Galanter, M. "Why the 'Haves' Come Out Ahead: Speculations on the Limits of Legal Change," 9 *Law & Soc'y Rev.* 95 (1974)

Galligan, D. J. *Discretionary Powers: A Legal Study of Official Discretion* (Oxford: Clarendon Press, 1986)

Gambitta, R. A. L., May, M. L. and Foster, J. C. (eds.), *Governing Through Courts* (Beverly Hills, CA: Sage, 1981)

Gavison, R. *Administrative Discretion in Law Enforcement* (Jerusalem, 1991)

"Jewish and Democratic? A Rejoinder to the 'Ethnic Democracy' Debate," 4 *Isr. Stud.* 44 (1999)

"The Attorney General: A Critical Examination of New Trends," 5 *Plilim [Israel Journal of Criminal Justice]* 27 (1996) (Hebrew)

Gavison, R., Kremnitzer, M. and Dotan, Y. *Judicial Activism at the High Court of Justice* (Jerusalem: Magnes, 2000)

Ginsburg, T. *Judicial Review in New Democracies: Constitutional Courts in Asian Cases* (Cambridge University Press, 2003)

Glikman, A. "The Attorney General Freezes the Appointment of the Chief Commissioner," *Ynet*, November 18, 2010

Gordon, R. "The Ideal and the Actual in the Law: Fantasies and Practices of New York City Lawyers, 1870–1910," in G. W. Gawalt (ed.), *The New High Priests: Lawyers in Post-Civil War America* (1984)

Graglia, L. A. *Disaster by Decree: The Supreme Court Decisions on Race and the Schools* (Ithaca, NY and London: Cornell University Press, 1976)

Green, B. A. "Must Government Lawyers 'Seek Justice' in Civil Litigation?" 9 *Widener J. Pub. L.* 235 (2000)

Grosman, G. "Ulmert Calls for Investigation of the OAG for Obstruction of Justice," *Walla News* June 23, 2011

Gutman, Y. *A Storm in the G.S.S: The Attorney General Versus the Government* (Tel-Aviv, 1995)

The Attorney General Versus The Government (Jerusalem: Edanim, 1981)

Handler, J. F. *Down from Bureaucracy: The Ambiguity of Privatization and Empowerment* (New Jersey: Princeton University Press, 1996)

Harvey, J. R. III "Note, Loyalty in Government Litigation: Department of Justice Representation of Agency Clients," 37 *Wm. & Mary L. Rev.* 1569 (1996)

Haynie, S. L. "Resource Inequalities and Litigation Outcomes in the Philippine Supreme Court," 56 *J. Pol.* 752 (1994)

Haynie, S. L. and Devore, J. "Judging in an Unjust Regime: South Africa's Appellate Division, 1950–1990," 17 *Am. Rev. Pol.* 245 (1996)

Hazut, R. "The Night on which the Supreme Court was Almost Conquered," *Yediot Acharonot*, May 14, 1997

Herz, M. and Devins, N. "The Consequences of DOJ Control of Litigation on Agencies' Programs," 52 *Admin. L. Rev.* 1345 (2000)

Hirschl, R. "The Political Origins of Judicial Empowerment through Constitutionalization: Lessons from Four Constitutional Revolutions," 25 *Law & Soc. Inquiry* 91 (2000)

Towards Juristocracy: The Origins and Consequences of the New Constitutionalism (Cambridge, MA: Harvard University Press, 2004)

Hofnung, M. and Weinshall-Margel, K. "Judicial Setbacks, Material Gains: Terror Litigation at the Israeli High Court of Justice," 7 *J. Empirical Legal Stud.* 664 (2010)

Horowitz, D. L. *The Courts and Social Policy* (Washington, D.C.: Brookings Institution Press, 1977)

The Jurocracy: Government Lawyers, Agency Programs and Judicial Decisions (Washington, D.C.: Lexington Books, 1977)

Ilan, S. "An Effort to Prevent Violence in the Ultra-orthodox and Secular Demonstrations in Jerusalem Today," *Ha'Aretz* February 14, 1999

"Inflation of Bills: From Four to Average of 40 Bills for Each MK," *Ha'aretz* October 30, 2000

"Rabbi David Yosef: 'Antisemistic forces in the legal bureaucracy calls the Shas people parasites'," *Ha'aretz* February 2, 1999

"Rabbi Ovadia Yosef: 'The HCJ Justices Are Worse than Non-Jewish Courts and Should not Be Regarded as Judges of Israel'," *Ha'aretz*, October 8, 1996

"Shas: Deri's Conviction is the Conviction of Shas," *Ha'aretz* March 18, 1999

Ilan, S., Alon, G. and Verter, Y. "An Extreme Ultra-orthodox Attack on the HCJ: 'Barak is the Enemy of the Jewish People'," *Ha'Aretz* February 10, 1999

Ilan, S., Alon, G., Moalem, M. and Krao, N. "Rabbi Yosef: The HCJ Justices are Villains and are the Cause of All the Suffering in the World," *Ha'Aretz* February 11, 1999

Jacobsohn, G. J. *Apple of Gold: Constitutionalism in Israel and the United States* (Princeton University Press, 1993)

Kagan, R. A. "Adversarial Legalism and American Government," 10 *J. Pol'y Analysis & Mgmt.* 369 (1991)

Adversarial Legalism: The American Way of Law (Harvard University Press, 2001)

Karp, J. "Basic Law: Human Dignity and Liberty: A Biography of Power Struggles," 1 *Mishpat Umimshal [Law and Government]* 323 (1993) (Hebrew)

Kedar, A. "The Legal Transformation of Ethnic Geography: Israeli Law and the Palestinian Landholder 1948–1967," 33 *N.Y.U. J. Int'l L. & Pol.* 923 (2001)

Kelly, J. B. "Bureaucratic Activism and the Charter of Rights and Freedoms: The Department of Justice and Its Entry into the Centre of Government," 42 *Can. Pub. Admin.* 476 (1999)

"Canada: Legal Services and the Role of Government Lawyers" (Paper presented at the Annual Meeting of the Law and Society Association, Budapest, July 4–7, 2001)

Krebs, S. "Lifting the Veil of Secrecy: Judicial Review of Administrative Detention in the Israeli Supreme Court," 45 *Vand. J. Transnat'l L.* 639, 689 (2012)

Kmiec, K. D. "The Origin and Current Meaning of 'Judicial Activism'," 92 *Cal. L. Rev.* 1441 (2004)

Kremnitzer, M. "The HCJ and Its Wide Concept of Its Role," in R. Gavison, M. Kremnitzer, and Y. Dotan *Judicial Activism at the High Court of Justice* (Jerusalem: Magnes, 2000)

Kretzmer, D. "Judicial Review of Knesset Decisions," 8 *Tel Aviv U. Stud. L.* 95 (1988)

"The New Basic Laws on Human Rights: A Mini-revolution in Israeli Constitutional Law?," in I. Zamir and A. Zysblat (eds.), *Public Law in Israel* (Oxford: Clarendon Press, 1996)

Kritzer, H. M. "The Government Gorilla: Why Does Government Come Out Ahead in Appellate Courts?," in H. M. Kritzer and S. Silbey (eds.), *In Litigation: Do the "Haves" Still Come Out Ahead?* (Stanford University Press, 2003)

Kronman, A. T. *The Lost Lawyer: Failing Ideals of the Legal Profession* (Cambridge, MA: Belknap Press of Harvard University Press, 1993)

Lahav, P. *Judgment in Jerusalem: Chief Justice Simon Agranat and the Zionist Century* (Berkeley: University of California Press, 1997)

Lanctot, C. J. "The Duty of Zealous Advocacy and the Ethics of the Federal Government Lawyer: The Three Hardest Questions," 64 *S. Cal. L. Rev.* 951 (1991)

Langevoort, D. C. and Rasmussen, R. K. "Skewing the Results: The Role of Lawyers in Transmitting Legal Rules," 5 *S. Cal. Interdisc. L.J.* 375 (1997)

Lawry, R. P. "Who is the Client of the Federal Government Lawyer? An Analysis of the Wrong Question," 37 *Fed. B.J.* 61 (1978)

Lemos, M. H. "The Solicitor General as Mediator between Court and Agency," 185 *Mich. St. L. Rev.* 2009

Levine, D. I. "The Modification of Equitable Decrees in Institutional Reform Litigation: A Commentary on the Supreme Court's Adoption of the Second Circuit's Flexible Test," 58 *Brook. L. Rev.* 1239 (1993)

Levit, N. "Megacases, Diversity, and the Elusive Goal of Workplace Reform," 49 *B. C. L. Rev.* 367 (2008)

Levontin, E. "*Representation of the State in Court*" (PhD dissertation, Hebrew University of Jerusalem, 2009)

Levontin, E. and Gavison, R. "The 'Binding' Position of the Attorney General," in A. Barak (ed.), *Shamgar Book*, vol. I (2003)

Lewinbuk, K. P. "Let's Sue All the Lawyers: The Rise of Claims Against Lawyers for Aiding and Abetting a Client's Breach of Fiduciary Duty," 40 *Ariz. St. L.J.* 135 (2008)

Likhovski, A. "The Invention of 'Hebrew Law' in Mandatory Palestine," 46 *Am. J. Comp. L.* 339 (1998)

Linowitz, S. M. and Mayer, M. *The Betrayed Profession: Lawyering at the End of the Twentieth Century* (Maryland: Johns Hopkins University Press, 1994)

Luban, D. "The Adversary System Excuse," in D. Luban (ed.) *The Good Lawyer: Lawyers' Roles and Lawyers' Ethics* (Totowa, NJ: Rowman & Allenheld, 1983)

Macey, J. R. and Miller, G. P. "Reflections on Professional Responsibility in a Regulatory State," 63 *Geo. Wash. L. Rev.* 1105 (1995)

Magen, H. "Aharon Barak: We Shall Fight Like Lions against the Individual Survey on Judges," *Globs* December 12, 2001

"Changes in the New Proposal to Implement the Or Commission Report," *Globs* November 22, 1998

"The Bar Rejects the Central Part of Or Commission Report," *Globs* September 9, 1997

Margalit, D. "Rabin and Peres of the HCJ," *Ha'aretz* December 9, 1994

Markus, Y. "The Malice, Not the Stupidity," *Ha'aretz* January 14, 1997

Marshall, W. P. "Conservatives and the Seven Sins of Judicial Activism," 73 *U. Colo. L. Rev.* 1217 (2002)

Mate, M. "Public Interest Litigation & The Transformation of the Supreme Court of India," in D. Kapsizewski, G. Silverstein and R. A. Kagan (eds.), *Consequential Courts: Judicial Roles in Global Perspective* (Cambridge University Press, 2013)

Mautner, M. *Law and Culture in Israel at the Threshold of the Twenty First Century* (Tel Aviv: Am Oved, 2008)

The Decline of Formalism and the Rise of Values in Israeli Law (Tel Aviv: Ma'agalei Deot, 1993)

McCann, M. W. *Rights at Work: Pay Equity Reform and the Politics of Legal Mobilization* (University of Chicago Press, 1994)

McCann, M. and Silverstein, H. "Rethinking Law's 'Allurements': A Relational Analysis of Social Movement Lawyers in the United States," in A. Sarat and S. A. Scheingold (eds.), *Cause Lawyering: Political Commitments and Professional Responsibilities* (Oxford University Press, 1998)

McCormick, P. "Party Capability Theory and Appellate Success in the Supreme Court of Canada 1949–1992," 26 *Can. J. Pol. Sci.* 523 (1993)

Meir, A. *As Nomadism Ends: The Israeli Bedouin of the Negev* (Boulder, CO: Westview Press, 1997)

Mellinkoff, D. *The Conscience of a Lawyer* (St Paul, MN: West Publishing Company, 1973)

Mendel, O. "On the Job of the Lawyer at the High Court of Justice Department," 2 *Ma'asei Mishpat [The Practice of Law]* 53 (2009) (Hebrew)

Miller, G. P. "Government Lawyers' Ethics in a System of Checks and Balances," 54 *U. Chi. L. Rev.* 1293 (1987)

Mishkin, P. J. "Federal Courts as State Reformers," 35 *Wash. & Lee L. Rev.* 949 (1978)
Mizrachi, S. "Dani Dankner to Face Indictment for Bribery and Fraud," *The Marker* September 5, 2011
Moalem, M. "A Wave of Intimidation against OAG Staff after the Ultra-orthodox Demonstration against the HCJ," *Ha'aretz* February 17, 1999
Nagel, R. F. "Separation of Powers and the Scope of Federal Equitable Remedies," 30 *Stan. L. Rev.* 661 (1978)
Note, "Developments in the Law: Conflicts of Interest in the Legal Profession," 94 *Harv. L. Rev.* 1244 (1981)
"Government Counsel and their Obligations," 121 *Harv. L. Rev.* 1409 (2008)
"Rethinking the Professional Responsibilities of Federal Agency Lawyers," 115 *Harv. L. Rev.* 1170 (2002)
Ogletree, C. J., Jr. and Sapir, Y. "Keeping Gideon's Promise: A Comparison of the American and Israeli Public Defender Experience," 29 *N.Y.U. Rev. L. & Soc. Change* 203 (2004)
Orgad, L. and Lavi, S. "Judicial Guidance: Comments for Legislative Amendment in Supreme Court Decisions," 34 *Iunei Mishpat [Law Studies]* 473 (2011) (Hebrew)
Pacelle, R. L., Jr. *Between Law and Politics: The Solicitor General and the Structuring of Race, Gender and Reproductive Rights Litigation* (Texas A&M University Press, 2003)
Parker, W. "The Future of School Desegregation," 94 *Nw. U. L. Rev.* 1157 (2000)
Paulsen, M. S. "Who 'Owns' the Government's Attorney-Client Privilege?," 83 *Minn. L. Rev.* 473 (1998)
Perry, H. W., Jr. "United States Attorneys – Whom Shall They Serve?," 61 *Law & Contemp. Probs.* 129 (1998)
Pierce, R. J. "Two Problems in Administrative Law: Political Polarity on the District of Columbia Circuit and Judicial Deterrence of Agency Rulemaking," *Duke L.J.* 300 (1988)
Polikoff, N. D. "Am I My Client?: The Role Confusion of a Lawyer Activist," 31 *Harv. C.R.-C.L. L. Rev.* 443 (1996)
Porsher, E. "Now It Is Official: Chief Justice Beinish," *Ma'ariv-NRG* September 7, 2006
Posner, R. "Enlightened Despot," *The New Republic*, April 2007 (Review of *The Judge in a Democracy* by Aharon Barak, 2006)
Postema, G. J. "Moral Responsibility in Professional Ethics," 55 *N.Y. U. L. Rev.* 63 (1980)
Provine, D. M. *Case Selection in the United States Supreme Court* (University of Chicago Press, 1980)
Reichman, A. "A Very Narrow Bridge: Constitution, Justice, Equity and Remedy," 37 *Mishpatim [law]* 701 (2007) (Hebrew)
Reinfeld, M. "The Movement for the Quality of Government to HCJ: Order the Bar to Discharge Hoter Yishai," *Ha'aretz* March 13, 1997

Roitman, Y. "The Public Lawyer and the Protection of Human Rights" (Lecture, 2004)

Roots, R. "Unfair Federal Rules of Procedure: Why Does the Government Get More Time?" 33 *Am. J. Trial Advoc.* 493 (2010)

Rosenberg, G. N. *The Hollow Hope: Can Courts Bring About Social Change?*, 2nd edn. (University of Chicago Press, 2008)

Rosen-Zvi, I. *Taking Space Seriously: Law, Space and Society in Contempoary Israel* (Aldershot: Ashgate, 2004)

Rotem, M., Noach, H. and Al-Ukbi, N. *The Arab-Bedouin in the Negev-Naqab Desert in Israel: Response to the Report of the State of Israel on Implementing the Covenant on Economic, Social and Cultural Rights (ICESCR)* (Shadow Report submitted by The Negev Coexistence Forum for Civil Equality, 2010)

Rubin, M. H. "The Ethical Negotiator: Ethical Dilemmas, Unhappy Clients, and Angry Third Parties," 26 *Constr. Law.* 12 (2006)

Rubinstein, A. and Medina, B. *The Constitutional Law of Israel* (Tel Aviv: Shoken, 2005)

Salokar, R. M. "Politics, Law, and the Office of the Solicitor General," in C. W. Clayton (ed.), *Government Lawyers: The Federal Legal Bureaucracy and Presidential Politics* (University Press of Kansas, 1995)

The Solicitor General: The Politics of Law (Philadelphia: Temple University Press, 1992)

Sandler, R. and Schoenbrod, D. *Democracy by Decree: What Happens When Courts Run Government* (Yale University Press, 2003)

Sarat, A. and Scheingold, S. "Cause Lawyering and the Reproduction of Professional Authority," in A. Sarat and S. Scheingold (eds.), *Cause Lawyering: Political Commitments and Professional Responsibilities* (Oxford University Press, 1998)

Scheingold, S. *The Politics of Rights: Lawyers, Public Policy, and Political Change* (New Haven CT: Yale University Press, 1974)

Schiff, Z. and Ya'ari, E. *Intifada: The Palestinian Uprising – Israel's Third Front* (New York: Simon and Schuster, 1990)

Schlanger, M. "Book Review: Beyond the Hero Judge: Institutional Reform Litigation as Litigation," 97 *Mich. L. Rev.* 1994 (1999)

"Civil Rights Injunctions over Time: A Case Study of Jail and Prison Court Orders," 81 *N.Y.U. L. Rev.* 550 (2006)

Schnapper, E. "Legal Ethics and the Government Lawyer," 32 *Rec. Ass'n. B. City N.Y* 649 (1977)

Schuck, P. H. "The Role of Judges in Settling Complex Cases: The Agent Orange Example," 53 *U. Chi. L. Rev.* 337 (1986)

Segal, A. "The Judgement of Edna Arbel [State Attorney] is Flawed," *Maariv* April 4, 2001

Segal, J. A. and Spaeth H. J. *The Supreme Court and the Attitudinal Model Revisited* (Cambridge University Press, 2002)

Segal, Z. *Israeli Democracy* (Tel Aviv: Ministry of Defense, 1990)

Shachar, Y., Haris, R. and Gross, M. "Anatomy of Discourse and Division in the Supreme Court: Quantitative Analysis," 20 *Iunei Mishpat [Law Studies]* 749 (1997) (Hebrew)

"Reference Patterns of the Supreme Court: A Quantitative Analysis," 27 *Mishpatim [Law]* 119 (1996) (Hebrew)

Shadmi, H. "The Government to Set Up Clinics for Bedouin: We Shall Build One Clinic," *Ha'aretz* March 21, 2003

Shalev, C. *Collective Punishment in the West Bank and the Gaza Strip* (B'Tselem Report, November, 1990)

Shamgar, M. "The Observance of International Law in the Administered Territories," 1 *Israeli Yearbook of Human Rights* 262 (1971)

Shamir, R. "'Landmark Cases' and the Reproduction of Legitimacy: The Case of Israel's High Court of Justice," 24 *Law & Soc'y Rev.* 781 (1990)

"Suspended in Space: Bedouins under the Law of Israel," 30 *Law & Soc'y Rev.* 231 (1996)

"The Politics of Reasonableness: Discretion as Judicial Power," 5 *Theory and Criticism* 7 (1994)

Shapiro, M. *Who Guards the Guardians?: Judicial Control of Administration* (Athens, GA: University of Georgia Press, 1988)

Shavit, A. "An Interview with Deri," *Ha'aretz* July 20, 2000

Sheehan, R. S., Mishler, W. and Songer, D. S. "Ideology, Status and Differential Success of Direct Parties Before the Supreme Court," 86 *Am. Pol. Sci. Rev.* 464 (1992)

Shetreet, S. *On Adjudication: Justice on Trial* (Jerusalem: Yedioth Aharonot, 2004)

"Reflections on the Protection of the Rights of the Individual: Form and Substance," 12 *Isr. L. Rev.* 32 (1977)

"The Critical Challenge of Judicial Independence in Israel," in P. Russel and D. M. O'Brien (eds.), *Judicial Independence in the Age of Democracy: Critical Perspectives from around the World* (2001)

Simon, W. H. "The Ideology of Advocacy: Procedural Justice and Professional Ethics," *Wis. L. Rev.* 29 (1978)

Solomon, R. C. "Wearing Many Hats: Confidentiality and Conflicts of Interests Issues for the California Public Lawyer," 25 *Sw. U.L. Rev.* 265 (1996)

Songer, D. R. and Sheehan, R. S. "Who Wins on Appeal? Upperdogs and Underdogs in the United States Courts of Appeals," 36 *Am. J. Pol. Sci.* 235 (1992)

Straschnov, A. *Justice Under Fire* (Tel Aviv: Yedioth Aharonot, 1994)

Strauss, D. A. "The Solicitor General and the Interests of the United States," 61 *Law & Contemp. Probs.* 165 (1998)

Strauss, P. L., Rakoff, T. D. and Farina, C. R. *Gellhorn & Byse's Administrative Law: Cases and Materials*, 10 edn. (New York: Foundation Press, 2003)

Sunstein, C. R. *Radicals in Robes* (New York: Basic Books, 2005)

Supreme Court of Canada: Statistics 2001 to 2011

Symposium: Legal Ethics for Government Lawyers, 9(2) *Widener J. Pub. L.* 199 (2000)

Tate, C. N. and Valinder, T. (eds.), *The Global Expansion of Judicial Power* (New York University Press, 1995)

Tidmarsh, J. and Trangsrud, R. H. *Complex Litigation and the Adversary System* (New York: Foundation Press, 1998)

Trapolin, E. W. "Sued into Submission: Judicial Creation of Standards in the Manufacture and Distribution of Lawful Products – The New Orleans Lawsuit Against Gun Manufacturers," 46 *Loy. L. Rev.* 1275 (2000)

Ugarte, E. E. "The Government Lawyer and the Common Good," 40 *S. Tex. L. Rev.* 269 (1999)

United Kingdom Ministry of Justice, Judicial and Court Statistics 2010

Utz, P. J. "Two Models of Prosecutorial Professionalism," in W. F. McDonald (ed.), *The Prosecutor* (Beverly Hills, CA: Sage, 1979)

Volcansek, M. L. "Exporting the Missouri Plan: Judicial Appointment Commissions," (in: "Symposium: The Fallacies and Fixables of Merit Selection and the Constituencies that Support Missouri Plan Reform") 74 *Mo. L. Rev.* 783 (2009)

Wade, H. W. R. and Forsyth, C. F. *Administrative Law*, 10th edn. (Oxford University Press, 2009)

Wald, P. M. "'For the United States': Government Lawyers in Court," 61 *Law & Contemp. Probs.* 107 (1998)

Wasserstrom, R. "Lawyers as Professionals: Some Moral Issues," 5 *Hum. Rts.* 1 (1975)

Weinshall-Margel, K. "Attitudinal and Neo-Institutional Models of Supreme Court Decision Making: An Empirical and Comparative Perspective from Israel," 8 *J. Empirical Legal Stud.* 556 (2011)

Wheeler, S., Cartwright, B., Kagan, R. A. and Friedman, L. M. "Do the 'Haves' Come Out Ahead: Winning and Losing in State Supreme Courts, 1870–1970," 21 *Law & Soc'y Rev.* 403 (1987)

Yashuvi, N. (ed.), *Violations of Human Rights in the Occupied Territories 1990/1991* (Jerusalem: B'Tselem, 1991)

Yoaz, Y. "The Labor Party: Friedman's Proposal Will Cause Coalition Crisis," *Ha'Aretz* November 16, 2007

Young, E. A. "Judicial Activism and Conservative Politics," 73 *U. Colo. L. Rev.* 1139 (2002)

Zamir, I. *Adjudication in Administrative Cases* (Jerusalem: The Harry Sacher Institution, 1975)

"Administrative Law," in I. Zamir and A. Zysblat (eds.), *Public Law in Israel* (Oxford: Clarendon Press, 1996)

"Editor's Note," in I. Zamir (ed.), *The Klinghoffer Book on Public Law* (Jerusalem, 1993)

"Evidence in the High Court of Justice," 1 *Mishpat Umimshal [Law and Government]* 295 (1993) (Hebrew)

Klinghoffer Book on Public Law (Jerusalem, 1993)

"Rule of Law and Civil Liberties in Israel," 7 *C. J. Q.* 64, 65 (1988)

"Secondary Legislation: Procedures and Directives," 11 *Iunei Mishpat [Law Studies]* 339 (1986) (Hebrew)

"The Attorney General: A Public Servant, Not a Government Servant," in I. Zamir (ed.), *The Klinghoffer Book on Public Law* (Jerusalem, 1993)

"The Lawyer in the Public Service," in Y. Dotan and A. Bendor (eds.), *Zamir Book: On Law, Government and Society* (Jerusalem, 1995) (Hebrew)

"The Role of the Attorney General in Times of Crisis: The Israeli Shin Bet Affair," in S. Shetreet (ed.), *The Role of Courts in Society* (Dordrecht: Nijhoff, 1988)

"Unreasonableness as Ground of Review," in I. Zamir and A. Zysblat (eds.), *Public Law in Israel* (Oxford: Clarendon Press, 1996)

Zarchin, T. "This is how Noam Solberg's Road is Paved to the Supreme Court," *Ha'aretz* October 27, 2011

Zaring, D. "National Rulemaking Through Trial Courts: The Big Case and Institutional Reform," 51 *UCLA L. Rev.* 1015 (2004)

Zelikovitz, M. "Ramon: The OAG Became Coercive," *Ynet* June 12, 2008

Zer-Gutman, L. "The Lawyer's Duty not to Mislead the Court," 24 *Iunei Mishpat [Law Studies]* 413 (2000) (Hebrew)

Zitrin, B. Z. "Hoter Yishai: The Judicial System is Frozen and Very Conservative," *Ha'aretz* February 25, 1997

Ziv, N. "Symposium: The Legal Profession: Looking Backward: Combining Professionalism, Nation Building and Public Service: The Professional Project of the Israeli Bar 1928–2002," 71 *Fordham L. Rev.* 1621 (2003)

Zysblat, A. "Introduction: The System of Government," in I. Zamir and A. Zysblat (eds.), *Public Law in Israel* (Oxford: Clarendon Press, 1996)

"Protecting Fundamental Rights in Israel without a Written Constitution," in I. Zamir and A. Zysblat (eds.), *Public Law in Israel* (Oxford: Clarendon Press, 1996)

INDEX